Quality and Me

Philip B. Crosby

Quality and Me

Lessons from an Evolving Life

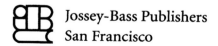 Jossey-Bass Publishers
San Francisco

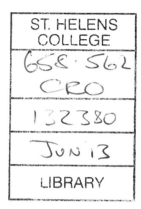
Jossey-Bass books and products are available through most bookstores. To contact Jossey-Bass directly, call (888) 378-2537, fax to (800) 605-2665, or visit our website at www.josseybass.com.

Substantial discounts on bulk quantities of Jossey-Bass books are available to corporations, professional associations, and other organizations. For details and discount information, contact the special sales department at Jossey-Bass.

Library of Congress Cataloging-in-Publication Data

Crosby, Philip B.
  Quality and me : lessons from an evolving life / Philip B. Crosby. — 1st ed.
    p. cm.
  Includes index.
  ISBN 0-7879-4702-4 (acid-free paper)
  1. Crosby, Philip B.   2. Total quality management.   3. Quality control.   4. Executives—Biography.   I. Title.
  HD62.15 .C764 1999
  658.4'013—dc21   98-58073
                                                                                   CIP

FIRST EDITION
HB Printing   10 9 8 7 6 5 4 3 2 1

—ɯ— Contents

—~~— Preface

One of the problems with writing a book is finding a title. All the titles I came up with for this book were too long. It seemed as though, as the subject of an autobiography, I should have my name in the title, but that takes up a lot of space. I have several hundred biographies and autobiographies in my library. About half of them have a title that doesn't give you a clue as to their content. *A Streak of Luck* is about Thomas Edison; Dean Acheson called his *Present at the Creation.* It is hard to file such books and difficult to find them if you don't already know what they are about.

My wife, Peggy, watching my struggles, finally asked, "What is the book really about?" I responded, "It is about quality and me." That struck us, and after a long discussion about "Quality and I," we concluded that "Me" was proper because it was originally part of a prepositional phrase. Anyway it rhymed.

Peggy has been my personal rock. She is ever pragmatic and knows when to let my thoughts pass by and when to get involved with developing them. We do not make trouble for each other.

I would like to thank Debbie Eifert, my assistant, who hangs in there better than anyone. She has patiently taught me how to use a computer and has rescued me from deleting the whole book from my hard disk several times. We have worked together fifteen years—from Philip Crosby Associates, Inc., through Career IV, Inc., and now into Philip Crosby II, Inc.

Writers need a lot of encouragement. My editor, Cedric Crocker of Jossey-Bass, showed me how to frame the text to make it easier to read. The "Learning" segments in italics were his idea. I appreciate the faith he had in this book.

When I began this book, I had retired from Philip Crosby Associates, and Peggy and I were spending half our time in Highlands, North Carolina, at our house in the Cullasaja Club. (Cullasaja is said to be an Indian word for "double bogie.") Giving a couple of speeches a month somewhere in the world and writing four books satisfied me. We worked with the India Quality Foundation and had made four trips to India to help the school system. (School systems in the United States were not interested in my assistance.) I liked to go to MBA schools and speak with the students. I was in excellent health, which is a lot of hard work, and I wanted to hang around for another twenty-five years or so. That way I could see my grandchildren and children mature. I was not interested in another career or even in trying to change the world, as in the past. Then I got Philip Crosby Associates back and found it to be a wonderful opportunity and challenge. Those who say they like golf and writing better than a corporate challenge will lie about other things too.

I had a lot of reservations about writing this book, but I enjoyed the process. Even if no one ever buys a copy, at least I will have put the story of my life down where it can be seen. I deliberately concentrate on the development of my ideas and describe my experiences as they occurred. Learning is what needs to be shared. I do not talk about the people I have known over the years except where they were part of that learning process. Someone would be left out for certain if I tried to include everyone, and the book would resemble a telephone directory. Most of all, I didn't want to hurt anyone's feelings.

I know of no one who stood in my path or tried to do me harm during my careers. Some thought I was wrong, and some thought I had no substance. I viewed that as their problem, not mine, and the results have borne me out. Essentially I have worked alone, even though many individuals have been involved in implementing my ideas. I am an information junkie, and what I knew about a situation was usually far ahead of what I could find out by asking someone. So this book, good or bad, is my responsibility alone. It is truthful and as complete as I can recollect.

At any rate, I am glad *Quality and Me* is on paper. I hope you will find it useful.

Winter Park, Florida   PHILIP CROSBY
January 1999

Introducing Me

"Read no history: nothing but biography, for that is life without theory," wrote Benjamin Disraeli. Disraeli's advice was practical, at least for me. My library shelves are stuffed with biographies, and I have read at least some of all of them. Learning how others spent their time, developed their thoughts, took action or shrank from it, sold their ideas, suffered from rejection, loved, hated, handled success and failure is a primary source of knowledge. Little that we see today is new; almost everything has been done or tried in some way at some time. It is not necessary to have everything happen to us personally in order to learn. We have to be aware of when the opportunity to learn appears; sometimes it is not all that obvious. Often it takes a while to learn the real reason for what goes on.

When I was sixteen I took the Red Cross lifeguard test in order to work as a lifeguard that summer. The test was no problem as I was a strong swimmer and had been taught all the methods of retrieving those in trouble in the water. But one of the criteria was floating. I could not float, went right to the bottom. My mother used to lie on her back, put an ashtray on her stomach, and float around the lake all day. I sank. However I learned how to fake floating and passed the test. All my life I felt inadequate about not being able to float and tried continually to master the art, which comes so naturally to others.

This spring I went to an antiaging clinic for a physical examination. Part of the protocol is a full-body bone scan. The result is a photo of the entire skeleton and a measurement of bone mass. The doctor showed me the chart produced by the machine. My bone mass was clear off the top of the chart. He said he had never seen such density. "I bet you can't float," he said. "You'll never break a bone." It had taken me fifty-five years to learn that it was not my fault; my body was not designed to float. And that is the way life is. There are all kinds of things that involve us for which we have inadequate information. Who knew about bone density? I was just the dummy who couldn't learn how to float.

Learned: *if no one understands how something works, then you don't have to feel inadequate just because you can't do it.*

That is the kind of information I would like to discuss in this book. I learned a lot in progressing through life. But I had no idea of where it was all leading. I just kept learning and plodding. The key is developing an open mind. Usually the conventional wisdom is wrong, about everything. By examining it we can make progress.

I have had a life filled with some disappointments and many successes and have been surrounded by opportunities to learn. It is only natural for me to think that knowing about this life could be useful to someone who wants to understand how others learned. I have always been full of ideas; some were great, some were lousy, but they all came about because of varied stimuli. I can recognize that what has happened to me is unusual in many respects. Those who handicapped the future of my peers and myself during childhood or young manhood did not pick me for achievement. There is no conventional explanation for my becoming influential in managerial areas or for my ability to create the opportunity to gain some wealth. There was no reason for this success in my background. It came about because I accumulated knowledge that resulted in an attitude and approach that made me useful. I was not born useful; my usefulness developed as I learned from life.

Learned: *people do not know enough about themselves or others to predict their future, good or bad.*

The idea of a biography is to get to know the person, not necessarily the events in their lives. We don't know how these events come about. For that reason I do not record conversations with anyone or quote others' thoughts or comments. Each time I am quoted in a book or article, there is always something wrong with the quote. People hear differently. For instance, I have always written and said that *quality* means conformance to requirements. At least six authors have insisted that I define quality as "conformance to specifications." Then they proceed to write a chapter or two on how stupid this definition is because specifications make up only a tiny part of what goes on in a company. Their interpretation gives folks a completely erroneous image of me that I never bother to contradict. So I will not do that to others.

I hate to have to thumb through biographies in order to put the subject's life in chronological order. My plan for this book was just to start from first memories and to follow events and thoughts. For that reason the chapters are arranged according to major events. If readers want to know about a specific time of my life, they can just look for the major event of that period. Inside those time periods I am not always chronologically consistent, having written what I remembered as it occurred to me.

Let me provide a rough overview of what is covered in the rest of the book. I include "learnings" from each event as we go along. Readers can then relate these to their own life experiences. We are probably not very different.

The book is divided into four parts to make it easier to deal with. The first is about growing up. I had a calm childhood, rather normal and quiet. This childhood was interrupted by World War II, which required that I finish growing up rapidly. I served as a medical specialist in the Navy, saw combat, and returned to my home in Wheeling, West Virginia, without even thinking about going anywhere else. I went to podiatry college, got married, was called back for the Korean War by the Marine Corps, and then decided to carve my own way, which led to going to work in a factory.

Learned: *the things we do in our first twenty-one years don't happen again.*

The second part of the book describes how and what I learned about the world of business. Most important, I learned that many things are done wrong and that there was a role for someone who could change the philosophy of management. I called the new way a "reformation" rather than a revolution. I worked my way up through three companies before winding up as a vice president at the ITT Corporation working for Harold Geneen.

Fourteen years of this relationship launched the third part of my life, starting a management-education company to teach the reformation based on a best-selling book that I conceived during the first two parts of my life. Running a company according to my own concepts and making it successful were a great joy. During that time I wrote six books and made some money—with the company, not the books.

The fourth part of the book describes how and why I left my company after selling it and then concentrated on writing four new books and speaking about leadership. Those who bought the company turned it the wrong way however, and I got it back. I discuss its rebirth in a new age.

I have tried to write the stories behind all these events in an interesting fashion. If something I did or didn't do helps readers in the evolution of their own life, then my writing this book will have been worthwhile.

To my Peggy

Quality and Me

PART ONE

Growing Up

CHAPTER ONE

From Wheeling to the Navy

I was born in Wheeling Hospital in Wheeling, West Virginia, on June 18, 1926, at 5:30 A.M. (I put that in so astrologers can cast my horoscope if they wish, although we Geminis do not believe in all that stuff.) My parents were Mary Campbell Crosby and Dr. Edward Karg Crosby. Dad was a podiatrist. My brother, David, was born in 1930, and that made up the family. Our parents were nice people, bright and interested in the world. They did not particularly like each other and eventually divorced when I was seventeen. But they showered us with a confident love and provided a solid family life.

Mom was a born aristocrat, although she never had any money. She played piano, sang, and was gifted with a sense of culture without attending college. She taught me to play the ukulele and encouraged me to attempt the piano. But I was never interested in it after realizing that I was going to have to learn bass clef.

Learned: *if you want to learn how to do something, just go ahead and dive in; nothing can stand the test of being picked apart.*

Mom's family was from Bellaire and the rest of Belmont County in Ohio. Her mother, Pearl Chambers Campbell, was a strong woman who lived with us part of the year and ran a hotel in Bethesda, Ohio, during the summer. We used to spend most of the summer there. I always felt that her living with us was the biggest source of disruption in our parent's relationship. She did not like Dad.

Learned: *children look at their family life as if they are in a movie theater; lots of stuff goes on, but there is no control lever for them, so they mostly observe.*

Our father was good at anything he wanted to do. He was a scratch golfer, a high-scoring bowler, and a pioneer photographer. He was recognized as an innovator in the field of podiatry. A large and pleasant man, he was well liked and had a comfortable life. However, although he knew how to make money, he was not good at hanging on to it; so he was always juggling things. We never did own a home, although we lived in nice neighborhoods. I looked exactly like him, but I never achieved his weight—or wanted to.

Dad came from Findlay, Ohio, where his father owned a shoe store. They lived a typical middle-class life in that flat, northern Ohio town of twenty thousand or so. His brother, Harold, a physician, had two kids and called himself "just an old country doctor." He was good at his work and was beloved by everyone. But he couldn't collect his bills and also had a drinking problem. Aunt Lucille, an authentic saint, took over the management of the office and helped "unkie" get along.

Dad's sister, Frances, taught the first grade. She and her husband, "Bus" (nicknamed after Buster Brown), also had two children. The whole family got together several times a year, and I have wonderful memories of dinners and outings. They were all nice people, very loving, and with quiet lives. None of them made much money, but they lived well enough and had a great many friends.

My brother, David, has the same memories as I, but he is still irritated that he had to sit with the younger children because we ran out of room at the big table. Dave was a flower child before there were flower children. When we went fishing in Bethesda together, he would take the fish off the hook for his delicate older brother. Today he has his own business and five children. We see each other regularly. We always call each other on our birthdays, and as we age we come closer together. When we were young, one of my jobs was to search the neighborhood for Dave each evening as dinnertime approached. He would be playing with a frog or doing some creative and positive thing. But he was always surprised that it was already time to go home.

His school was three blocks from the house, and it often took him four hours to make the trip.

As the first grandchild, I had a special place with my father's parents, whom I called "Daddy George and Momma Nell." When I visited them as a pre-teen, I worked in their yard doing little-boy chores in order to earn enough money to buy pulp books like *G-8 and His Battle Aces*. Fortunately those in charge of me approved of reading even if it was not the classics. However, I was often tossed out of the house to "go play" rather than read. My problem was that my playmates were not interesting enough for long enough. It was not their fault; I have always been that way. What I was thinking about pulled me away from what we were doing. For that reason I have had few close friends in life—a lot of people I know well, but few to whom I am close.

Learned: *all this is really about being self-centered.*

I was always a little shy about imposing myself on others. That made it difficult to ask someone to go somewhere or to do something. The impression I gave was of an outgoing, happy boy, which was accurate. However, this same boy held himself back a lot and would not step out to do something, even if he wanted to do it. Not a good practice.

At home in Wheeling, Woodsdale School did well by me up through grade 8. It was located about three-quarters of a mile from our house, a distance that my children were delighted to discover in later years because at some point I had apparently mentioned walking miles through the snow and sleet to school. The streets in the neighborhood were named after the trees that lined them—Poplar, Maple—and for most of those years I rode a bike to school with my friends. Once we ice-skated to school only to be stuck when the afternoon sun melted everything. We had neglected to bring shoes, and one did not call one's parents in those days. So we walked home on our skates. That experience led me to begin thinking ahead a little bit. If my grandmother Campbell (Nana) had been living with us at that moment, she would never have let me out of the house on skates.

Early in school I discovered that if you did not appear to take things seriously, then you could not be accused of failing. This belief led to my acting as though I did not care about many things and predictably resulted in my teachers and fellow students believing me. No one took me seriously. These sorts of attitudes feed on themselves, and so when I did do something right, on purpose, they felt it to be an accident.

Relationships can get off on the wrong track easily in this type of environment. After a while I began to believe it myself. So there I was, a kid who actually thought about things in some detail but whom every one assumed was quite shallow. I wasn't insecure, but my self-image was low. My fourth-grade teacher turned me around for a while by getting me interested in math, but in fifth grade the teacher viewed me as a "silly boy," and that settled it.

Learned: *people take you for what you present yourself as.*

We went to Bethesda, Ohio (about twenty-five miles west of Wheeling), each summer and lived in a cottage near Nana's hotel. One reason was to escape the polio epidemic, which hit Wheeling each year. I lost several friends to that disease over time. I almost lost my own life to an infection in my foot one summer. There were no antibiotics then, and I can remember the red streaks starting up my leg and my mother frantically putting hot compresses on the sore. I also went through St. Vitus Dance, which is a manifestation of rheumatic fever; it left me with a heart weakness that has been around all these years but wasn't a problem until I was over fifty.

I also did chicken pox, scarlet fever, measles, whooping cough, and several other routine diseases. Somewhere along the line I developed a tic in my cheek, which apparently came from the rheumatic fever. I think now that it became a habit because over the years I have developed little twitches like that and have learned to overcome them by force of will. When people begin looking at you strangely, you learn to quit doing such things.

My summer jobs at Bethesda taught me the pattern of work life. Most of them revolved around Nana's hotel. It had about forty rooms, no serious plumbing, and a large dining room. I emptied chamber pots (there was one under each guest bed) early in my career and worked my way up to washing dishes. One summer I ran the concession stand selling ice cream, candies, and burgers. All these jobs were supposed to prepare me for the responsibilities of the real world. But they only convinced me that the real world did everything the hard way. The family had informal meetings on "what would become of Phil" because I seemed not to take life as they viewed it seriously.

Learned: *it is OK to be different as long as you are not different about it.*

Later I became the lifeguard at the lake. That is one job I would have been willing to pay to have. Bethesda housed Epworth Park,

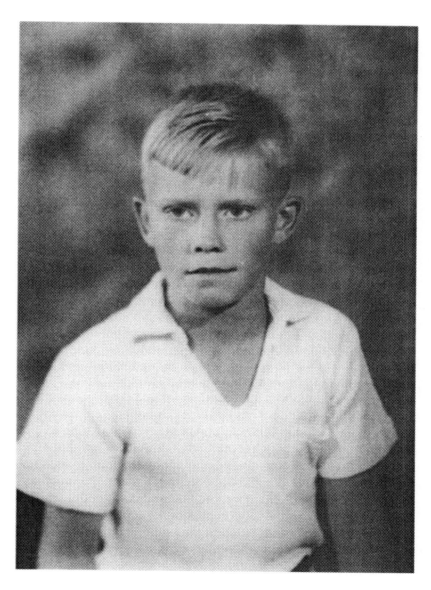

Me at age nine. My mother made me pose for this photo.

where the lake, cottages, and hotel were. The park was used by the Methodist churches in Ohio for outings and recreation. Each Saturday a Sunday school group from a church somewhere in Ohio arrived, and the previous group left. Thus, a whole new bunch of boys and girls would appear at the lake on Saturday afternoon. By Sunday afternoon I would have them taking care of the boats and cleaning out the place. The girls needed to be instructed in the use of a new product called suntan oil. I took on that job personally.

Hymn singing and prayer services were held most nights in the outside theater, and for two weeks each year the chautauqua came to town. It included music, magic, a play, and preaching; it was something to look forward to. One year I ran the record machine for the magician and got to watch from backstage. When he picked the guy out of the audience to help him unload his car in order to show that there was nothing in the box, I knew for sure that life was not always as it was supposed to be.

There was a hamburger, coke, and jukebox place downtown, about a hundred yards from the park gate. We went there a couple of nights a week and hung out with the other teens. Then couples took the long walk through the dark park back to the cottages. I had the same conversation with a different girl each week. By July I was good at it. That is about as great as life ever gets; at least we thought so.

When the dining room at the hotel served a chicken dinner on Sunday, it began with the hired man and me chasing chickens around the backyard. The ladies in the kitchen prepared everything from scratch. My grandmother baked apple pies by the dozen while clad in a long dress with long sleeves with a lace cap on her head. She and Mrs. Chapman did all the cooking, and it was wonderful. Dinner was announced by striking a triangular bar of steel on the front porch with a rod. The hired man could make it sing; I could only get it to gong. He tried patiently to teach me, but somehow the lesson never took. Even fifty years later that failure pops into my mind; I call up the memory and intently watch him ring that device, searching for the secret. I get the same feeling watching a great golfer swing through the ball.

Bethesda was a great place to learn about yourself. I read a lot and watched what went on. My mother used to say that I was born forty years old. I figured out early in the game that if I took a few moments to do the things adults wanted done, they would leave me alone to do the things I wanted to do. Also I learned that I did not have to let them give me a lot of trouble. Walking around looking busy, with a smile on your face, is the best defense against adult control. I wanted to do things my way and did not respond well to procedural direction. This approach proved to be valuable when I went to work for real.

We belonged to the Cedar Rocks Country Club, which was up Big Wheeling Creek a few miles. The creek wound through the golf course and offered players the opportunity to dump balls into its clear water. My dad was the club champion, and I learned how to play when I was about eight, which has been wonderful for me. Unfortunately I never got as good at it as I could have because competition did not interest me. Still doesn't.

However, at Cedar Rocks I spent most of my time as a caddie, which paid seventy-five cents per round of eighteen holes for an A caddie and fifty cents for a B caddie. We had badges indicating which we were. Promotion to A came when a B took the badge from the shirt of the A. Tell me about the dog-eat-dog world of international management. The bags were light in those days, and I enjoyed the work. What I did not enjoy was taking off my clothes and diving into the creek to retrieve balls that had found their way into the ponds. The golfers did not expect to lose something you could see.

High school was a great experience. I can still remember more about those four years than perhaps any comparable period in my life. In those days the biggest problem was being caught in the hall during classes without an excuse in your hand. I was an 80 percent student, which was high enough to pass but not so high that they expected a great deal from you. I did get good grades in world history and algebra, just because I liked them. One teacher told my mother at a conference that she would like to get me to read two books a year. My mother replied that I read a book a week and that she spent all her time going to the library and back. When pressed I wrote up a list of recent reads for the teacher because she obviously did not believe us. Some of the books were Hardy Boys, some were history, and some were whatever was lying about. I just liked to read. Teachers often form their opinions of students without asking for the real story. Youngsters who are good at public relations keep adults informed about the wonderful things they are doing. They become Eagle Scouts; inefficient daydreamers like me remain Tenderfoots.

My dad had a lot of different interests at the same time; once he was the boxing commissioner of the state. This unpaid job resulted in enormous, and sometimes uncouth, people appearing at the house for dinner or a visit. My brother and I thought they were fascinating, but

Mom was not thrilled. One day Jack Dempsey came home with Dad. He was impressive. Somehow or other this visit led to our being invited to a special musical performance at the state penitentiary in Moundsville. The prisoners were performing a minstrel show. We went each year to the Elks minstrels in Wheeling, and I assumed that these were the same, which turned out to be an accurate guess. Most of the actors wore black face, which was the style, but they never let the black prisoners in the show. The talent displayed in the prison was better than in the Elks show. My dad and his friends commented that it was good for a youngster like me to see the prison. I would learn how bad it was to be in jail. However, it looked to me as though the performers were having a great time. I thought it would be a lot of fun to spend time doing plays and such. Later this experience helped me realize that it is dangerous to make assumptions about how someone else views what we both see. Those adults never understood that prison could appear to be an attractive place to a boy—no parental supervision, no school, and apparently a lot of fun things to do. Thank heavens I accumulated enough general knowledge later on to realize my error. I acquired that knowledge during my Navy years, when I conducted sick call in the brig.

In my senior year of high school I needed only two credits to graduate but was required to take four courses. So I selected typing as one of the extra subjects and manual arts as the other. Both were freshman courses. Manual arts consisted of three different studies: electricity, where we learned to hook up doorbells and such; mechanical drawing; and woodworking. I learned something useful in those classes. As the only boy in the typing class, I was under constant pressure to keep up. Seeing all the keys covered with black caps to hide the letters was a shock. But I liked typing; and although I never got good at setting margins or other regulatory skills, typing has come in handy. I would never have become a writer if I had had to depend on someone to type from my handwriting. And in this day of computer keyboards it is a decided advantage. I made a wooden clothes spoon for my mother in woodworking. It was used to pass clothes from the hot-water tub to the cold-water tub during washing. My kids have no idea what that is all about. Mom loved that stick and kept it with her even when washing machines became automatic.

My father did not want me to play football even though he was still remembered in Findlay as an all-star running back. He thought I would get hurt. So I was team manager for my freshman year and learned a great deal about laundry and water buckets. But the next year I disobeyed and signed up for football. I weighed 160 pounds, which was large enough in those days. We had a single-wing offense, like everyone else, and I played blocking back on the reserve squad. When Dad found out, he said he was disappointed in me but let me continue. Later I learned that he was proud that I had stood up to him, which I had a hard time understanding. My brother thought I was sneaky.

Becoming a member of the football community was a major learning experience for me. I enjoyed practicing, looked forward to scrimmage, and didn't care much about the real games. The next year, when I was second-string fullback and played enough to get a letter, I still enjoyed the practice workouts the most. Getting dirty together and pounding into each other helped us get to know ourselves while building a bond. The girls had a difficult time understanding the need for this male rite. But they pretended to. They just sort of put up with us in order to have escorts, I think.

About this time I worked up the nerve to ask a young lady to go to one of the Friday night club dances in the gym. She turned me down a couple of times but finally gave in, and after a while we went steady, which lasted for a couple of years, until I graduated. My initial reaction when she accepted my invitation was, "Why would she go out with me?" Romance with one's steady in those days consisted primarily of long embraces and closed mouth kissing. As far as I knew hardly anyone ventured far past that. After all, not much else happened in the movies with the actors we all used as role models. Married couples didn't even have double beds in the films, and everyone was fully dressed even when shipwrecked. Nobody ever went to the toilet in the films; they spent days together and never even stepped behind a bush.

One day I sought out a girl with whom I had a personal friendship that began in grade school. We were not romantically attached in the least but enjoyed each other's company. She didn't have a brother and I didn't have a sister, so we sort of filled those roles for each other. I asked to walk her home from school, and during that stroll I commented that as far as I could see no boy and girl, and no adults for that matter, had an honest relationship. They just did not know enough about the opposite sex to say what was on their mind. My misunderstandings with my steady had motivated this conversation. I wanted to see whether my friend and I could open up to each other, and then we would both be in a position to understand others better. I just didn't know what women thought about or what they wanted us males to do to them or about them. She considered my proposal until we reached her house. Then she kissed me on the cheek and stated that women wanted the same things that men did; they were just shy about it. She went inside and closed the door, smiling. I knew what men wanted, and I could not accept that women had the same low thoughts. We never talked about it again.

The school had dancing at noon in the gym, usually sponsored by one of the clubs. Admission was one cent, and the jukebox was pulled out of the closet to provide music. That was the era of the big bands, and the music was wonderful. The single-play 78 rpm records of Glenn Miller, Tommy Dorsey, Harry James, Benny Goodman, and others were all well known to us. We didn't mind the limitations that the war economy put on us; we didn't even drink many Cokes. Boys and girls danced together, arms around each other, in the traditional fashion, with appointed teachers watching carefully that bodies were not pressed too energetically together. Once in a while a couple was called aside and cautioned about this matter. Actually it just felt good; we didn't know about lewd.

The summer before my senior year of high school, 1943, I was able to get a job at Oglebay Park in Wheeling. This public park of several thousand acres had many cabins, two golf courses, a large swimming pool, a hundred picnic sites, and miles of nature trails. People came from all over the tri-state area to spend time at Oglebay. The park hired thirty or so boys to perform various tasks. All of us summer boys lived in a brown wooden building in the park called the White House, wore uniforms, and got paid little. But it was wonderful; I drove a pickup truck and cleaned up trash around the picnic sites.

Learned: *supervisors are always right; the supervised are always wrong, even when they are right.*

The new football coach had a summer job there also, and he started working with me on a formation he had dreamed up. The fullback (me) would receive the ball from the center and either run with it, spin around and hand off to the tailback or wingback, or throw it. We worked on the routine all summer, and when football practice began, he taught the rest of the team all about it. It worked well in scrimmage and gave us a versatility that did not exist in the plain single-wing formation.

However, when the scheduled games began, I learned about politics. The tailback, who called all the plays, did not like to have anyone else deal with the ball. He never called any of those fullback-spinning plays and told the coach that I had hurt my arm or something. For some reason the coach never insisted, and, of course, I would not speak up about it, which is a personal characteristic I have never understood.

Learned: *everyone has his or her own agenda.*

We didn't have a good year, winning only one game. But I still enjoyed myself because in those days the players played both offense and defense. I liked defense and was good enough to get honorable mention on the all-valley team. Several of my teammates thought it was a mistake, that the judges had confused my uniform number with someone else's. Things like that build self-confidence—not.

My internal priority machine worked in a somewhat strange manner. I observed its workings as if from a distance because there did not seem much I could, or should, do about it. I have never liked conflict or confrontation, and as a result I have never been very competitive, even today. It never made much difference to me if I won or lost at anything. I always did my best and worked hard at my assignment, but the outcome was not important to me. The things that I consider important usually are not obvious. I hardly ever keep score when playing golf, for instance. I can remember the score if necessary, but recording how many shots it takes to play a hole does not interest me. Executing good shots does turn me on, and just being out on the course is a great pleasure.

When it came to work performance, I wanted to do well, better than anyone had ever done; but if someone didn't notice my contribution and take advantage of it, I would never bring it up. Rather than promote myself I would just look for another situation. As a result, later in life I was able to advance quickly through the ranks of business without ever asking for a raise or promotion. But I was also disappointed when I worked for people who did not know what was happening around them.

Learned: *it is important to teach those in charge of you how to take good care of you.*

During adolescence I became convinced that I would be an eternal underachiever. The teachers considered me a daydreamer, with a quick wit when nudged, not much trouble, but not properly respectful. I wasn't insecure enough to be an authentic class clown, but I was probably close to it. I never got elected to anything or chosen to be something. My lighthearted view of the world convinced everyone that I was not all that bright. Because they all had authority and obviously knew more than I did, I accepted their opinion.

My father was one of those "idle hands are the devil's workshop" kind of people. In my early teen years he was after me to get a newspaper route to learn responsibility and make some spending money. But whenever I got any money, I just spent it. I found out that I was just as happy with it as without it, unless I needed it for something specific like a movie. The problem with going steady was that you had to buy the girl a ticket. But if you were just dating, it was permissible to meet inside the theater. For this reason a considerable amount of time was spent determining the exact state of relationships between couples. I liked to pay if I had any money; girls did not seem to care. They had a different relationship with their fathers than boys did. They could always get money and help.

Because Dad seemed determined about the newspaper route, I checked it out with a friend whose brother had been distributing papers for a year. The report I got was not encouraging. First of all there was the getting up at 5 A.M., meeting a truck on the corner, folding the papers (I failed this completely), then walking or biking around the route, rain, snow, or shine. On top of this people didn't pay on time, so the carrier had to retrudge the route each evening in order to pick up a few pennies. The newspaper company, however, always wanted to be paid on time. Digging up the money was not always easy.

With this fate about to be laid on me, I explained to my parents that because my brother was too little, they would have to deliver the paper any morning I was ill or away from home. We would also never be able to take a vacation or even go away for a few days. They were beginning to get the message about the paper route, but my father made it clear that I had to provide my own money from then on. He did not seem to care how or have any ideas that were usable. His world was an adult one where things were rational and documented. Mine was sort of mushy.

The A&P grocery chain had just opened the first of what we came to know as supermarkets at the end of our street. When I went there one day to get some things for Mom, I noticed that the carts were all over the parking lot. People left them there after loading groceries into their cars. When I pushed a few of them to the front of the lot, a young man motioned to me. He was the manager of the store and wondered whether I would like to round up baskets and do odd jobs. We agreed that I would do this job after school and on Saturday. Stores weren't open on Sunday, of course. Forgetting the urgency of buying the items on my mother's list, I started right away. I was so excited I forgot to ask the manager how much money I was going to earn. It turned out to be thirty-five cents per hour, which let me earn enough each week to take my steady to a show and put some gas in the car.

Not every family had a car in those days, and when they did, the father drove it to work. My mother was one of the few women who could drive. She took the car once in a while to do her errands and shopping. Sons, like me, got the car for a date when no one important needed it. None of the girls I knew were able to drive or showed much interest in doing so. But they got around by just asking and without having to pay the eighteen cents a gallon for gas. There wasn't any place to go in Wheeling anyway, so most of the gas was used driving around pretending not to look for a place to park and pet.

One day when the Ohio River was rising during the spring flood season, Dave helped the dock tender with a problem. A large houseboat with a floating dock attached to it served as the mooring place for all the boats. It was tied to the shore at Wheeling Island. The manager decided that he needed to measure how much the water was rising, but he couldn't make his yardstick stay in the ground. The water kept shaking it loose. Dave nailed it to the side of the houseboat for him, and he sat there watching it while the houseboat floated up over its moorings. My brother still smiles a special smile when I remind him of this trick.

While working at the A&P, I often carried groceries from the store to the homes of older ladies. Usually that was good for a tip, but mostly I did it because I didn't see how they were going to make it otherwise. One day one of these ladies said she would pay me fifty cents an hour to drive her where she needed to go after school and on weekends. She was particularly concerned about Sunday morning because she wanted to go to church on Wheeling Island. Public transportation was difficult to use at that time. I worked for her the last two years of school. My dad thought this was "sissy work." He felt that if you didn't sweat or suffer, it didn't count for much. I pointed out that he did little sweating and suffering in his job, but he attributed that to having gone to college. It was not a good policy, I learned, to question adults' logic.

Learned: *it is not to your advantage to go into the cave and poke the bear with a stick.*

The war effort was in high gear as I was preparing to finish my senior year. All the boys were talking about having to register for the draft when they turned eighteen years old. But I wanted to make my own choice; so I went down to the Marine recruiting station at the post office. The officer in charge took one look at my glasses, put his arm around my shoulder, and led me next door to the Navy station. The chief petty officer there explained to me that if I volunteered I would get the Navy but if I waited for the draft I could be in trouble. He also pointed out that if I did wait for the draft, it would probably be a year before I went into the service. I did not want to miss the experience, I told him.

It was apparent that I was healthy in all respects, but the Navy did have some requirements in regard to vision without glasses. Because I wanted to go to hospital-corps school, the officer thought I would always be in a situation where glasses could be worn. In preparation for the test he put me in a side room and said he would be back in twenty minutes. The test would require that I read the fourth line down on the chart on the wall without my glasses. When he left, I took off my glasses and the chart disappeared. It took me ten minutes to realize that he had left me there so that I could memorize the line, which I promptly did. When he returned I passed forward and backward. We pretended I had my parents' permission, needed at age seventeen, and he swore me in. This was in January 1944.

Learned: *being an adult is a lot more fun than being a kid.*

He instructed me to go back and finish high school. I would receive orders to report the morning after graduation. Did I want him to put my enlistment in the newspaper? That was absolutely against my wishes, so we kept our little secret. Frankly I was getting tired of the orderly life I led, where the most important thing was who was dating whom or who was not, and why not. There had to be a lot more out there in the world, and the service offered a way to see it. In later years as I became fascinated with history, I realized that boys who thought this way supplied the armies of Frederick the Great, Napoleon, and other adventurers. When you are seventeen, not many choices are available to you. I didn't say a word about my new career to a soul until just before graduation. Actually, I did tell the lady I was chauffeuring, but she wasn't too clear about there being a war and all.

Our parents were formalizing their divorce at this time. There was not much to distribute in the way of assets, and it became apparent that Mom was going to have to learn to support herself. She had obtained a job selling newspaper advertising in Columbus, Ohio. A friend had supplied the lead, and my mother made all the arrangements over the telephone, even finding a place to live. The judge asked Dave and me to state with whom we would like to live. Dave nodded to Mom, and I said that I was going into the Navy the next week. This announcement surprised everyone but solved a big problem. Supporting a woman and a small boy was one thing, adding a never-filled-up teenager, quite another.

Sure enough my orders came. The morning after graduation I went to the bus station accompanied by four of my friends, all boys. I have a photo of that group, taken by Dad, hanging on the hall. Each time I see it I marvel at how young we all were, although we all considered ourselves quite mature and sophisticated. Such perceptions are based on limited knowledge and experience. I did not consider that I "knew everything," but I was not the least bit worried about being able to get along in the real world. Life always looked like a movie to me anyway.

I had begun to experiment with smoking around this time, and when I found that an entire carton of Camels cost forty cents in the Navy, I figured smoking was a good way to pass the time. I began to smoke a pack a day and maintained that standard for some time. There is a lot of standing around in military life, and the procedure of lighting up and smoking helped pass the time. It let you think you were doing something. Who knew how harmful it was to us.

Navy boot camp was an experience for me in many ways but the most significant way was obtaining a new concept of myself. It turned out that I could run faster than most others my age (which I never thought I could do back home); it turned out that I finished in the top 4 percent of the Navy in intelligence tests; it turned out that I had no trouble doing all the drilling and exercising. Perhaps I wasn't a complete clod after all.

This newfound confidence was eroded a bit by my problem with recognizing enemy aircraft. They put us in a dark room and showed us a dozen photographs, one at a time, of these planes. I always wondered whether enemies traded photos or spies had to get them or just

Graduation photo, Triadelphia High School, 1944.

exactly where they came from. We were expected to be able to call out the names of the planes as soon as they appeared on the screen. I just couldn't get interested enough in airplanes to tell them apart. The same problem had presented itself with automobiles in civilian life; they all looked alike to me. One day, when it was apparent that my company was going to graduate without me, I realized that the slides were getting quite old and had cracks and other marks on them. I couldn't tell one plane from another, but those cracks spoke to me. They were different on each slide, so I learned which crack related to which plane. I scored 100 percent the next time. When I did come upon some real enemy planes during the Okinawa invasion, they went by so fast I could barely see the red circles on the wing tips. There were no cracks in the sky around them.

Boot camp probably made a larger impression on me than any other single institutional event. The completely different way of life, the personal challenge to make it in these circumstances, and the intensity of living with 119 strangers who became best friends were dramatic. I still know my serial numbers, the manual of arms, and all the other stuff we were taught. And I remember being the first in line, thanks to the alphabet, on the tower over a flaming swimming pool. We were in dungarees and life jackets and the idea was to hit the water and swim to safety without being burned. I was really uncomfortable with that. When the chief leaned over and told me to jump, pointing out that everyone would think I was a coward if I didn't, I jumped.

Like everything else we did in that line, it wasn't as bad as I had anticipated. But then it had been possible to figure that out in advance because thousands of men and women had already done it and they didn't die. As I was the only high school graduate in the company, I was regarded as something of a scholar and was asked to help read and write letters. We all took tests for several days to determine what we were going to do in the Navy. I was given the option of going to one of two schools: fire control or hospital corps. I thought fire control had to do with turning wheels in the engine room, so I quickly picked the medical services. It turned out that fire control was about aiming guns and that the fire-control school was in Fort Lauderdale and took six months. However, I was happy with my choice.

When I returned home from boot camp, resplendent in my white uniform, my girlfriend informed me that we couldn't be together because it would ruin her social life for the coming senior year. We hugged and parted friends. By this time I had discovered that girls liked the Navy uniform and were willing to accept that it came with a sailor. It was apparent to me that everyone in that small town was hopelessly provincial and behind the times. Six weeks made quite a difference. When Mr. Wolfe talked about being unable to go home again, this must be what he meant. I couldn't wait to get back to the real world.

Learned: *everything changes as soon as you change.*

A lot of ex-boots were going to San Diego from Great Lakes Training Center for one reason or another, so the Navy found four railroad cars from the First World War to get them there. The cars were mostly open but did have enough bunks; they were not uncomfortable provided you were seventeen or so years old. Tacked onto the back of an Army troop train, these cars set out for California. The Army train had its own canteen car but was all coach. The troops had no bunks as we did; they sat up with all their gear for five days. I was delighted that I had selected the Navy, even though the Army showed up better in the movies.

Hospital-corps school in San Diego was next. It was held in what had been an exposition park, near the zoo. I realized that I would have to try hard; the Navy took its medical responsibilities seriously. The key consideration was prevention. More soldiers and sailors had died from noncombat causes in all the wars of history than from enemy action. If we could keep our service people healthy and heal their wounds quickly, we would reduce the death toll. Inoculations against many diseases were routine, and penicillin and sulfadiazine were now available; using them helped cut down on the effect of wounds. We were expected to know how to maintain a health chart on every person within our command. We also learned nursing techniques and had a good survey of the contents of the body and its operating systems.

Learned: *the war movies are about the fighters, which is reasonable; but the ones who keep everything going are the functional people.*

Preventative medicine isn't all chemicals; there are social aspects of it also. Venereal disease, particularly gonorrhea, was prevalent in the Navy at the beginning of the war. Catching it meant a court-martial.

While you were in the hospital being cured, you received no pay, and the incident went on your service record. Someone finally figured out that no one was reporting the problem until he could not stand it any longer. The disease was then hard to cure, and the person also could be spreading the disease in the meantime. Making venereal disease a medical problem, like a cold, rather than a discipline charge meant that the condition could be found and treated quickly. We learned to recognize the symptoms and how to identify the disease early. As a result venereal disease became a small problem in the Navy.

In the fall of 1944 I joined my ship, an attack transport, the USS *Kenton (APA-122)*. It was brand new, and we were taking it on its first voyage. The ship was designed to carry about fifteen hundred soldiers or Marines, as well as the twenty-six attack boats that would carry them to the beach. Our medical department was larger than such a ship would normally have so that we could take care of casualties brought back from the beaches. This system worked out well during the cleanup of the Philippines and the invasion of Okinawa. Much of my time during combat was spent assessing the wounded as they came aboard to determine their place in the priority system. This was a heady responsibility for an eighteen-year-old, and I took it seriously. People could die while waiting for attention if their problem was not calibrated properly.

During noncombat times I worked in the sick bay each day seeing those of the ship's company or troops who had a problem. To my pleasure I found that I was rather good at this and could remain calm regardless of the situation. I liked people and enjoyed helping them feel better. I began to think about a career in medicine after the "great unpleasantness," as the guys called it, was over. We adapt to the environment as it exists. Thinking about the future while at sea during a war has little to do with reality. None of us had any information about what we could do except resume the lives we had left. It never occurred to us that things were changing back home. It was sort of frozen in time, like the movies we saw over and over. *Going My Way* was shown twice a week for six months until we were finally able to exchange it for *The Spirit of Stamford*. In a couple of weeks the crew was asking for Bing Crosby to come back. Death was about us all the time, but we never thought of dying. One of our group fell over the side one night during a storm. A year later I was still expecting him to stroll into sick bay.

Learned: *you can put a couple of thousand men in close quarters for a long time with no problems if they are convinced it is for a good reason.*

After the hostilities ended we traveled between Japan and San Francisco, returning veterans and taking new people out. We did not get much liberty in Japan, but we came to know Frisco well. We also enjoyed being welcomed home every month after our round trip. I still don't know why I didn't stay in California; it just didn't occur to me, and no one suggested it.

When the ship was scheduled to be decommissioned, we sailed to Norfolk via the Panama Canal. We counted everything that was left and shipped it to a warehouse, where I guess it still sits. Each day someone else's number was up, and they went home. I wound up with six weeks left to go and accepted an offer to join the Naval Reserve in return for being let out early. That was not one of my better deals.

Just before being discharged, I got home on leave for Easter. As we were eating dinner that day in Columbus, I had an attack of appendicitis. My family took me to an osteopathic hospital, and the surgery was done right away. In the Navy, where I participated in all kinds of surgery, we had a practice of keeping patients in bed for a few weeks after this operation. They suffered a lot of gas pains, but they got well. In Columbus it was different; they dragged me out of bed as soon as the anesthetic wore off and stood me on my feet. I protested that this was against modern medical science as practiced by the U.S. Navy. They were not impressed. When I walked out of the hospital four days later, I realized the Navy was behind the times. My experience since then has been that every big organization gets behind and suffers from it. So do their employees, customers, shareholders, and, in some case, patients.

Learned: *if you just accept what everyone else takes as the way to do things, you soon become brain-dead.*

CHAPTER TWO

A Podiatrist
in the Marines

he Navy offered a structured life. You always knew where you were supposed to be and what you were supposed to be doing. It wasn't always fascinating, but the system did eliminate the need to fend for yourself. Coming home was different. My plans were to go to college, but I wasn't certain which one or to do what. The GI Bill ensured that veterans could attend college, and I was entitled to a full education.

In that summer of 1946 many of my buddies signed up for West Virginia's "52-20" unemployment program, which gave them $20 a week for a year. They would meet at a tavern, and the person whose day it was would lay $10 on the table for beer, keeping the other $10 for his own expenses. As I said, this was a long time ago. I never got around to applying for it. I was waffling about what to do for schooling.

Dad took the initiative; he had arranged for me to enter the Ohio College of Podiatric Medicine in September, provided I could gain a full year's credits of pre-medicine that summer. The college was willing to accept my Navy medical work as half of it.

Learning: *if you don't have a plan, someone else will have a plan, and you probably won't like it.*

Because I had been practicing medicine in the Navy, which is what the sick-call corpsman does, I thought this was a good deal. So I went to West Liberty State College and took a bunch of accelerated courses all summer. I can remember only three things about that period: my roommate opened a fresh bottle of booze each morning and spent the day emptying it; the psychology professor taught us that the purpose of child psychology was to "help all these boys and girls do better all the worthwhile things they are going to do anyway"; and there was a blind woman in our class who took notes in Braille and typed her reports on a typewriter. As a result, I resolved never to be dependent on booze, to learn to help people rather than control them, and to start taking studying seriously. If that young lady wanted to learn that badly, then there was no reason for my being such a slouch.

In the fall I went to Cleveland and to the Ohio College of Podiatric Medicine. The dean and my dad were thick as fleas, which made my acceptance certain. There were only a hundred in each class. But it was apparent that I would have to work, and I found to my surprise that everything was easy if one listened and considered. All 206 bones of the body became my friends, especially the funny-shaped 26 in each foot, although I did memorize the histology slides by remembering imperfections in the glass. I always did well at benefiting from the past. However, podiatry was not like holding sick call in the Navy. It was far less interesting, but I stuck it out.

Learning: *when you decide you are doing the wrong thing, quit doing it because it probably is not going to get much more interesting.*

The college was situated next to Western Reserve University on the east side of Cleveland up past 105th Street. My roommate, Roy Harmon, and I found jobs moving lumber around a lumberyard and got a room near the college. (Roy and I had gone to Triadelphia High School together, played football and other sports on the same teams, and dated in the same circle. He didn't have a plan for his life either, so when I suggested foot-doctor school he thought it was a good idea. He is still practicing in Wheeling.)

Learning: *what is a good idea for one is not necessarily so for another, but that doesn't make it a bad idea.*

We ate most of our meals at a little joint where they sold meal tickets, which were then punched each time the holder sat down to eat. Pay for ten and the ticket credited you with twelve. One of my fellow eaters described it as "just right," meaning if it were any worse he couldn't eat it and if it were any better he couldn't afford it. The Navy trains you to eat whatever shows up and not to be too concerned about flavor.

The school was neat, efficient, and hard work. We spent the next three calendar years, four school years done thirty-six months in a row, in class and clinic. The professors were mostly practicing physicians and podiatrists who mixed the academic with the practical. Because of my recent Navy medical experience I had no trouble understanding the language of the professors or the material, so the subjects themselves were easy for once. However, I needed more credits for my pre-med work and had to attend Western Reserve University for a couple of classes and then Cleveland College, which was downtown, off the public square. All of these classes took a lot of time. At Cleveland College I was able to take two optional courses: abnormal psychology (called "nuts and sluts" by the students) and music appreciation ("clapping for credit").

Learning: *college is about going to classes, and the real world is supposed to tread water while the students immerse themselves in this artificial learning life; as a result they wind up with blank spots on the experience tape.*

A fellow student, Shirley Jones, and I fell in love and were married in 1947. Shirley quit school and went to work; I sold shoes at Higbees downtown; and we got along. She became a wonderful home manager; we lived in a place with a pull-down bed and an icebox that had ice delivered to it. When we went home for a holiday or such, she rode the bus and I hitchhiked.

I entered school broke, and I graduated below broke. I had taken state boards during the last weeks in school, so I was licensed to practice in West Virginia and Ohio. Other states were available on a reciprocity basis, except Florida and California, where the podiatrists were hostile. We decided to return to Wheeling so that I could work with my father for a while and learn the realities of the business.

This was good news in that we were now able to settle down a bit, but it was bad news in that we were still without the choices that money can bring. It is hard to build a practice from scratch, and the fee structure did not lend itself to earning significant income. The typical office visit was $3. Podiatrists were not permitted to do surgery at that time, and the work was not covered by insurance. We had a steady stream of patients, most of whom did not mind having to deal with a young doctor. But it was slow, and it was not easy working with Dad even though he was patient and generous.

Learning: *father and son have a hard time working together if they are doing the same thing; if one is the carpenter and the other is the plumber, they can do well.*

So I decided to set up shop in Moundsville, which was down the river twelve miles. We obtained a house using the GI mortgage at 4 percent interest. The house cost $7,000 and had three stories. We put the office on the first floor, we lived on the second floor, and we scratched out a little game room on the third. Money was short. Shirley went to work at Marx Toy Company, and that helped. But it was a losing proposition. Dad had bought a park and saloon five miles down the river at Fish Creek. I worked there a few nights a week, but all of this was going nowhere. We couldn't figure how to pull ourselves out of the pit we were sinking into.

Learning: *little towns don't have many patients in them.*

The only bright spot of this era was some new friends, Harry and Mary Hamm, who lived on the next street. Harry was editor of the *Wheeling News Register,* Mary was a writer, and they knew everyone. We met at the Wheeling Civitan Club, which I had joined in order to drum up some business. We attended the christening of their second baby (they eventually had twelve) and soon became very close. I wrote some pieces for the paper and found the newspaper life fascinating. It sure beat fixing feet. But there was no job for me there, and no one took my desire to write seriously. Eventually I just wrote until my work got published.

Learning: *you don't need someone else's approval to do what you want to do.*

Early in 1951 I received notice that I was going to be recalled to the Navy because the Marine medical corps had suffered many losses in the Chinese invasion of northern Korea. We both felt that this was a way out of our debt and dead-end business, and I went off willingly. Shirley would go back to Pittsburgh for a few months until I got settled or shipped out. She would work to support herself, and we would use the allotment money to pay off our debts. The house was sold for exactly what we owed by a lawyer who may be the first person I ever decided I did not like. We had a few farewell parties, I delivered Shirley to her parents, and I went off to Norfolk, Virginia.

Learning: *people take advantage of you when you don't have any money; they equate that with lack of power.*

The train ticket the Navy sent me had a coupon attached that was good for a meal in the dining car. As I looked at the menu, I saw that amount of money specified on the coupon covered most of what I wanted to eat. From my previous experience, I knew that the dining-car people would take my coupon and give me a substandard meal in return. So, after eating, I used the coupon to pay most of the bill and added enough to cover the remainder plus tip. The conductor went ballistic. A Navy captain sitting across the way straightened him out by saying that the Navy did not specify any meal and noting that he had done the same thing with his coupon.

When the furor died down, the captain asked me to tell him what I was about. He was a veteran of the South Pacific also, and as we chatted it became apparent that we had been in many of the same places. He had heard of the *Kenton* and shared a can of beer on Mog Mog with some of her officers. Mog Mog was a strange little fleet recreation isle in the Ulithi Atoll. After hearing my story, he wondered why I did not ask for a commission instead of returning as a third-class petty officer. He was serving in Washington in an administrative post and offered to introduce me to the proper person if I could get up there. I agreed to take that suggestion under advisement because officer life was much better than enlisted life. When I said that I was almost certain to be assigned to the Marines, he told me to be careful because the Korean conflict was not going well and it was dangerous over there.

Learning: *if I had accepted the offer made in my first real conversation with an authority figure, I would now be retired from the Navy and would have missed the next couple hundred pages.*

I decided at that moment that I must be maturing because I received the first cold tremor of fear ever to invade my mind and body. During all those World War II months of living with enemy planes crashing into ships and handling the wounded or dying, I was never afraid.

Apparently that is why young warriors are the best. Now, suddenly, I was scared, but I shook it off. Later that evening I decided that this must be a rite of life like the first sexual experience.

When I reported to the receiving station at Norfolk, the Navy came rushing back to me; I remembered everything. But this time I knew what I had to do and what was not required. I had my physical, received a sackful of clothes, and found my bunk. The master at arms (MAA) told me that I had a day to get settled and then would be processed for a week or so before being assigned. He also noted that I would need to get my uniforms tailored, which consisted mostly of having the pant legs cut and sewed, by the next afternoon. He also told me that the tailor shop was backed up two weeks. The Navy had not changed.

In my previous internment this would have stumped me. But, being an old salt, I just selected two outfits from the duffel bag, took a piece of paper from the bulletin board that looked like a regulation, and walked out the gate, waving it at the guards.

Learning: *a confident stride and purposeful look can get you anything in the service.*

I knew that there would be a tailor shop or two just down the street, and as it turned out there were four of them. The last one in the row looked to be the least busy so I went in and arranged to have the tailoring done while I went to get a beer and a sandwich. They offered to make me a set of "tailor-mades," which every sailor needs because the standard-issue uniforms don't fit that well. But I told them I was going to be an officer or a Marine, or both, in a few days, so we agreed to wait.

Two hours later I marched back in the gate in full uniform, including rates and battle ribbons, with my civies under my arm. The guards and I waved at each other. The MAA didn't say a word when he saw me, just handed me a schedule of events for the next day.

Three days of testing and probing resulted in an interview with two officers. They reported that I was in the top 4 percent of the Navy (I was beginning to wonder whether they told everyone that), including admirals, and that they would like to offer me a deal on the base. They would assign me to the hospital-corps school, get me base housing, and have me promoted to chief petty officer on a temporary basis. It would become permanent in a year. I could bring my wife down, and they would guarantee that I would never get out of Norfolk for the remainder of my enlistment, which was fourteen more months. I accepted immediately and was told to come back the next afternoon at 2 P.M. to begin processing.

Learning: *in a strange place, with unknown people, it is easy to assume that everything is going to be as they say it is going to be.*

Back in the barracks the MAA handed me a packet of orders to report to the 2nd Marine Regiment at Camp Lejune, North Carolina, for assignment to the field medical service school. The bus was leaving at 6 P.M. that night, and I would be on it. I told him about the offer I had just received, and he suggested that I go see those officers and get released from these orders. Like the wind I dashed over to the office only to arrive at a scene from *Gaslight*. No one there knew exactly who those guys were; they had just used the office to talk with me. Calls to the hospital-corps school were to no avail. I returned to the barracks, where the MAA offered to help me pack. He thought that they would track me down and I would be coming back in a few days. That was forty-six years ago, and I have not heard from them yet.

The Marines get their medical services from the Navy. Each platoon has at least one corpsman living with them, and the company has a couple more. Battalion headquarters (H&S company) has a doctor or two and a small mobile hospital. When the operation goes into the field, which it does all the time, medical care goes right along with it. The first purpose of the field medical service school was to teach us how to do that part; the second part was to make us tough enough to accomplish the first part. This was the master's school of boot camp. We marched Marine-style, pretended to fight, dug holes and slept in them; we learned to eat a meal from a little package; and in a few weeks we were certified "jarheads," which only Marines can call Marines.

Learning: *we can never assume that people are prepared to do a job different from the one they have been doing; training is a must for everything.*

It was difficult work that lasted three months, but I rather liked it. There were no bill collectors, no patients coming or not coming; and everyone was in the same boat. We lived simply, in the field most of the time. I became a master at cutting up a cookie can to create a stove on which to heat cans of beans and spaghetti or brew coffee. We attacked the beaches of North Carolina, froze in the bushes, and got to know more about ourselves. In the midst of one concentrated set of war games we heard a bell and were delighted to see Happy Dan the Ice Cream Man and his truck cruising through the woods. We cleaned him out.

Learning: *you can deal with anything if you don't have a hidden agenda.*

Upon graduation I reported to the 2nd Marines and was promptly assigned to hold sick call in the H&S hospital. It wasn't long before life was moving along smoothly. Shirley was comfortable with her parents, and I was able to get to Pittsburgh every other weekend by driving earnestly with a few other people ($15 round-trip) for twelve hours each way.

People kept coming and going all the time. The 1st Division was in Korea, and it needed replacements. Each day I had several Marines who needed their health record brought up to date by receiving shots or getting physicals. I found that I would not be going to Korea because I had been on active duty in the previous war.

Learning: *don't question anything that helps you even if the reason seems stupid.*

I found an apartment in New Bern and brought Shirley down. We were able to get an old Dodge, and I drove it up to Pittsburgh. On the way back, in Cumberland, Maryland, the car blew a ring and quit working. This was Sunday afternoon, and I had to be back in the camp the next morning. We found a garage that was part of a used-car lot, the only one open in town. The man there said it would take several days to get my car fixed, so I asked him about a Studebaker Champion he had for sale. He took pity on us, and we worked out a deal that involved signing a lot of papers with no transfer of money. After he bought us a lunch, we were ready to be on our way. When we thanked him, he just said that perhaps we could do something similar for someone else one day. I said we would. I think I have never had a car I liked as much as that one.

Learning: *the seed was planted in me for helping those who need a little help.*

In May 1952, when my time was up, I was sent to Charleston, South Carolina, to be ready for discharge, which took only a few days. My mother came down to join us, and we had a wonderful weekend in Charleston before driving to Columbus, Ohio. We had agreed that we were not going to spend more time in the medical field because it just didn't turn me on enough. I wanted to do something with my life, and we were tired of never having any money. We were able to get jobs with firms in Columbus—Shirley with an insurance company and I with an editing group that was classifying the equipment in the Columbus Army Depot. I never understood why they were doing it or who was going to use the information, but it was a job. We were able to settle our debts, get some furniture, and begin to feel like real people. However, we needed to find career jobs, so I began to look around.

Learning: *there is a defining moment when one takes charge of one's life rather than being part of an organization.*

PART TWO

Learning the Need for a Quality Reformation

CHAPTER THREE

Discovering Industry

The Crosley Corporation's plant in Richmond, Indiana, about ninety miles away, was looking for technicians. I learned that from the Ohio State employment office. So I wrote to them, and they invited us over for an interview. While I talked to the people at the plant, Mom and Shirley looked over the town; they liked it. Mom was going to stay in Columbus, but we would be going back and forth. The company offered me a job, at $315 per month; we found a one-bedroom apartment inside a big house, and everything was settled. I was going to be a junior electronic test technician working on classified government equipment. Everyone was polite enough to avoid commenting that I knew little about electronics. I told them my degree was in pre-medicine and didn't bother mentioning being a podiatrist. I thought they would figure I wasn't serious about their job. When it came time to get a security clearance, I had to come clean only to find that they didn't have the slightest interest in my education.

Richmond was the typical midwestern small town in 1952. Everything revolved around friends, homes, and jobs. I don't remember going to a movie all the time we were there. Even though both of us had jobs, we were still skimping along. Our biggest expense was the car payment, but there was no way to have life without a car. However, I felt that I could grow in business if I could just find the right set of levers.

Learning: *the greatest gift my parents placed in my DNA was the gene for being an optimist.*

The Crosley plant was a large operation with two separate buildings. In one they built the Crosley refrigerator, three a minute, and the whole process was vertically integrated. I worked in the other building, where we built fire-control systems for the B-47 airplane. This system consisted of a gun turret and an antenna with a revolving dish. It was mounted in the tail of the plane and fired automatically from the cockpit. It was the only armament on the aircraft. I guess they figured there was no need to fire anything forward.

The first time I looked down on the machine shop from the walkway I knew that I had found a home. Here were people planning and making things. You could get your arms around this place, or at least I thought you could. My work area was in a windowless large room where the antennas were assembled. The people in there all were much more experienced than I and used a language that was not familiar to me. I imagined that they would be just as lost in my sick bay. So I listened carefully and tried to follow what the boss was saying to me. All the instructions were verbal; nothing was written down. My comment that we dealt with folklore rather than science was not appreciated; it became a companywide joke that no one seemed to get.

Learning: *when coming to a new place it is good to be quiet and pleasant for a while; if you are smart, they will figure that out.*

Fortunately he assigned me to the collimating device, which was not electronic. The key to the rotating antenna system was a casting that had machined holes in all four sides. This configuration let them hook up azimuth and elevation-movement gimbals. It was necessary to know how far away from being exactly perpendicular the unit was. Then an adjustment could be made in the gun sight. This whole operation was done with a set of mirrors. The entire antenna was mounted on a platform, and the mirrors were looked at through scopes. It took me a while to learn how to do this, but soon I was able to perform about two of these adjustments a day. In the meantime I began to study electronics and found that there was not a great deal to it if one could understand the vacuum tube. That was like saying medicine was no big deal if the cardiopulmonary system was understood.

Learning: *complex tasks are made up of a concept and a bunch of little steps; if you can understand the concept, the task is yours.*

As I was trying to fit into this new life, an accident changed my situation. The engineering supervisor was adjusting one of the antennas while it was whirling. These antennas were made of magnesium and were very hard and sharp. As he moved the antenna into an elevated position, it snapped back and the edge sliced an artery on the inside of his wrist. Blood spurted across the room. Nothing panics people like spurting blood, but to me it was old hat. I grabbed his wrist, stopped the bleeding, got him up on the table, and went to work trying to prevent shock. In the meantime I asked someone to call for an ambulance. They took him away bandaged and smiling. I went back to my bench.

All of a sudden people began to treat me differently. I was no longer just another fumble-fingered technician; I was an individual worthy of some respect. After that everyone helped me learn, and I received several opportunities to assume additional responsibilities. When I suggested that we could measure just the central casting for alignment rather than the entire antenna, which saved thousands of dollars in rework costs alone, the idea was accepted immediately. A month earlier the same suggestion had been greeted with disdain. The Lord always looks out for me in ways like this.

Learning: *suggestions, to individuals or organizations, have to be made in a context that doesn't make the suggester look too smart.*

I was asked to join the American Society for Quality Control (ASQC) section in Richmond. This group was made up of quality-control people from various companies in the area and was part of the national organization. At my first meeting the speaker was a nationally known consultant who talked about the laws of probability and the concept of acceptable quality levels (AQLs). Because worker errors are inevitable, and it would cost an enormous amount of money to get everything right, companies need to determine the quality level they can afford and work toward that goal. He talked about statistical quality control and suggested that we learn how to determine standard deviations and such. There was a bright future in quality control everyone thought. We were the army that protected the customer.

I told Shirley that night that I thought we had found the niche in life we were looking for. The concepts they use in quality control are exactly the opposite of those used in medicine. Instead of preventing problems or curing a disease, they keep great records of who died and what they died of. The whole thing is hard to understand, I noted, and management has not a clue of what it is all about. If someone could sort out the ideas of quality control and explain them so that they made sense, that someone would be well received. The conventional approach to quality needed to be reformed.

Learning: *those who are truly expert in a field live in the past and keep adjusting what they already know in order to meet the needs of the present; they have a mental block about the future.*

On the assumption that this opportunity might be mine one day, I visited the Toastmasters Club to see whether they could help me learn to speak. My first assignment was to stand up in front of a group of strangers and give a two-minute talk on "mirrors." When I sat down, in a little under the allotted time, my socks were soaking wet and my shirt dripped water on the seat. It was terrifying but exciting. I knew that I needed a lot of work, so I joined. The club met weekly at a restaurant that served fried chicken dinners for $1.25. Most the time I could not afford the dinner so I timed my arrival for when everyone had finished eating. As time went on we became more financially secure, and I was able to join the others on most occasions. Toastmasters changed my life. I began to gain confidence in my thought process and started a little club newspaper entitled *Speak Up*. Everyone liked it; we bootlegged it through the Crosley mimeograph machine.

In these years many useful opportunities arose, including my first supervisory job. I included a few stories about these experiences in my 1992 book, *Completeness*. One I did not mention was about my first tour in the press shop as a supervisor. Understand that this was a temporary job because of lack of work in the antenna-test area. I received the same pay as I did for my regular job—so that they wouldn't have to lay me off, I guess. I found that few of the operators could read blueprints or do the math necessary to set up the machines properly. This explained why the material-disposition area was so busy. I started an informal after-hours school to teach blueprint reading, and it was well attended. The company did not like it at all.

After the first year I got a $20 a month raise and the same after the second year. I was not going to get anywhere here, that was obvious.

Also I was not certain that the place would be around too long. We had had a strike the previous summer, and relationships were not good. Managers showed up only once in a while to hassle us and left things to the foremen. It was becoming apparent to me that I was going to have to move on.

Learning: *organizations do not have feelings; they do not actually exist.*

I had been taking evening courses and reading biographies of people who had become successful. The one thing they all seemed to have in common was the ability to communicate. All that took was work and having something to communicate about. No one was the slightest bit interested in my thoughts on quality. The reason, I decided, was that I did not have it clear in my own mind. So I quit talking about it and began to concentrate on what would happen if someone actually tried to prevent problems. I began to make little changes to see how they worked. None of the bosses were interested; they concentrated solely on getting fire-control systems out the door.

I began to realize that no one had a definition for the word *quality.* The ASQC as well as the company treated it as meaning "goodness." That definition made everything a matter of opinion. It took only a small trip through the shops to realize that those little groups of arguing people were trying to decide whether products had quality. One person would say a part was fit for use; another would say that it wouldn't work. Finally a decision would be made, and the part would move on. I thought that we should be producing products that matched the drawings and specifications exactly. If that was not feasible because of inadequate equipment, then we needed to change the requirements. But that change would eliminate opinions, and no one likes that possibility at all.

Learning: *quality is conformance to the requirements, not "goodness"—my first Absolute of Quality Management.*

During a strike we were kept out of the plant for a few days, which we put to good use playing golf on the Elks course (nine holes) on the east side of town. However, one morning we were waved into the plant (while we were sitting in the car with golf shoes on) and told that we were not permitted to do our regular work but would be loading refrigerators in boxcars. This was a good deal because we could easily have been laid off until the strike was over. The refrigerators, packed in cardboard boxes, were sent on a conveyer belt from the warehouse to the boxcar siding. When they reached the designated boxcar, they were tipped and put on a handcart to be taken inside the car and stacked. The plan was to put sixty-six in each car. Three of us worked together in each team.

The foreman told us that his teams did four cars a day and that we would certainly not be able to keep up with that rate but should do the best we could. We asked him whether we could leave when four cars were full. He found this to be chuckling funny but agreed and strolled off to tell his buddies about us. The secret of loading cars is to receive a constant supply from the warehouse, so we went there and talked to our colleagues, who were plucking boxes from the five high stacks and placing them on the belt. They went to their boss and asked whether everyone could leave when each gang had stuffed four cars, and their bosses agreed. The second day we all left before lunch with four cars full and no more to load. The supervisors came back, opened the cars, and counted the machines to make certain we had done our work. We thought getting paid to play golf a good incentive and besides the job was not very interesting. When the strike was over, the schedule went back to four a day: one before coffee break, and one after; one before afternoon break, and one after.

Learning: *people perform to the standards of their leaders unless an alternative standard is more important to them.*

When the refrigerator line was rolling, I used to like to slip over and watch the three guys who fitted the doors. They opened and closed each door and then used rubber-coated bars and sledges to adjust it to a tight fit. They were masters at it, but I often wondered why someone did not design the machine and the process so that the door did not need this adjustment. The assembly area there also had an office up in the air where the superintendent sat looking at a graph of the work line that was the size of a Ping-Pong table. Each station was indicated on the graph by red and green lights. If something stopped working, the red light went on, and the superintendent rushed to the floor. Everyone said you had to get it fixed before he came down and fired you.

In Wheeling I had joined the Elks Club (BPOE), to which Dad had belonged for some time. The organization was good for business and social contacts and, in more practical terms, was one of the few places you would choose to eat in Wheeling. But I discovered its real value as we entered this new life. Because of the BPOE there was a place in almost every town where I would not be a stranger. It was possible to drop in at the Elks and chat with businessmen who quickly provided an accurate picture of what that town was like and what was happening. The Richmond group made it clear to me over a period of time that I would not be able to carve out a future there. We were going to have to move on when we were ready.

Learning: *real people have real information.*

The doctors had told us that we would not be having children the old-fashioned way, so we decided to see whether we could adopt a child. It seemed a forlorn hope; we were barely getting along financially, had no savings, and had no profession that promised future growth. However, we applied anyway, and much to our surprise we were accepted. In due time we became the parents of an eighteen-day-old boy whom we named Philip Jr. I hated to saddle the kid with the "Junior" part but I wanted to make certain that he knew he was wanted and that I was proud of him. Shirley quit work, we got kicked out of our apartment because of the child, and I realized for the first time in my life that I had to get serious about working. It was February 1955.

The strategy that had evolved in my mind was that learning everything about some function like engineering, manufacturing, marketing, or finance was not the way to get ahead. The key lay in being considered useful and reliable. I found that I was good at understanding problems and that people would tell me things they would not share with management or others. By nature I was always on time and careful about completing the tasks I had agreed to do, and I was always where I was supposed to be. These are not remarkable traits, but they are unusual.

Learning: *don't get typed; I was considered eccentric by the quality professionals, which saved me from that.*

The machine-shop foreman asked my boss to lend me to him for a few days. He was concerned about the low productivity in his shops compared with that of identical shops in Cincinnati. Weeks of study by the industrial engineers and other folks had not revealed the answer. He thought I was "intuitive" and might come up with something. I finally realized that the operators had the habit of going to the rest room three or four times an hour to grab a smoke. There was no smoking in the shop because of an agreement made earlier. The thought was that smoking slowed productivity. The operators went back to smoking on the job, and productivity went back up. The general foreman sent me back upstairs, and that was the last I heard of it.

Learning: *the solutions to complex problems are not complex.*

By searching the Indianapolis and Chicago papers in the public library and by networking as best I could, I turned up a few options for new jobs. My salary at Crosley was now up to $345 a month, and I had a couple of other jobs. One of these, admittedly seasonal, was selling Christmas trees. However, one year I made $40, which was enough to take us to Pittsburgh for the holidays.

I had made up my mind to become an executive. I wanted to change the way companies worked, and I wanted to make a proper living for my family. That was never going to happen on an assembly line. I would have to learn how to be so useful to management that they would take me into the tent. Toastmasters and writing were helpful, but I needed a job where I could learn how to get things done. I searched the papers from the Midwest looking for it.

Learning: *no one is going to find a job for you.*

That place turned out to be Bendix-Mishawaka, the Bendix missile plant located in the twin city of South Bend, Indiana. They offered me $460 a month, and we were able to find a two-bedroom house in Twyckingham Hills. The name was classier than the neighborhood, but we really liked the area.

Learning: *when it comes time to move, move everybody because sending the person with the new job to find a house and then moving everyone is a distraction; kids, and adults, handle the move better than the uncertainty.*

Bendix and the Navy were making the TALOS missile, which was a surface-to-air, radar-beam-riding ram jet. I was going to be a reliability technician in the assembly area. This job involved investigating defects found by the inspectors and testers, then classifying them according to seriousness, cause, and responsibility. After that I would try to get permanent corrective action. By now I had learned that no one was expected to know everything and that it was all right to ask the most basic questions. The key was to be able to understand the answers enough to pull the complete story together. If one was pleasant about it and didn't accuse anyone of anything, the truth would work its way out. Then the problem could be approached with the idea of preventing it from happening again. I quickly learned that nothing was ever as it was supposed to be, and no one was ever going to admit being personally responsible for anything that went wrong. As in every other place, I found hard-working, dedicated people busily meeting AQLs. Worse, they believed that they were thinking about quality in the proper way.

Learning: *the way to achieve quality is through prevention, not detection and correction—my second Absolute of Quality Management.*

The failure data that the other reliability people and I created went into an IBM machine via punched cards and was used to analyze the worth of the missile and the systems that made it up. Reliability, as they defined it, was a new approach to statistical quality control and used equations to determine how good each system had to be if the missile was going to accomplish its mission most of the time. It was like awarding the World Series rings after spring practice based on statistical assumptions. It drove me nuts, but I kept my opinions to myself.

I made up a flow chart of the missile's assembly and testing. In this chart I listed the most frequent defects and determined whether they were caused by workers, design problems, component failures, or the process itself. When these causes were examined one by one, it was apparent that each could be prevented. Workers could be trained, designers could have information that showed them what caused the problem, and suppliers could get their processes straight. My message was that problems were not caused by the laws of probability or statistics. We caused problems ourselves and could stop doing it. I detected a brief glimmer of light, but no one was really interested in prevention; fixing things was much too interesting. The customer also paid for it, premium money at that. There was little motivation to make things right when we were being paid to do it over again.

Learning: *when you are on a crusade, go by yourself; some disciples may abandon their boats and follow you, but don't count on it.*

The Navy decided that it wanted some films on reliability and sent in a crew to do a few shots. They did one scene with a naval officer behind a desk insisting that the missiles had to be better. I stood around watching it and during a break pointed out to the director that the actor was wearing an Army officer's shirt. I immediately was appointed to provide technical support, which was a lot of fun. A bit later they decided to do a thirty-minute film called *TALOS, Deadly When Reliable.* I wrote much of it and got a nice exposure to film-making through the course of its production. However the theme still was "we're trying hard but we're only human." I just didn't have the words and experience to change their minds. An artist, Bill Johnson, and I created some posters and booklets trying to explain reliability to the world of TALOS, but it had little impact.

Learning: *providing education about quality was going to be the key to any success I would ever have in changing the philosophy of managing.*

The family's financial status was a little more secure, but with Shirley being at home it did take more to live on than we were making. We both felt that our child needed a parent with him in person in order to have a proper base in life. So I got a part-time job at Gilbert's, a men's store in South Bend. Working on commission, selling shoes and whatever else Mr. Gilbert wanted me to, I was able to bring home $50 to $60 a week, which Shirley translated into food, clothes, and a nice warm home. Gilbert's was an education in itself, which I have written about elsewhere. I was good at retail sales because I liked dealing with people who came into the shop on their own. I never was comfortable in situations where the salesperson went out and bagged customers, talking them into wanting to buy something. Helping them find what they needed and showing them how to use it I liked.

Learning: *the success the retailer had was the result of hard work by managers who stayed close to the customers; industrial management does not take customers that seriously.*

When I first set foot on the assembly floor in Bendix, I went around and introduced myself to all the manufacturing managers. From the superintendent down to the assistant supervisors they were positive and professional to work with; they took good care of me and were patient with my learning process. I didn't find out until later that none of my colleagues in the quality and reliability department had ever done anything like that. They contacted superintendents only when there was a problem. Understanding the impact of politeness came in handy as I moved along in my career. It wasn't that I was extra considerate; it was that hardly anyone else was considerate at all. The comparison was beneficial and helped me be recognized as someone who had empathy with working folks.

Learning: *treat people with respect and they will return the favor.*

My mother had died earlier in the year (1956) from heart failure. Dad was sick; he had had a stroke while on a boat in the Ohio River, fell in, and was pulled to safety by a friend. But he never fully recovered and died on his fifty-eighth birthday, that same year, at his sister's house in Findlay. My boss said I could take a couple of days off for the funeral, with pay, so we drove to Findlay for his services. When I came back the personnel department reported that I had not been there long enough to earn time off so they were not going to pay me. But the boss, Dick Dertinger, went around to the other members of management with a hat in his hand and took up a collection, saying that their word had been given. He forced me to take the money, which did help us, but I have always remembered his gesture more than the cash.

My brother and I borrowed some money from the Ohio Bank in Findlay, with Uncle Harold as cosigner, in order to pay for our parents' funerals. About a year later an insurance company in Columbus called Dave and told him that Mom had had a policy with the last company she worked for and they wanted to send us $5,000. We paid off the bank and split the remainder, getting about $1,800 each. I used my part as a down payment on our little house, which we purchased for $10,750. It was 1,100 square feet, and it was ours. I mowed the grass with a hand-powered mower. Skip (our nickname for Philip Jr.) had a toy mower that was about as effective as mine, and we worked together each weekend.

Learning (again): *family is much more important than work.*

After I had been with Bendix a few months, the manufacturing superintendent invited me to join the monthly poker game at his house. They played nickel and dime draw poker, "guts to open, trips or better to win." This meant that if you dropped out of a pot, you were out until it was settled. I learned to play cautiously so I could enjoy the fellowship and still buy my lunch once in a while between paydays. When I sat down to play the first time, the host said that they should clean me out quickly because I would not be sticking around the company for long. They kidded me that I was destined for better things, although I had never said anything along that line to any of them. In fact I didn't even think about it. My goal was more like making a thousand dollars a month. That would be a fortune.

A few weeks later my boss was promoted. He had a little glass office, and we all sat in a row of desks outside. He moved upstairs; the guy in the first desk, who was most senior, moved into the office; and we all moved one desk forward. I was now six desks from the office. In only ten years or so I could be a supervisor. I had been there a little over a year and half; I realized that it was time to get moving.

Learning: *coworkers can recognize talent when they see it, but personnel and top management can't tell one of us from the other.*

Part of my work was to go to suppliers' plants to see whether we could help them send us more reliable components and materials. The contacts and travel involved let me learn a great deal about what went on away from the plant floor. Most of the folks I dealt with spent little time on that floor and did not have much of a relationship with workers. I took our film to these plants and showed it to the people who were working on products for TALOS. This part of the job gave me some speaking experience. It also let me know that the dedication to making a few things wrong in every operation was as sincere a belief as any in the American Dream. Machine shops issued 10 percent more raw material than necessary in order to cover what would be wasted. No one I met felt that this was a problem at all. The thought leaders of quality control grew irritated with me when I brought that up at ASQC meetings. I was admonished to listen more carefully and study harder. It was becoming clear to me that I was on the right track. None of these people had any medical experience, few of them ever worked on a line, many were college professors; there was no reason they should know any different. Besides, if the concepts and techniques of quality control were so complex they could not be understood by management, we were assured of a living. But we were wasting a lot of effort and making a lot of extra work in the process.

As far as my own career was concerned, I was learning that companies were not prepared to recognize that people could learn how to do much more than they were doing. They had no mechanism for recognizing that Albert Einstein was working in the mailroom and should immediately be made chief of research. If you came in at a low level, you would always be viewed at that level even if you made progress in how you performed. Performance reviews and personality evaluations were no help. I took a day's worth of tests only to learn that I could be considered stubborn or at least "firm." I already knew that. No one had any faith in the reviews because they were tied to raises. If the supervisor wanted to give you a 6 percent raise, it was necessary to provide an "above average" rating.

Learning: *personnel-rating systems are to personnel rating as military music is to music.*

I wanted to be an executive, and Bendix-Mishawaka was not where it was going to happen; there was only one good job there, and even it wasn't too important as far as the corporation was concerned. Gilbert's offered me a good salary to work for them, but it would be the same work for the next fifty years, although Mr. Gilbert might eventually let me stand in the front of the store and greet customers. We liked South Bend and had many good friends there, but it was a tough place to live. I often say in speeches that Mishawaka is an American Indian word meaning "begins to snow on Labor Day and quits on Memorial Day."

I constantly read the help-wanted pages in the major newspapers and the trade magazines, and kept my senses working as I traveled about. In February 1957, on a trip to Boston, I read in the want ads of the Boston paper that a company was looking for reliability engineers and they were interviewing right there in the Statler Hotel. During an hour's chat, in which I was able to show them the material we had developed, they indicated they were interested. We arranged that I would meet my potential boss at the O'Hare Airport the following week for an interview. When that went well, I was offered a job as a senior quality engineer for the Martin Company in Orlando, Florida. The salary was $640 a month plus the usual benefits.

Learning: *in an interview one sells oneself; the attitude one presents is 99.86 percent of the deal.*

It was obvious that the Lord wanted all this to come about. Someone walked up to our house and offered to purchase it for $11,200, which was a little more than we had in it. We accepted immediately, and I gave notice at Bendix. They were beginning to thin their ranks, so no one even asked me to stay. That was reassuring. We packed the contents of our house and took off for Orlando with Skip's tricycle in the trunk of the car. Its bell rang each time we hit a bump. The car was a year-old Chrysler. I had realized that we were not in a position to pay for repairs on a car, so I traded every couple of years for a new one before breakdowns began. About twenty thousand miles was where problems began, according to my anecdotal research. If you did it right, trading in cars this way also gave you relief for a couple of months from car payments. So the key was not how much the cars cost; it was the amount of the payment. I dreamed of not having a car payment.

We arrived in Orlando in May 1957, checked into a motel, and set about finding a house. We needed one that was empty because our household goods were on the way. We didn't want to spend more than a couple of days doing this. We were able to come up with a brand new one at 2800 Vine Street on a lot with no grass and eight aging but productive orange trees in the backyard. Of course it was built of cement block; but it was raised off the ground a couple of feet so the builder could lay hardwood floors, which were unusual for Florida. It cost $16,500 and required a little more of a down payment than we could muster, so we wound up with a small second mortgage. The whole street was new; the neighbors were mostly beginning at Martin, which was in the process of moving to Orlando from Baltimore. We planted grass plugs and learned to deal with the summer heat. No one had air conditioning; they all said you didn't need it, but actually they couldn't afford it.

Learning: *it is a good idea to buy a little more house than you actually need; it saves at least one later move, and paying for it motivates the wage earners.*

Life began again in a new place, with new people, with new opportunities.

CHAPTER FOUR

On the Road to Comprehension
The Martin Company

T he Martin Company was founded by Glenn L. Martin, who, like other founders of corporations in that era, was an original. He had an apartment inside the Baltimore plant, was a baseball fanatic, and helped create an entire industry. The company did well in World War II, and afterward it ventured into commercial aircraft production. It designed a two-engine, unpressurized passenger plane called the 202, which worked out well. Then Eastern Airline's Eddie Rickenbacker wanted a new plane, so Martin agreed to build a 404, which was planned to use something like 80 percent of the same parts as the 202, be pressurized, and fly higher and faster.

The contract was at a fixed price for each aircraft, and Rickenbacker appointed himself the unofficial program manager. He appeared regularly at the plant to keep track of what was and was not happening. One of the stories about him concerns the time he came to the assembly line and walked to the back of a framed plane. There, with everyone watching, he dropped his pants and sat on the toilet to make certain he would fit. Not being satisfied with the arrangement, he demanded a refit. These sorts of demands, coupled with the fact that only about 20 percent of the parts from the previous plane were compatible with the new one, made for economic disaster.

Learning: *the people who are successful with government work go down in flames doing commercial projects.*

When everything was over, Eastern had its planes and Martin was bankrupt. The bankers took over, removed Mr. Martin, and put George Bunker in charge. Bunker wanted to get out of the aircraft business, where Martin had no products, and into missile weapons systems. The Baltimore facility, one of the world's largest, was so steeped in aircraft construction that management felt it would be hard to switch to electronics. Bunker decided to build a new factory somewhere warm—a facility that would concentrate on military electronics and missile-based weapons systems. Bunker and his engineering director, Ed Uhl, came to Orlando and looked around. According to the story, they wore Hawaiian shirts and seemed rather ordinary to those they met. Orlando was just a small citrus town in 1955. Nothing much ever happened there, and the two executives soon realized that.

The president of the First National Bank (now Sun), Linton Allen, had a custom of standing at the front door of his bank and greeting people. He did that with me when we moved there and lent me $250 at a time when that seemed like a fortune. Today that bank handles all the money I can send its way because of his participation. Anyway, he determined what these two tourists were up to and arranged for them to see 6,500 acres of land southwest of town. When they returned north, Mr. Allen wrote his personal check for a couple thousand dollars to take an option on the property. Bunker was so impressed that he decided to build his plant in Orlando. After Martin was all settled a few years later, they held a party for Mr. Allen and thanked him for the "vision that brought Martin to Orlando."

Learning: *bank presidents who want to meet people stand in front of the bank; those who don't want to meet people stay in their offices.*

When I joined the company, the Orlando operation consisted of a thousand people who had been transferred from Baltimore. The idea was to staff the plant with a key group of technical and managerial people who had experience and then hire and train local people to complete the population of Martin-Orlando. Many of the transplants were afraid alligators would eat their children. Probably 15 percent turned around and went back north after a short time. However, the rest immediately fell in love with the area and settled down. They worked in old buildings around town while the plant was being constructed. When I left in 1965, there were over ten thousand employees.

The quality-assurance operation at Martin had been put together with the idea that it would be the most modern in the field. All involved were enthusiastic about the opportunity to begin from scratch; they were determined that Martin quality would be the best in the business. The individual members had come from different aerospace companies and together created a pool with a great deal of experience. Procedures were developed, defective-material tags were designed, people were recruited, organizational charts were drawn, and meetings were held. The basic philosophy was to find errors as early as possible and then implement corrective action in order to wipe them out. The material-review crib was set up early in the operation in order to identify components and parts that were not in compliance with requirements. Also it was taken as fact that the manufacturing, engineering, purchasing, finance, and other divisions were the natural enemies of the quality division, as well as of quality in general.

Learning: *people who show up in combat attitude can expect combat.*

I listened carefully to all the discussions in order to learn; everyone else seemed much more experienced and confident than I was. The company was so new and unstructured that there were not a great many ironclad processes, procedures, or customs. The employees were so determined not to be like Baltimore that they tossed out some good ways of doing things. The director of the quality division reported to the general manager like all the other directors and had an impressive office in "checkerboard row," so named because of the black and white linoleum floor.

Learning: *creating a hard-to-get-to executive area creates hard-to-get-to executives.*

Life was beginning to be comfortable for the family; grass was actually growing in the yard, which had to be cut and edged each week year round. My neighbor Bud Blandford was the Eastern Airlines manager at the airport. He was also skilled at taking care of his yard. He tried his best to transfer these talents to me, but I never got very good at it. We were furnishing the house and developing some real friendships. Three neighbors and I had formed a car pool, which allowed each of us to leave our only car home for the family to use most of the time. One of the riders, Bill Weaver, was responsible for beginning a new employee-orientation program. I asked whether they discussed quality in it; he said they didn't but they would be happy to have us participate. The managers in the quality division were not interested in taking part in the program because they felt it was premature to talk to people about quality until they were involved in specific work; so I did it on my own. For several years I stood in front of each new group of employees for about ten minutes and told them about their personal responsibility for quality. It was obvious this subject had never been mentioned to them in their previous work lives.

Learning: *it takes only a few moments and some choice words to impart important concepts; everyone can understand and relate to "doing it right the first time."*

All the other presentations—on security, benefits, personnel requirements—were heavy, so I kept my presentation light and friendly. I had stolen one of the stories I told from comedian Ernie Kovacs. A young princess met a frog and was told that the frog would become a prince if he were permitted to spend the night under her pillow. She let him, and the next morning the handsome prince was right beside her. The punch line? "To this very day that girl's mother does not believe this story." One time a lady raised her hand and asked whether I knew where she could get one of those frogs.

These sessions taught me again the value of learning to communicate information while being interesting at the same time. The group always reacted when I emphasized that someone was going to use the output of the plant to defend us. Only later did I realize that management had not gotten the same message. I think that people who make weapons of destruction never believe that anyone is going to use them. The weapons are for making, testing, and storing. No thought is given to the destruction they can cause and how important it is for them to be safe. These are the same work habits of most people whether they are making space machines or typewriters.

Learning: *people think that space workers are particularly careful because of the potential loss of life; but lots more people die in cars than spacecraft, and the subject never comes up in auto plants.*

As a senior quality engineer my first assignment was on an air-to-surface missile being made for the Navy. I shared a drawer in someone's desk with another quality engineer in our temporary location, which had been an orange-processing plant in its previous life. The rafters were several inches deep in bird manure when we took it over, but all that was cleaned away. I got involved in the assembly process and quickly determined that most of the units required rework after test and inspection. After making a list of the most frequent problems, I sat down at the general foreman's desk and started discussing it with him. I had taken time to get acquainted the previous week, assured him I was there to help, and assumed he would be interested in my analysis.

When I explained that the workers apparently did not understand the process clearly enough because they were doing several assembly operations wrong consistently, he blew up. He leaped from the chair, screamed at the top of his voice, accused me of spying on his operation, and tossed in his opinion of staff people who didn't have real jobs. This was a new experience for me but was apparently common in aircraft manufacturing, where intimidation was everything. He had been raised in that world. For lack of anything better to do I just sat there and stared at him. He had a large stomach, which was bouncing up and down. People stopped work to stare at us. Just then the telephone on his desk rang. I considered answering it since he was busy but decided to not get anymore involved. Hearing the ring, he stomped over to the desk, picked up the phone, and spoke into it just as sweetly as if he had been sitting reading Shakespeare. When that brief conversation was over, he sat down and looked at me. I smiled and asked whether he felt better; he nodded. I laid the data sheet in front of him and said I would come back and help him work out a corrective-action plan when he was ready. He could call me if he wanted to do something; otherwise I would just disappear.

The next day he did call, and we started to work on a way to prevent the defects in the process. He began to realize that I had not shown the analysis to anyone but him. Neither of us ever mentioned the blowup (apparently it was just a way of testing my sincerity), and we became tenuous friends after a while. Many senior executives use the same technique as the foreman did because it is so different from what one would expect in offices. In their case it is pretend, but in the factories they usually mean it. Even the gentlest souls learn one day that most staff people are not to be trusted.

Learning: *those in charge of an area will always defend it.*

After a while I was running a small group of quality engineers who were supposed to help the projects identify their problems and take corrective action. My focus was on the production process, but quality management was more interested in the quality-assurance process. We held extensive philosophical discussions as we searched for the system that would let us become effective. However, all these discussions started from the assumption that the world was full of errors and deviations. (Three Sigma—99.73 percent right—was the quality-control standard.) Finding and then controlling those errors, while containing the assumed evil intent of the manufacturing, engineering, and purchasing people, was the purpose. It was sort of the same strategy of deterrence that the government was using against the Soviet Union. If you are bad we will blow you up, and we get to decide what bad is. My efforts to encourage quality education that would promote prevention were dismissed as being hopelessly romantic.

My group concentrated on corrective action, but it was hard to nail down the specific actions that would prevent a problem from happening again. The same problems kept taking different forms. However, we were able to begin a corrective action that later became known as configuration control. Senior inspectors known as planners kept logbooks of the changes made to equipment as it progressed through the system. These logbooks were the only fairly complete record of what we were making and the government was buying. By gaining some cooperation from all, we were able to formalize this record keeping. Those who have not worked in a defense plant would never think that a factory could go to all the effort of making complex products and not know exactly what the content was, but it happens all the time and causes a lot of trouble. Prevention is the cure.

Learning: *keeping neat records of incidents of nonconformance is not quality management.*

In early 1959, I think, we moved into the new plant in southwest Orlando. It was a great place, with close to a million square feet of manufacturing and office space. There was one big cafeteria for all, each of whom swiped a spoon the first day. I finally got a desk but couldn't think of anything to put in it. They would not let me have a typewriter of my own because I was a member of management now. It was hard to do any creative work in the office anyway. But we got settled and began to reorganize the quality division one more time. A sure sign of this reorganization was that someone was asked to design the defective-material tag again. The thought seemed to be that we could document our way to efficiency.

Learning: *all the actions to organize are often based on opinion only, "what should work," and are aimed at getting others to do their part properly; "what actually works" is a pragmatic program.*

After the company grew so quickly, managers wanted a little breathing room, so they began to look around for a way to reduce costs. In manufacturing those who touch the product in a way that adds value are known as "direct" labor. Those who evaluate or move things along are "indirect" labor. Direct labor is charged to the customer, the government in this case, and indirect labor is charged to overhead. The customer pays for overhead, but it is a percentage of another factor that is not easy to document. Inspectors and testers are indirect labor, a fact the financial wizards soon figured out.

The senior managers determined that if they could turn the inspection process over to the manufacturing people, they could eliminate all those costs. The company was still hiring, so eliminating jobs would not result in people being laid off; they could fill some of the openings personnel was having trouble with. This was considered the perfect solution, except that the company would not spend any money to train the manufacturing people how to incorporate the inspection and test operations into their process. It also was necessary to record results in order to know what the configurations were. But these were considered small problems, and the deed was done.

Learning: *people who devise a reorganization often have never worked on a manufacturing floor; they had no idea what they were bringing about.*

The customer objected but had no valid reason for requesting that the change not take place. Within a few weeks it was apparent that anything that fit into a box was considered acceptable and thus shipped off to the government. After a couple of months the customer threatened to shut the plant down, several senior executives were fired, and the quality division was directed to get back into the inspection and test business. A new quality director was selected, an experienced and proven executive, Jim Dunlop Jr., who was serving as a product-line manager. He didn't know much about the quality business, but he set about learning and took quick action to eliminate those who had caused the previous problem.

At the same time G. T. (Tom) Willey took over as general manager. Tom was a long-time Martin executive who had been running the Cape Canaveral operation for a while. He was a lay preacher in his spare time and was oriented toward people. It was difficult to find him in his office; he was out on the floor and into the operation. He was approachable and reached out to people. He was also tough. I remember him picking up a cigarette butt in the machine shop and shoving it into the pocket of the general foreman's white shirt. He thought everything should be clean, including the machine and press shops. He eliminated coffee drinking at desks and vending machines from around buildings. This decision left everyone with no use for their personal spoon, so suddenly the cafeteria was awash in them. His way of looking at it was that everyone should work at work and eat at lunchtime. We loved him.

Learning: *an operation mimics the attitude of the senior executive.*

Personnel was asked to evaluate the people in the quality division and recommend someone who could provide Jim Dunlop with professional assistance. They picked me because, as they told me later, the psychological tests built into the employment application showed I was resourceful. "We need someone who can both create and implement," they said. I never figured exactly how such information came from a test, but I was delighted with the opportunity to help get us on the right track. (Basically I think I was selected because I had objected to the previous plan.) We made clear policies, we restructured the division to eliminate roadblocks, we started quality training, and we made it clear that product quality was not negotiable.

The quality division quickly went from being a place of shame to being the bright star of Martin. After a year or so, Jim felt that he had done his job and wanted to return to project management. We gave him a plaque appointing him an honorary quality engineer. Jim Halpin, who had been director of facilities, took over. He was the best manager I have ever seen. He was careful and methodical, and he maintained good relationships with everyone. He taught me a great deal, and not just about management. He took time to help me present myself better, for instance. He told me to get rid of the white socks everyone in the shop wore and got me to roll down my sleeves and put my coat back on. He taught me about timing and how to deal with people who bullied others. He backed me up when my ideas were different than everyone else's, and he made certain that those higher up in the company knew of my contribution. Few bosses do that. Mr. Willey had confidence in Jim and let him do it his way. Our quality reputation with the government grew quickly. They trusted us now.

With Jim Halpin (left), Martin quality director, 1961.

Learning: *those who know a lot usually look for someone to mentor, but the person mentored has to be capable of learning.*

My thoughts about my career were still evolving. It was nice to be on a fast track with promotions and raises, and it was nice to have the confidence of senior management; but I wasn't getting into a position to change the world. It was impossible to reach the press or find any way to influence national leaders, let alone the world. Also running a staff operation was boring; I wanted some action. When you have a lot of ideas, people think they come easily to you and that you are merely facile. I was slowly beginning to understand that my outlook was different from others' and that it was best to be patient. The people I was working with were not going to understand me, although they gave me no problems. Senior people, at least some of them, seemed to think that I was "original" and appreciated my efforts. It was not necessary for me to feel appreciated all the time. I could take care of that myself, and my family appreciated me in real terms.

About this time we were beginning to bid on designing, developing, and producing the Pershing Weapon System. It was to be a two-stage artillery missile with a range of two hundred or so miles and capable of being fired in the field by ordinary soldiers. The Army Ballistic Missile Agency (ABMA) of Huntsville, Alabama, would be the technical director. The core of ABMA was the German missile team under Wernher von Braun, the folks who had been trying to blow up London a dozen years before. I was assigned to the project as the section chief, which was the number two job, to help Murray Hack, who became the Pershing quality manager. Four or five of us from quality were on the program, and each of the other divisions had similar teams. Engineering was all over the job, of course. The quality and reliability laboratory of ABMA was the responsible agency as far as we were concerned, and we got to know the people there well. They knew the missile business. We made certain that all their requirements were in the contract proposal.

One day when I was visiting their lab, they showed me a new specification for soldering. Many missile failures in those days were due to bad soldering. Their specification was completely different from what was happening throughout the aerospace industry. They told me that it had been rejected by several of the large aerospace companies that were bidding against us. The techniques involved made sense to me, so I volunteered to try it out in a production area by setting up a training operation and then using it. They were delighted and offered to help teach. This way of soldering was a true breakthrough. (In fact, during the life of the Pershing, which was at least twenty years, no failures were attributed to soldering.) The quality and reliability lab became close to us as a result of this cooperation, and after we received the contract, we got along well for years. I learned that the customer can be correct along with being right. The companies who did not want to consider changing were within their rights because the development contract did not require it. Big mistake. Von Braun himself was one of the idea people behind the solder specification.

Learning: *customers sometimes have good ideas; it makes sense to listen.*

After Martin received the Pershing contract, we began to assemble mockups of the hardware so the Pentagon and Martin executives could see it. Engineering sent drawings with a big stamp on them stating, "Do not use for manufacturing or inspection." Naturally the manufacturing people began to build the mockup units right away and offered them to our inspection supervisor. He would not have anything to do with it. Soon I received delegates from engineering, who said the stamp meant nothing, and from manufacturing, who questioned my manhood and waved large bellies at me. There was a list of engineers who could make changes; the whole system was called "green engineering" and had been used in aircraft manufacturing for years. When I said we would have clean drawings or none, they all stomped out, and their leader went directly to Mr. Willey to report that the mockups would not be ready on time if I did not relent. Also, he noted, the first phase of development was done with such drawings, and that would be late also. Mr. Willey told him that they should comply with their own rules, that nothing was ever done properly when green engineering was used, and that the engineering department was being paid in real money so they should produce real engineering. I always liked that line.

Learning: *people don't respect those who help them do the wrong thing.*

Mr. Willey's decision caused the project to be the most change-free in anyone's memory. It was courageous, and it was correct. Sometime later, when he and I were alone in the middle of the plant for a moment, I thanked him for his support. He let me know that he did it for the company, the customer, and the soldiers who were going to use it. If I got some good out of it too, that was just added benefit. Then he smiled at me.

When the project was well under way and Pershing was beginning to take over most of the facility, it was divided into three programs: airborne, ground equipment, and field test. I was appointed quality manager of ground equipment. When I came back from Jim's office, after being notified, my secretary was packing. She knew before I did; so much for security. Here was my chance to build prevention into an organization or at least to find out why it was so difficult. The management team for ground equipment included a project director, Jack Libby, and a manager from each of the divisions. The ten managers and the director would be responsible for 80 percent of the hardware of the Pershing system.

The only way to learn what works in real life is to try it in real life. Research is useful, of course, and theory has to be the beginning of everything. But real life is where it is at, and being the most junior manager in the company was a good place for me to start. It would not do to begin launching lectures on what I came to call "quality improvement through defect prevention." I had to be more subtle because people were not interested in improving; there just was too much work to do. I began to develop a plan.

In June 1958 we were fortunate in being able to adopt the baby who became Phylis B. Crosby. Her name had one *l* in it just like her brother's and mine. She was a delight and has continued to be. The counseling we received this time emphasized that we should make it clear that our children were "chosen" and not leave their finding out why they were in the family to chance. One result was a bedtime ceremony that went on for years. The adult would say, "Once upon a time there were a mommy and daddy who didn't have any children. Jesus told them that they could choose any boy and girl in the whole world to be their child. And do you know who they picked?" The children answered by smiling and then pointing to themselves; later when they could talk they would shout enthusiastically "me" or "us." We also had discussions on the subject as they asked about it, but it never seemed very important to them. To my knowledge, neither of them ever had a problem with being adopted. They considered it natural and certainly have been secure in the love their parents have had for them.

Learning: *solid relationships are built on love and respect, which are not automatically transferred genetically; they are self-generated.*

At work I was continuing to have new experiences. The subcontractors for ground equipment were beginning to develop the contracts for the production phase of the system, and their representatives came to work out the details of the quality part of the contract. They were consistent in one respect anyway: they all wanted AQLs on their products. They gave me a list of statistical requirements for their process of production and then numbers concerning the product we would receive. Typically we would agree that they could make a certain percentage of errors, like 2 percent. I took the position that we were not going into this project committed to nonconformance before anyone had even chipped a chip. This was not a popular approach, and our contracting people soon descended on me. They said that AQLs were a traditional part of government contracts and that it would double the cost of the program (at least) if we didn't use them. The contractors were contending that they would need hundreds more inspectors and testers in order to get everything exactly perfect. It would be an incredible waste of money and time and would cause the government to reopen the prime contract. They quoted the quality-control authorities and gurus and offered to send me to school with one of them.

The other managers on the project hit on me also; they said that I was making a big deal over nothing, that no one paid attention to the quality part of the contract. What passed the test passed; what didn't pass was reworked until it passed. They were describing reality. But I didn't want to deal with what existed; I wanted us to do things properly because I knew that then the product would serve its announced purpose, we could produce it for much less than the usual price, and the company would build a great reputation with the customer as a result. I still had not figured out how to explain my proposal in a way that would light up managerial eyes. They all thought I was "bright but flaky."

Learning: *if you want an idea to be understood, you have to describe it concisely and clearly, particularly if it is a new idea.*

The way my mind processed new ideas was beginning to become clear to me. It can be described as an ever-decreasing circle of concentration. As I understand one sweep of experience, the next sweep begins to reveal itself, sort of like the layers of an onion. Most of my ideas come from intuition, listening, and observation. After a while confidence that the sweeps will happen begins to build. I know that an answer will be revealed to me if I am just patient and keep poking. I worked on that antenna-columniation problem at Crosley for weeks before it dawned on me that the key was the central gimbal. At Bendix it became apparent to me that the entire manufacturing industry had a built-in commitment to the inevitability of error. Processes were planned and executed so that making errors became a self-fulfilling prophecy. One example was the plan for assembly floors. Areas were set aside for rework, which of course meant a commitment to have some; no one had empty rework stations. When I asked why this was part of the plan, I was told that "we have to be practical."

The management team for ground equipment took its responsibilities seriously and planned the delivery of the equipment down to the last detail. There were several hundred separate pieces, which were either line items or spares. The planning department kept track of each of them, and meetings were held daily to make certain progress was being made. Quality was considered the responsibility of the quality department, and if a part failed to pass its test, I got yelled at. No one thought the finance manager was responsible for profit. The job of quality manager was a precarious one because the customer could be mollified in times of trouble by moving or firing the quality guy. I learned to point out the cause of problems clearly before attempting corrective action. Engineering designed things, purchasing bought them, manufacturing assembled and created them, and marketing sold them. All the quality department did was measure what was happening and report on it. We made a few feeble attempts to demonstrate the cost of all this corrective action but to no avail. The urgency of having weapons systems overrode the cost of producing them. The U.S. Defense Department assumed that money was something to feed to the furnace, that the Soviets were going to attack if we didn't get it done on time. Most of the contracts Martin had were based on cost plus fixed fee. Consequently, we didn't make more profit by spending more money, and cost was down a bit on the priority scale. Making schedule was first, second, and third. Then came cost and, finally, quality.

Learning: *managers talk quality as though they covet it, but they have no idea what it means.*

One of the problematical responsibilities of the quality department was running the material-review board (MRB). Material that could

Martin Company, 1962. The only thing worse than not getting invited to a meeting is getting invited.

not be reworked to its requirements was sent to the MRB. Engineering, the customer, and a quality engineer then looked at it and decided whether it could be reworked enough to be useful, could be used as is, or had to be tossed out. Detailed records were kept. The biggest management problem was getting engineering to make these decisions. They just didn't take this responsibility seriously; we had rejected items in the MRB crib for weeks sometimes. So I notified the management team that we were going to scrap everything that was there more than three days. This announcement was met with a dull silence, which was broken when we sent a big pile of items to the engineering director's office. That received a lot of attention, and people began to take the MRB seriously.

Learning: *doing what you said you will do, without rancor, is important when you are at the bottom of the managerial food chain.*

After that we reduced the number of hours the MRB crib would be open for business. I also shrank the size so it would not hold as much. This made the manufacturing folks get their wounded in on time. They didn't like having to do that and were even less enchanted when I suggested they learn how to produce materials that did not need to be judged. This was viewed as a "noncontributing remark," and I received a mild lecture from Halpin after the manufacturing director complained about my attitude. Halpin agreed with my opinion; the lecture was about the clumsy way I shared it.

As a department manager I found my time well scheduled and a lot of work to be done. I learned several lessons in this first senior role that have stuck with me since that time. First, it was not necessary to work long hours. I went home each day at quitting time in order to be with my family. If it was necessary for me to travel, I arranged it so that I was gone only as long as necessary, and I called home each day. The company policy was to call only twice a week, which I ignored.

Second, it was not possible to do any real work in the office, so I carried a briefcase home with me each day, and after the children were in bed, I spent an hour or so processing the paper that had accumulated during the day. If I had a paper or report to write, I did it on my typewriter at home and had my secretary redo it at the office. I would give her a box full of stuff in the morning; she would give one back to me at night. If something important showed up, she tracked me down (her system for knowing my exact location was impeccable) and read it to me. I didn't accept material classified as secret; instead, I read it while the messenger stood there and gave it back. When I received an assignment or request from senior management, I stopped what I was doing and accomplished the assignment right away and completely. It never took much time, which always surprised and pleased them, so they left me alone.

Learning: *if you get your work done well, you can do it on your own terms.*

Third, managers are not as dumb as the lower-level folks think they are. As a quality engineer, even as a group leader, I thought that management just didn't care about the problems of quality. But when it comes down to the priorities of the company and the project, it becomes impossible to stick to every detail when something is a little bit wrong. There are too many other aspects involved. This was the first glimmer I had that prevention could become a reality if management could be helped to think ahead a little. For instance, we had two suppliers who failed the quality evaluation, yet their products were completely acceptable. Management overrode the evaluations in order to use the products, the lack of which was holding up delivery. The quality-control professionals were furious. When the dust settled, I got the process changed so that it concentrated on product conformance to requirements instead of the subjective items normally used. The ineffective procedures for evaluation that I eliminated back then have been retrieved for use in government quality-award programs. Some things die hard.

Fourth, and most important, although some people were effective in their jobs, some were not, and their effectiveness had little to do with intelligence or education. Relationships were the whole thing. I developed the approach of trying to help the other managers achieve their goals; this approach did not require giving up principles or rewarding bad behavior, only being a considerate person and being interested in others.

After about a year it was decided to bring the three project teams together into one Pershing project. Coordinating the three was becoming too difficult, and we were about to get into the flight-test program at Cape Canaveral. We all assumed that Murray Hack or one of the senior quality managers would take the Pershing job. However, Jim called me in and said something like "I have decided to make you the grand high pubba of Pershing. I want Murray to run quality engineering." Later he commented that I was the only one who didn't know exactly how to run the operation, which made me his choice. Jim was the only other person I knew who felt the accepted quality system was fatally flawed. No one in our industry delivered products or services exactly as ordered because they didn't believe that doing so was important. Yet everyone complied with the government's specifications (Mil-Q-9858) on the subject. If the recipe is wrong, then the result will be disagreeable no matter how many pretend to like the taste of the stew.

Learning: *having the same set of golf clubs as Arnold Palmer does not guarantee you will play as he does.*

As a result of Jim's decision, I suddenly had as subordinates several people for whom I had worked at one time or another. I went to each of them and asked whether that was a problem for them; each said it wasn't. A couple were not sincere when they answered, but after all it was only business. Nobody held back in doing their job, and I didn't treat anyone with kid gloves. We set up the department and went at it. The project director was Herman Staudt; the other managers were all the senior people in their divisions. With one exception, besides myself, they all came from the Missile department.

Learning: *in business, people are promoted or selected based on the job they had in the past, not necessarily on their performance in that job.*

I made it a point to get to the subcontractors' plants regularly to see that they were paying attention to quality. We had inspectors on site, but a couple of guys in a five thousand–person plant were not much protection. Also I quickly learned that their loyalty drifted over time. We do tend to love those who are near regardless of what the poets say. We did a poor job of ensuring supplier quality, and it showed in our assembly results. Again quality came in a poor third—probably fourth actually, after the field people's expense reports. Those seemed to me to be the main concern of that department's management.

As it got closer to the time for the first flight tests, it became apparent that we had a big bottleneck in the final test. The engineers were doing the actual testing while trying to make the automatic test equipment work. The strategy was to keep the testers paid who were paid by the hour out of that area because of union complications. However, date after date was missed, and when a few missiles were finally released for a flight test, they arrived at Cape Canaveral needing additional verification.

Mr. Willey became frustrated with the lack of progress and decided that a change of direction was in order. Without consulting anyone he announced that the final test was being transferred to the quality department immediately. When asked about the other test areas, he said "that too," and my department suddenly tripled. A few minutes after I found out about this change, the four test managers appeared at my office. They wanted me to know that they would take care of everything, and I wouldn't have to do anything about it. They realized that I had little experience in these areas and wanted to assure me that I could depend on them. I expressed my thanks and suggested that they come back at 7 A.M. the next day with their scheduling plans and that we would spend as long as it took in order to have a plan Mr. Willey would like. They agreed grumpily. It was well known that each of them thought the other three were the problem.

Learning: *never show uncertainty even if you are not certain.*

The personnel director agreed to see me on short notice so I could ask about my idea of bringing the testers who were paid by the hour into the operation. He said that there was nothing against it but that I should recognize they would be a lot of trouble. Because nothing was getting out now, it didn't seem that things could get much worse. He agreed to have one of his people work with us on this move.

On the way back I stopped at Jim's office, but his secretary told me he left word that I was doing fine and should leave him out of it until the end of the week. He had decided that I was grown up, I guess.

The next morning I told my four test managers and the chief inspector that we were going to have a new strategy. The new testers would operate the test equipment exactly in accordance with the test procedure. The test engineers would stay on the balcony, or wherever, and not come to the test floor. When we got a red light, we would bring the test engineer, design engineer, and process engineer together. They would determine whether the problem was the missile, the test equipment, or the process. Then we would do the necessary corrective action and proceed until the next red light. Once a missile went through the process, we would be able to test it in just the few minutes it took the automatic equipment to go through all its steps. If we did it right, we would be able to take the missiles right from the end of the line and do our test quickly.

The reply was that this new procedure was going to take a long time and that we would blow all our schedules. They wanted to hear from Mr. Willey and the project director that they agreed with what I wanted to do. I said they could go ask but there would be no jobs in this department for them on their return. There was a pause while they calibrated whether I meant that or not. Having decided I did, they relaxed and we all went to work on the problem.

Learning: *we have to simplify a task if everyone is going to understand it; when only a few know how to do it, it will never get finished.*

In time I learned that my consistent attitude and lack of explosiveness had led many to think that I was an intellectual wimp. But when people probe for your strength or weakness, it is best to let them find the real person. One of my coworkers said of me that "beneath that calm exterior beats a heart of solid granite." I don't think it was that bad, but stubbornness has always been a family trait. It is possible to be just as firm when you are wrong as when you are right. The more experience people get, it seems to me, the more often they think that it must be right because they think it is.

We were missing delivery dates right and left, the Pentagon was screaming, the people at the Cape were threatening to come over and run test operations for us. No one would sit next to me at the project-team meetings for fear they might get hit by flack. The pressure did not bother me because these people were not important to me. Halpin and Willey knew there was no other way but to get the testing problem fixed once and for all. The main thing was that my family not know from my actions or reactions that all this was going on. I left it all on the desk when I walked out of the plant. Eventually all the red lights turned green; the test equipment drawings were stamped; and the procedures were signed. Now we could test a missile system quickly and accurately. Before long the birds were lined up waiting for the Cape to be able to accept them.

Learning: *a sensible plan will work if distractions are kept out.*

Martin was a wonderful place to work then. It had all changed after Mr. Willey took over the plant. Before that, morale was low, and several of us had been looking around for other jobs. I had contacted my old Bendix boss, who was now in Massachusetts with an aerospace company. He flew two of us there for interviews with his company. On the way back from Boston, in mid-winter, we were bumped off the plane. We went into Manhattan, stayed overnight, and saw *My Fair Lady* with Rex Harrison and Julie Andrews. The next day the only ride we could get home was on the initial flight of National's 707 jet plane. That was a thrill and to me a glimpse of the future; even driving a rented car back from Miami did not erase it.

Back when the customer was beating up on us about quality, as I noted before, the place seemed to be drifting. We were bidding on the Pershing at that time. One of the actions Willey took in order to build morale when he first arrived was to have family nights. About four hundred employees of all levels were invited to come to the plant one evening each month with their spouses. There was a reception in the area of the director's offices, and each person could conduct a personal plant tour. A few places were off limits, but not many. All the senior managers were commanded to be there, and a dinner was held in the cafeteria. I was asked to be on the program each time in order to give the predinner prayer. When people arrived, we had a reception line at the front door. Mr. and Mrs. Willey, the personnel director and his wife, and Shirley and I greeted each and every person. It took me a while to realize that this was Willey's way of showing that he considered quality important. Complaints about my screwy ideas decreased with each session. Harold Geneen did much the same thing several years later at ITT. In both cases they wanted to send a message about something that was important to them and indicate that they had trust in a person, without having to say or write it. Others picked up on this practice before I did. The other half of the equation is that the person involved works harder and deeper. The unwritten part is that the person should never mention what is happening or that he or she realizes what is going on. All the magic disappears when the lights are turned up.

Learning: *study people's intent before condemning what they are doing; they might be up to something that will help you.*

Willey and I exchanged few words during our time together, and I never worked directly for him, but he has always been an inspiration to me. Among other things I realized that one could practice Christian principles and still be successful in business. It was not necessary to be a preacher or even to speak up about one's beliefs; people watched how others acted and treated people. What was said mattered little.

I kept working on my personal development by reading and speaking. Philosophy books helped me to learn that some of my "original" ideas were hundreds of years old. It was not necessary to subscribe to only one philosopher; they complemented each other and offered alternate suggestions. Henry Ford, Alfred Sloan, Harvey Firestone were all philosophers of business to me. Their results came through understanding leadership and principle. Ford raised the national wage level, doubled it in fact, in one swoop. He also cut the price of his product each year. Sloan organized a company so that it could be run by people who were not as smart as he was. Ford didn't understand the need for that. Darrell Huff's *How to Lie with Statistics*, Steven Potter's *Lifemanship*, other books along this line, as well as Parkinson's Law, led me to understand that life did not have to be ponderous. We also began attending a church whose pastor was a great teacher; he helped me to relate the scriptures to real life.

Learning: *the key to a successful life is a strong personal faith.*

Speaking was a little harder to make happen. I talked to a few ASQC sections and, of course, to different company and customer meetings. Then Carl Foster, my friend from across the street and car-pool companion, offered an idea. Carl was in public relations and kept getting requests from service groups, churches, and the like for someone to explain Martin to them. I volunteered to do a few talks for him; it turned out they offered a wonderful opportunity to learn to speak to real people. In order to make it all understandable, I recruited Bill Johnson, my artist friend from Bendix who had come to Martin recently. I explained to the audience what kind of missile systems there were: air to air, air to ground, ground to air, ground to ground. The audience selected one of these and named the system. Then they picked the propulsion system, the control system, and launch type after I described the options. I also told them how Martin worked and something about the company. At the end of my talk Bill came forward with a color drawing of their missile with the name they had chosen and the Martin logo on it. We did dozens of these pictures, and everyone liked them. The most popular name for the weapon, particularly in churches, was "killer."

When speaking to professional groups I included a funny anecdote every page or so. These were truly amusing tales, not jokes, that added to the audience's understanding of the subject. However, it didn't take me long to learn that the audience was more interested in the humor than the message I had in mind. They asked about the anecdotes after the talk and wanted me to write them down. As a result, today I never tell a story that does not include the message. Also I told no off-color anecdotes or other stories of questionable taste. The most important thing in any talk is to be interesting, and talking to the audience about something that interests them appears to be the way to do that. That observation seems obvious, but I listen to many speakers who think that the subject speaks for itself.

Learning: *tell stories, not jokes; jokes lessen your image.*

Our first six Pershing flights in 1960–1961 were successful; the seventh failed when the second stage ignited and set off the range safety package on the top of the first stage. This accident occurred because a shielded wire had been replaced by PVC as part of a cost-saving package. No one had checked the replacement through the regular change board because it was not tactical equipment. Unfortunately, it was the first time we had exposed the bird to the press and some Defense Department senior people. I had been sitting in the viewing stands with some national press people. When the sky lit up with the explosion, the person next to me was revealed to be an instantly recognizable network anchor. He glanced at my badge, smiled, and patted my shoulder. "Don't worry, Phil, this happens now and then." "It doesn't have to," I said. He smiled patiently at me.

Now that we were on schedule it was possible to put increased emphasis on quality. The project director gave me a lecture one afternoon about the number of defects that were being found when the missile was delivered to Cape Canaveral—an average of ten per missile. Most were insignificant, but now and then one was important. I explained that these defects were inevitable because of the AQL mentality and actual requirements. We had to learn to prevent, I noted, and that was not possible under the current concept of quality. He said that I should install the right concept and that he and the rest of management would support me all the way. He also led me to believe that if quality did not improve, mine would be the scalp sent to Washington and Baltimore (corporate headquarters).

The realization that I could get fired sent a shock through me that reminded me of the shock I received when the naval officer on the train told me how dangerous it was in Korea. Each year I received the biggest incentive compensation in the quality division. I was the golden boy. How could they fire me?

Learning: *in business, as in sports, your past has little to do with your future; how many hits you can produce today is what matters.*

This nudge gave me the incentive to do what I should have been doing anyway: change the way quality was managed, not just complain about it. This has been a pattern of mine through life; I needed a challenge to get me moving. I knew they probably would not have kicked me out of the company, and if they had, I could have gotten another job quickly; but they could have removed me from Pershing. That would have been a real blow.

I had been complaining and writing about the conventional concepts of quality control and quality management for years, but I had never done anything about it. I had offered no alternative, just readjustments of solutions that had not worked. I needed some time to think by myself, so I went out the front door and walked around the fence, which must have been three miles, in the September heat. It was apparent to me that I was the problem. I had gone along with AQLs when what we needed was to get everything right the first time. The problem was not the workers; it was the standard of performance that management provided and insisted on that needed change. We had to get no defects, zero defects. Instead of AQLs and "that's close enough," we had to go for zero defects (ZD).

I liked the words and my spirits improved immediately. I went back to the office and called my senior managers together. After explaining my experience of the afternoon, I shared the idea of ZD. I knew I was onto something when all the faces were blank. We discussed it for a while, and they began to warm up. The brief meeting ended with my promise to write a description of the ZD concept that everyone could understand. I stopped by Halpin's office on the way home and outlined my concept to him. He almost jumped out of the chair and said that it was exactly what we had been needing. He asked me to bring him the concept the first thing the next day so we could prepare a strategy of implementation and explanation. He also predicted that the quality establishment would not like this change and said that I would become famous and respected in the field but would always be considered an iconoclast. We looked iconoclast up in his office dictionary to make certain we both knew what it meant. It was just right for me in his opinion. History is full of iconoclasts; however, most of them never got away from being considered simply weird. I didn't mind being considered weird, but I did want to see my ideas considered before they were rejected.

Learning: *because I did not realize what a good idea ZD was, I lost control of it.*

CHAPTER FIVE

Getting Serious About Reforming Quality Management

By early 1961 the family had determined that we needed a larger house, which in turn absolutely had to be air-conditioned, and a pool wouldn't be too awful either. Those who say one becomes accustomed to heat and humidity are not playing with a full deck. Also Philip Jr. was about to enter the first grade, and we were becoming concerned that some of the kids in our part of town were a little more undisciplined than necessary. Many housing developments were being built around Orlando, so the good news was that it was possible to find a good buy on a new home; the bad news was that it was hard to sell an older house. Also the builders were easier to deal with than owners. We had some equity in the house, of course, probably $1,500 if we could get its value. We had no savings and little money left over at the end of each pay period.

Today I often think of what would have happened to us if I had been fired or laid off or had become incapacitated. We would have been able to live about two weeks. It never occurred to me to be concerned at that time. As near as I could tell my future looked good. I was getting promoted as quickly as decency would allow. My salary four years before was $7,680 a year with no bonus; in 1961 my total would be about $18,000. That was good progress I thought. The rapid growth at Martin required that management take a chance on people. Every time I got a new job managers remarked that they weren't sure I could do it but they had no one else. Even with this vote of little confidence I had worked out for them. As a result we could pay for better housing if the monthly expense was not too much.

Charlie Clayton was building a new subdivision in Maitland, which was north of the city and about eighteen miles from Martin. The interstate (I-4) was in the process of being built and would make the trip quicker if not shorter. Charlie magically arranged for us to trade homes, and we moved into a five-bedroom house in Dommerich Hills for $31,500. He bought our house, and we bought his house; it all worked out, just like trading cars. We arranged to slide wall-to-wall carpet and drapes into the mortgage. It didn't make financial sense, but it was the only way we could buy a new house. The pool would come along in a year or two; we couldn't work it in at the time.

Learning: *there is always a way to make something happen sensibly.*

I staked out the small bedroom of the new house for my den. While the moving people were arranging furniture, I stood guard to make certain a sewing machine or something else didn't get in there for "temporary" storage. When the dust cleared, I had my first "library," which consisted of a card table, folding chair, my manual typewriter, and a dozen books. I was as proud of that room as of any I have had since. Within a few months I had obtained a secondhand desk and chair plus a small bookcase. Several photos of work-related subjects had found themselves a place on the wall. I worked my hour in there each night and often on the weekend, but the family wandered in and out at will. They knew that I would stop what I was doing in order to chat with them as long as they wanted or get down on the floor and wrestle. My dog Foxy the Doxie sat in there with me. Sometime during the evening he and I, plus anyone who wanted to go, took a walk around the neighborhood. Now and then I rode a bike with Foxy running alongside the front wheel. How he knew when the bike was going to turn was a mystery to me. He was like the dolphins that ran ahead of our ship in the Pacific. We quickly felt comfortable in the home, and I could see that the family were all closet aristocrats. They were emerging rapidly.

I wanted to get some articles published. It is hard to get magazines interested in your pieces when they have never heard of you, but they will print letters. I decided to write a few letters to the editor of the ASQC magazine to see whether I could generate some interest in improving quality. Perhaps they would invite me to write an article, which I could then use as a sample for a real magazine. The 1961 letter that got the most response, all negative, stated that if the quality professionals didn't get to work on improving quality, it would not be long before the worldwide definition of U.S. quality would be "tacky and unreliable."

The established leaders of the profession told me personally and in print that this was a dangerous and inaccurate attitude based only on my inexperienced opinion. This controversy generated some invitations to speak around the country to ASQC and business groups. When the speech could be tied in to a company trip, I accepted; however, although audiences always applauded and encouraged me, it was obvious that there was no agreement. I learned that people would like others to improve, but they had little motivation to alter their own actions. If you wanted to get something changed, it was necessary to pull levers that dropped people into patterns. They would follow patterns whether they understood them or not. An analogy is trying to get someone to accept God because it is reasonable, logical, and good for them—a difficult task. That is still true today. Not everyone is interested in improving, except, of course, on their terms. Lots of people have made careers out of putting Humpty Dumpty back together again, even though they were the ones who pushed him off the wall.

Learning: *if it were easy to have new ideas accepted, life would be a Disney movie.*

Back to ZD. Responding to Jim Halpin's desire, I went straight to the typewriter after dinner and started to work on the concept of ZD. I began by reminding myself of the obvious: if you can't explain something so that any ordinary person can understand it, then you don't understand it. ZD had to be simple. The idea was to get things done right the first time by making that the way the organization worked on a routine basis. This is the description of ZD that I devised:

> We are conditioned throughout our private lives to accept the fact that people are not perfect and will therefore make mistakes. By the time we seek a business life, this belief is firmly rooted. It becomes fashionable to say, "People are humans, and humans make mistakes. Nothing can be perfect as long as people take part in it."

And people do make mistakes, particularly those who expect to make some each day and do not become upset when they do. You might say they have accepted a standard that requires a few mistakes in order to be certified as a human.

The question must arise, then, as to whether people have a built-in defect ratio. Do they always make the same percentage of errors in each thing they do? Like cashing their paycheck, for instance. Can we assume that people who err in 5 percent of their work activities will be shortchanged on 5 percent of the checks they cash each year? Will they forget to pay their income tax 5 percent of the time? Will they go home to the wrong house several times each month?

If these assumptions are wrong, then errors must be a function of the importance that a person places on specific activities. People are more careful about one act than another. They have learned to accept the fact that it is all right to make mistakes at work but not permissible to defraud the government. In short, a dual attitude has developed. In some things people are willing to accept imperfection; in others the number of defects must be zero.

Mistakes are caused by two factors: lack of knowledge and lack of attention. Knowledge can be measured and deficiencies corrected through tried and true means. Lack of attention must be corrected by the person himself or herself, through an acute reappraisal of his or her moral values. Lack of attention is an attitude problem. The person who commits himself or herself to watch each detail and carefully avoid errors takes a giant step toward setting a goal of zero defects in all things.

Learning: *zero defects should be the performance standard— my third Absolute of Quality Management.*

Everyone liked the essay and was enthusiastic about it. Jim read it to all the directors and laid plans to form a team that would implement ZD in the company. The government personnel hopped on it immediately, and within a few days there was a meeting of important people. They asked me to explain the idea, and I was able to show them some of the preliminary results that we were getting on Pershing just from talking about it. I was happy that quality was receiving so much attention until the missile-command people, the Martin executives, and the Washington folks all began to talk about employee motivation. I was saying that management was the problem because they insisted on the wrong performance standard, which in turn produced a negative attitude in employees and management alike. They were saying that the employees had a lousy attitude from birth and that motivation was the way to change it. They also wanted to add to my concept that there were three causes of error, the third being lack of the proper tools. I insisted that the one who provided the tool made the mistake in that case and that if they took this position ZD would become a blue-collar program exclusively. I also snarled about it, the only time I can remember doing that. The idea disappeared for the moment but kept popping up as others thought of it later.

Learning: *people have to be carefully instructed to understand something different from what they know, but they will not take time to obtain this instruction on their own.*

A ZD team was formed, without me on it, and a program was laid out to introduce the concept. The results were a large event and a well-orchestrated set of brochures. Executives from defense contractors all over the country came to see what was happening and went back to do the same. I kept running around the country talking about prevention and was asked to make many speeches. But all the managers wanted to know about was how to get employees to stop making mistakes.

Time magazine came by to do an article on the Martin program. I was the last person they interviewed after eight hours of talking to senior management and taking hundreds of photographs. I was called down to the public-relations office for a ten-minute talk. When I sat down to be photographed, I deliberately picked up a missile model that was on the director's desk. That was the only photo *Time* used, and they wrote the story entirely about me and how ZD was my idea. They also pointed out that motivation was a temporary expedient and that prevention was the hope of quality improvement. The article caused a few corporate brows to be furrowed in my direction, but my only comment was that I never knew *Time* was so smart. I was beginning to see ZD as my way out of Martin, and I didn't want the world to get mixed up on where the idea originated. They could create a screwed-up education program, but the concept was solid.

Learning: *it is not necessary to let others define your personal agenda.*

Several Japanese executives, from NEC (Dr. Kubayshi) and other companies, came to visit. While the U.S. executives wanted to know about bands and speakers, these people wanted to know how to get all managers to understand the concept. They could not afford to do things over; they wanted to "do it right the first time." It was a pleasure to talk with them even though they never seemed to get enough information.

Early in 1962 the Department of Defense held a big quality meeting cosponsored by the National Security Industries Association. I spoke to the senior executives of all the defense contractors as well as their Defense Department counterparts at that meeting. I tossed out the company-approved speech and told them that they, the executives, were the problem and had to change their ways. I talked like a person who was independently wealthy, really laying it on them. After the speech there was a great deal of applause and congratulations, but little action on their part. It was becoming obvious to me that they thought I was talking to the person in the seat beside them. From this meeting I learned never to prepare detailed handouts; people just take them home and hand them to someone else. Make them take some action by asking for the information.

Learning: *you cannot talk people into the need for improvement; they have to make up their own minds, and then you must be ready to help.*

The result of the meeting was that most of the executives wanted to send people to learn how to do the ZD "program." The missile command took charge and began to hold seminars across the nation. They did not ask me to speak at any of them, but they did ask me to write some of the material that was distributed. I did so, and it was changed only a little bit, nothing of substance anyway. No one was able to understand why I didn't like what was happening to my own "program." But I am loyal to those who employ me and did nothing to embarrass Martin; in fact, I was able to help them gain a reputation as a national leader in quality.

I still had Pershing quality to run, of course, and that took a lot of time. But because my den was functioning at home, I was able to write my first real article, "Quality Control from A to Y," which was illustrated by my brother, David, who was working at the plant now. *American Machinist* published it and paid me $400, which the family insisted I use for an electric typewriter. I then wrote a follow-up article: "The Z Is for Zero Defects." One result of these articles was continuous character assassination from the old guard of quality control. They never bothered to ask me what I was talking about or to wonder why they were suddenly getting so much attention from management or why quality managers were getting moved to the head table.

All they saw was this "silver tongued iconoclast," as one called me. Jim was right apparently. I thought it was funny so it did not bother me personally, but I did find it frustrating that the profession was not benefiting from the beginning of this reformation. It was the same attitude the medical profession exhibited when it rejected vaccinations and bacterial control.

Learning: *knowledge and understanding do not always go together.*

I was beginning to realize that I had made a big mistake by just dumping the concept of ZD into the melting pot of business philosophy. I decided that if I ever had another useful idea, I would develop a strategy for promoting it on my terms and with my definitions. This from a guy who was introduced as a "fanatic" and who had a moderator thank him by saying, "Mr. Crosby speaks symbolically; he doesn't seriously expect things to get done right the first time." I returned to the platform and corrected the statement, but most people just could not accept such a different stand.

Pershing was a success by any measurement. It was on schedule, below budget, more reliable than any other system, and the recognized quality leader. Now that the entire customer crisis was past and everyone loved us again, Jim asked me to recommend a better way of organizing the quality division. Working with two other managers I drew up a plan to improve communication, increase efficiency, and move some people around without hurting feelings. I had no problem with finding my successor on Pershing; Garth Meyers had been the real operating chief of Pershing quality for some time. He had been running the machine shop when I talked him into coming over as test manager. I asked him whether he knew anything about electronic testing and he assured me that he did not. I had enough people who understood electronics and couldn't work with their employees. Garth knew how to manage people, and that was our problem. I put him in charge of my four test departments, and he took the mystery out of them.

Learning: *pick your own people; don't let personnel or the boss do it.*

Murray Hack's move to a new program, Sprint, motivated Jim's reorganization. I wanted to run quality engineering so I could have the opportunity to install prevention in the organization. All was well until Jim showed the new organization to Tom Willey, who asked Jim what he thought the biggest problem in quality was. Jim replied that, as Tom already knew, it was supplier quality so Willey said he should assign me to that rather than let me retire to quality engineering. Jim told me that because his biggest problem was listening to everyone complain about supplier quality, he was going to give it to me since I was the main complainer. I knew all along that supplier quality was where I should go next, but it seemed like an out-of-the-way place; I would have to make it into a main-line operation.

My dad used to say that there were only two things to do in work life: "make big things out of little things, or little things out of big things." Martin bought tons of little things, from capacitors to castings, to make big complex things. The purchasing department bought all this stuff, and their natural enemy was the quality department. Everything that came in was checked by the quality people in receiving acceptance—everything, toilet paper to rocket motors. It was a real mess. Most shipments were late, so expediters were all over the area trying to get the products released into the shops. Government inspectors and testers examined the products after we did our evaluations. Between us we found more than a third of purchased items to be nonconforming in some manner. They were rejected and sent to material review, which found a use for most of them. Often the supplier came in to do some rework in our area. Little was sent back. There were also thirty or more field inspectors and quality engineers out evaluating the subcontractors. Still little was received exactly as ordered.

Managing the supplier-quality department let me deal with the entire Martin organization for the first time. Everything up to now had been contained in one way or other. The Pershing project management concentrated on an agreed list of items with an agreed list of people. The quality division consisted of people united in a common cause, even if they did not agree about how to reach that goal. Everyone was assigned friends and enemies along with a common language. The managers were all "types," as in "finance type" and "planning type." They played these roles to the hilt and were marked with them in the middle of their forehead. The quality people talked about how their purpose was to put themselves out of a job, but no one believed that for a moment. The loyalty of individuals was to their home function, not to a project or the company. Just as a dentist concentrates on being a dentist long before thinking about being a citizen of Chicago, so the engineering person is an engineer before everything else. Those who would bring people with different roles together in a team or staff forget the loyalty problem at their peril. The Pershing project director,

The trick is to look as though you understand what is happening.

Herman Staudt, worked hard at building a team atmosphere. He held weekend meetings where we evaluated each other and sought out areas in which we could provide support. These were helpful and effective. However, I kept thinking about the guy who says, "Enough about me; let's talk about you. How do you like my new suit?"

Learning: *people are so concerned about themselves they do not pay much attention to what others are doing—just like golf.*

The problems of supplier quality were several: the department itself had a low self-image; the purchasing people hated both quality and the suppliers; engineering didn't trust anyone so they made specifications tighter than necessary and relaxed them as asked; the suppliers were cynical about dealing with the company because of the arrogant way they were treated. There was a tendency to blame the suppliers for problems because they were not there to defend themselves. All of these problems presented a wonderful opportunity to learn how to cause a social revolution when no one knew they needed one. My strategy was to reestablish the supplier-quality department first, build a relationship with purchasing, get the suppliers on our side, and then convince everyone else that the scheme was working.

Learning: *there is little awareness of what goes on inside another department; outsiders don't know you are conspiring against them.*

I brought in a few key people. Bob Vincent, who had been with me on Pershing, came over to run the supplier-quality engineering operations. New supervisors were obtained for a couple of areas including the field operations. The field people were told that they should concentrate on the product, that expense accounts would just be scanned in my office, and that if they disobeyed accounting's rules, they were on their own. We never had any trouble with them. I also set up a schedule to see all of them in regional meetings. They needed to know that no one loved them but us.

We put a desk outside the receiving-acceptance area and told the expediters they could no longer roam around inside. After that the expediters reminded me of the people who used to hang around the gate of a naval station offering to provide services of all sorts to the sailors. The expediters' requests were logged in, and we kept them up to date on status. We took equipment off the top racks in the area so the supervisor could see everyone working, and we had a couple of meetings with the inspectors and testers to ask for their input. These meetings let them begin to feel as though they belonged. I discovered that they wanted their department head to wear a suit and to deal with the other managers. They didn't want another buddy; they were after some respect from the other employees. This was the only area I ever ran where no one called me by my first name. They just quietly refused.

I told the government inspectors that they were too easy and needed to become more consistent. They loved that request. One of their main complaints was about the "certificate of compliance" that suppliers were supposed to send in with each order. This form stated that what was in the box met all the requirements. It was a useless regulation. After all how dumb would you have to be to send in a letter saying the stuff was no good? This same logic is applied today in corporations that ask suppliers to send along process-control charts showing that the product is within the proper range. As far as I know no one has ever sent in a chart saying things were wrong. The automobile companies have tons of these charts.

Instead of complaining about the certificate of compliance, we learned to help the government people find the form or have a new one mailed in from the vendor. A couple of suppliers offered to send us a stack of certificates so we could just take one from our pile and put it in the box. I never answered their letters. Relationships with the government people improved because of this attitude, and we even began sharing acceptance data. This step caused an immediate improvement as far as senior management was concerned; the numbers could be trusted now. I also had nonconformance reporting broken out by departmental responsibility, which cut down the casual complaints from other areas. For the first time everything was not the fault of the quality division.

Learning: *management is a one-person job.*

When the department began to operate more smoothly, Bob Vincent and I went to see purchasing management, meeting with the four top managers. I took a notepad, told Bob not to say anything under any circumstances, and went in smiling. We asked them what we could do to help them be successful and what problems they had with us. They unloaded about fifteen problems. I wrote them all down while Bob writhed in pain, thanked them for being so candid and open, and asked that we meet again the next week. During that week we worked on these problems, which involved pushing orders through inspection and responding to critical situations. The problems were procedural for the most part and involved a lack of trust. They indicated that we had not been paying enough attention to them and their troubles.

Having been in a hundred or so supplier plants and having worked for several companies, I did not find the lack of trust unique. In no place I had ever been did the workers trust the management or did the management have respect for the workers. No matter how well they appeared to get along, no matter how much effort was made for everyone to be equal, workers knew they were not treated equally. One of the main reasons I decided to aim at becoming an executive was to get away from the patronizing attitude management is injected with. Well-meaning efforts to "empower" workers crash on the rocks of this demeaning approach. Power cannot be given to all; choice cannot be given to all. Nothing will work if the resources are that evenly divided. However, being nice to each other, understanding the other's situation, and not making unnecessary trouble for each other is the beginning of a useful relationship. I thought the supplier-quality system would become valuable if it was calm and purposeful. I proposed to be the catalyst for this change in attitude.

We took the list of complaints that purchasing provided seriously and took action to eliminate them as problems. The main reason items were late getting out of our area was usually because they were late getting in. This is one of the great truths of management that the airline people have never absorbed. If you want to land on time, you must take off on time. However, we didn't mention this mitigating factor; we just worked on streamlining our operation. I spent some time with the buyers and production-control people learning about their jobs. If ever there were people no one loved, here they were. It was not possible for them to do anything right as far as others were concerned. When a worker reached for a part and it wasn't there, one of these two groups was considered to be at fault. If a worker did get the part and it didn't work right, then quality was considered the culprit. All of us were at the bottom of the food chain for certain. While I was in their area, they kept asking me whether I had lost my way. When I was invited to the production-control golf tournament, it was apparent that a breakthrough had occurred.

Learning: *anything can be worked out if credit is given and blame is withheld.*

After our third meeting with the purchasing managers, they ran out of complaints. Everything wasn't fixed yet, but we were all agreed on the actions to be taken. During a pause in the conversation, I asked whether we could bring up a couple of items. When they expressed interest, we began to talk about change orders. A third of the purchasing contracts had changes made during their lifetimes, some of which were only a few weeks long. The main reason seemed to be that the initial contract was placed verbally rather than in writing. Purchasing's response was that people were always in a hurry and that was the reason for verbal orders. But could an organization devoted completely to planning be operating in such a haphazard way? It seemed that a great many needs were generated by engineering groups with no involvement in the big plan. We ordered guidance systems and serial-numbered components with great ceremony and documentation. Ordinary products just worked their way out into the ordering system. Purchasing knew the old system was bad but had never been able to get anyone interested in correcting it. We made a list of exactly who it would take to change such a process and made phone calls to them at that moment in order to set up a meeting for the next morning in the planning director's office. At the meeting I sat quietly by as everyone complained to each other and arrived at an agreement that was implemented on the spot. Each manager called in the appropriate subordinate, explained the process that had been agreed to, and asked them to become a team to document the procedure and arrange to train everyone involved. This solution was arrived at and implemented because each group benefited from it. They also knew that I would make sure senior management was aware of how civilized they all had been, which I did by dropping by each director's office and telling them how wonderful the agreement was. And it was wonderful. This was a breakthrough for me personally; I realized that I could cause the social changes that would bring solid improvement. A new control system could become the basis for systems integrity.

The next people we had to involve were the suppliers. We asked each project to invite its specific suppliers and subcontractors to special meetings. The agendas included quality and schedule considerations. All these seminars were planned with only one flat spot. When I asked for money to have a reception for the first one, Jim refused. He said we weren't allowed to entertain. He did offer to help me ask Willey but suggested that I let him do the talking. His approach was to ask whether it would be all right to serve hot appetizers at the reception. Willey refused that as an extravagance but agreed to pay for the rest. This was Jim's way of teaching.

We introduced the suppliers to real-world ZD and asked them to commit their companies to achieve that goal. They all wrote their names on a big chart I had made up. We made photocopies of the chart, attached a signed picture of them taken with me, and sent it to them. They all hung the pictures in their offices and started using the same technique on their own suppliers.

Jim taught me to not write a draft letter for people; give them a real one to sign, he said, and they will not pick at it. He taught me to recognize the inevitable and act accordingly. He taught me to ask questions that could be answered in the positive and to refrain from mentioning that which was not going to happen. He taught me a lot.

Learning: *I am a good student when the teacher has something worthwhile to teach.*

I was becoming bored with what I could do at Martin. It was a big plant, with a lot of people and a good cash flow, and it was a wonderful place to work. Martin had been good to me, and I believed I had paid the company back many times over. The ZD effort had saved a lot of money and gotten Martin a worldwide reputation for quality. My personal reputation in the field of quality was firm. Many people, particularly the old guard, thought I was a charlatan with concepts based on false premises. However, because I was a practitioner, they could not deny the results. Management people thought I was a pragmatic person who could break complicated processes down into steps they could understand. My speaking schedule grew, with invitations from other functions, like purchasing and engineering. I wrote another large article for *American Machinist.* My title was "The Great Supplier Quality Mystery." They changed it without asking to "How to Manage Supplier Quality." It was well received and with the other two articles formed a large part of the book I was writing: *Cutting the Cost of Quality.*

In mid-1964 I started looking around for another job, with the family's permission. The Martin personnel people had let me know, kindly, that there was no other place in the corporation for me. Headquarters jobs required more experience and education than I had, and the plant in Orlando had no other opportunities. I looked hard, reading all the advertisements and making a few networking calls.

When I am bored, I become dangerous, much like a small child. Jim sent me to a proposal-review meeting as his representative. The project, a Navy one, was for a new weapon, and the company wanted

Receiving an Army medal for creating the zero-defects concept, 1964.

to win it. The instructions we had were to bid the work on the basis that everything would be done right the first time. But when the manufacturing director laid out the assembly operation on a flannel board, he placed three blocks labeled "rework stations" in the line. I objected and was told that I should be practical. I said we would lose our shirts on the project if we didn't plan to learn how to do things right. Several of the directors glared me into sitting back down, and a few comments were made about "impractical youth." Being almost forty, I took that as a compliment. But there were little hints that I was not respectful enough of my betters. It was never my intent to be that way toward anyone, so I took time to mend fences and looked harder for another opportunity.

Out of the blue I received a call from International Telephone and Telegraph Corporation (ITT) in New York. They were interested in finding a corporate quality director and wondered whether I would like to talk about it. They sent me a package of material and said they would call back to arrange an appointment when the senior executives were there. I was impressed with their tone. The material showed that ITT was a worldwide corporation being grown by Harold Geneen into a conglomerate. "Hurry Up Hal" the magazines called him. ITT had plants all over Europe, and the world headquarters was a big building on Park Avenue at 50th Street in Manhattan, looking right at the Waldorf Astoria. ITT was bigger than Martin by a factor of six, and they thought I could work there. I felt as though I had given birth. The caller, Pat Stokes, didn't even ask whether I had graduated from high school. His interest was all based on my reputation. He had first heard about me from a senior executive at a large company that had been one of the Pershing suppliers. Then they had done enough research to discover some of my articles. After years of tiptoeing around my education, or misdirection of it, I was hopeful that it would not become a roadblock.

The second call didn't come for two months, at the beginning of 1965. Someone at ITT had been fired, someone had been transferred, and someone had set the quality job aside. However, Mr. Geneen had apparently asked about it, so the search was on again. Pat wondered whether I could come and meet the appropriate people. I went to Jim and told him my situation; he had always been straight with me. He said he understood that I had been told there was no future for me at Martin but he did not agree with that analysis. However, he was willing to go along this time and let me see what ITT had to offer. He did not doubt that they would want me and that I could do the job. He was much more confident than I. He also let me know that he didn't want to know anymore about anything. So I traveled to New York; I was well acquainted with the theater district but knew almost nothing about the rest of the city. Every time I got there on business I used my meal money to see plays. Suppliers were always wanting to take us to dinner and a show, but I felt it would not appear to be proper. I didn't think it was wrong. After all, who can you buy for a show and a meal? And would you want them if you could? However, it looked improper, and so I didn't do it. On occasion I slid into a theater at intermission and watched the second act from the standing-room area. I saw a lot of half shows, but in musicals that was usually the best part.

Pat introduced me to the vice president I would work for, and he took me to lunch with a few of ITT's worldwide staff organization. We went to the Waldorf, which was about a hundred yards away. The boss hopped in a cab and drove over there, about 150 yards by that route, and the rest of us walked. No one mentioned the cab. We all met in front of the hotel and walked through the lobby to the restaurant. I was always impressed with the place and expressed that opinion as we walked, which is something that real New Yorkers never do. The purpose of having a world staff organization was to have experienced specialists in areas like inventory, purchasing, and manufacturing who would help the units needing assistance. They would also set up worldwide systems for improving those areas. During the lunch each of the staff members took turns grilling me on quality. They were all nice guys and knew their areas well, but their idea of quality was old-fashioned, the policeman concept. They told stories about shutting down lines because of quality problems and of building cars with three doors and about stubborn and stupid inspectors. I let them understand that my approach would be prevention, which would make money for the corporation. We all got along well. I also spoke to a couple of executive vice presidents, and by now I had learned not to contradict their ideas about quality. There was plenty of time for that later.

Pat called me with an offer early in May. It was not as much as I had expected; the salary would be $25,000 plus incentive compensation, and the vice president I would be working for didn't think a "quality guy" could contribute a lot. However, I wanted to go there. Knowing that I did, Pat arranged for me to get a moving package that would provide the equivalent of three months' gross pay. Anything I didn't spend was mine to keep without any need to report it. He also got an allowance that would cover the realtor's fee for selling my house and also curtains and wall-to-wall carpet in a new home. By the time he got through, I had enough money to move, so I accepted.

Learning: *I always figure the Lord has a plan for me, so when an opportunity arises I just hop right in.*

After I had told Jim and Willey about my plans, I received an invitation to Martin honors night, which was held in Washington each year. Winners from all over the corporation were invited, with their spouses, and given medals for achievement. Most of these medals were awarded for technical improvements, and the engineers were always the big winners. The big award, which always went to engineers, was the Purple Martin, a little bird pin for the lapel. Jim, Willey, and I had been nominated for different awards because of ZD. I suggested to Willey that I not attend because I was leaving the company; but he insisted, and we went to Washington. The award dinner and ceremony were well done, but it was obvious the senior executives were not very interested. They partied, related to each other, paid little attention to the nervous attendees, and sort of mumbled through the program. I decided that I would have an award system one day that would give everyone positive vibes or at least no negative ones. There seems little use in going to all that trouble in order to turn people off.

The housing market in Orlando was depressed at that time, and it was hard to get attention for resales. However, I had a stroke of luck. A mysterious buyer had been snapping up land on the southwest side of town—thousands of acres; my Los Angeles resident inspector called me to say that he knew for sure it was Disney. Anyone with some money would have taken advantage of this information by running out and purchasing a few lots in the right place. I had no way of doing that, but I did go to see a friend on the newspaper. I offered to tell him who the buyer was if the newspaper would advertise my house in a little block on the front page. After some discussion, the newspaper agreed. They didn't believe me, but they kept their part of the bargain. I sold for a little less than I had paid for the house and added pool, and pocketed the realtor fee.

We had two cars at this time, an Oldsmobile station wagon and a little Plymouth convertible that I drove to work. When someone approaching forty buys a convertible, look out for major changes. We were able to trade the two of them for a year-old Cadillac, which we were embarrassed to admit was ours. The car was in perfect shape, but our lower-middle-class background was hard to shake. We dispatched the moving van to Greenwich, Connecticut, and drove north in the new used car. Family tradition says that when we drove past our church on the way out of town, seven-year-old Phylis called out, "Good-bye God. We're going to Connecticut."

CHAPTER SIX

ITT and Mr. Geneen

O nce in Greenwich, we checked into the Steamboat Inn and found a realtor. We told him how much we could afford and said we wanted an empty three-bedroom home with some woods. He noted that people with our amount of money usually migrated closer to Westport, but he did have three houses that met our requirements. We picked one that cost $45,400 and was on a wooded acre in a development that had lot restrictions of that size. It was about 60 percent of the size of our house in Maitland and had no pool. No one could afford to build a pool there, too many rocks. We paid a little down and arranged to close on Tuesday because the van would arrive on Wednesday. Movers do not drive on the weekend. How was I going to arrange for $10,000 by Tuesday? The house in Florida would not close for a month or so and even then would not come close to yielding that much money. I called my new boss, who lived in Greenwich, and he invited me to ride to work with him on Monday morning.

ITT had a deal with Chrysler at that time where executives could lease a Continental for $90 a month. As we drove into the city, he told me about his adventures during previous drives and about the company operations in Europe. We had a useful chat and developed a working rapport. We parked the car in an underground garage, and he delivered me to personnel, where I wandered around until I came to Pat's office. He checked me in and then walked me to the ninth-floor office where the world staff lived. After introducing me around, he led me to a small, windowless chamber that also housed a large drawing board. It would be moved out soon, everyone said. However, it had been there for a couple of years, according to maintenance, so I called the facilities department and asked them to get it. To encourage their response I folded it and slid it into the hall, where it blocked everything.

I asked Pat where I could get the use of $10,000 for a while, and he suggested that I ask my boss to introduce me to what is now Citibank, across Park Avenue. They did all ITT's banking and loved each employee dearly, he said. I went down the hall and made the request, which was implemented right away. Citibank welcomed me and offered me a "bridge loan" to get us through the house purchase and closing. The local bank in Greenwich was going to do the mortgage itself. They also gave me a personal line of credit of $3,000 with special checks, opened a checking account into which my pay would be deposited each month, and insisted that I open a savings account. My pocket contained only four dollars, and I gave it all to Citibank. (They must have a checklist that has to be completed in order to get their bonus.) As a result I had to borrow $20 from the boss's secretary in order to have some lunch and buy a train ticket home. I got good at taking the train in and back, but that is a whole other story.

Learning: *commuting is commuting; it is all solvable.*

My second day there I discovered the policy and procedure books, including a ten-pound one that described how the ITT logo could and could not be used. They were in genuine-leather three-ring binders and contained also a complete set of organization charts for all the companies in the corporation. No one was much concerned with my personal education at that moment, so I thought I could use the books to do it myself. There was only one mention of quality in any of the blocks full of names, and that was in LMT, a French company. To make a list of quality departments worldwide, I had to call all of them. The fact that none were important enough to formally exist on headquarters paper made the job interesting. I decided then that everyone in the business world would look at ITT as the standard for quality before we were through. The aerospace world had no idea about quality because it didn't have to deliver anything that worked right now. All its products went to a depot or other area where they were reworked before being given to the user. In the commercial world real people gave real products and services to real people, who were usually using their own money or money for which they were accountable. I was eager to get on with it.

Learning: *nobody knows what is going on everywhere in any business.*

I had found a publisher for my book *Cutting the Cost of Quality,* and it was released soon after I got to ITT. It was aimed at the quality professionals and had only modest sales. The few reviews did not take the idea of prevention seriously. I realized right then that I should concentrate on management, with an emphasis on executives. The conventional wisdom of quality control was too deeply imbedded in my professional colleagues to change during my lifetime.

I conducted a telephone tour of the U.S. companies in order to find my quality managers. To a man, and they were all men, they were delighted that I was at headquarters and wanted to be of help to them. To a man they politely let me know that it was not possible to rescue them or get through to their bosses. None of them reported to the top of their organization except a few in the defense group. None I talked to had any idea of how the business was doing financially. The quality professionals I thought were backward at Martin were looking better to me all the time.

I then examined the corporate policy and procedure books, and I realized that there was nothing to build on. The company needed an original and concerted quality effort beginning with a policy on quality. It would have to be built on the basis of a corporate statement that would eliminate the arguments and confrontations up front. I wrote one: "The quality policy of the ITT Corporation is that we will deliver products and services to our customers and coworkers that meet the agreed requirements, or we will have the requirements officially changed to what we and the customer really need." Then I added a couple of paragraphs that required every unit to have quality management reporting to its senior executive and performing tasks agreed to by the senior executive and the corporate quality director (me).

I took these statements down to the policy and procedure department on the next floor and asked that they be issued. In the process I learned that New York buildings had limited access from the stairwell. You could get into the stairwell, but the doors were locked from that side; they didn't open onto a floor. I had to walk down to the lobby and take the elevator back up to the eighth floor to reach the policy office. Things like this keep you humble.

The policy people were most cooperative; they noted that I could sign the statements but Mr. Geneen had final approval. They would send the final forms up to him on the twelfth floor unless I wanted to carry them personally. I thought we would just let them do it, and he signed the statements right away. I didn't expect a revolution from these policies, but they laid a foundation. I made certain that copies were sent to each quality manager worldwide. Most of them would have never seen it otherwise.

Learning: *big, important companies are manned by ordinary people.*

Writing memos and letters in this big world headquarters was no where near as easy as in my former life. Secretarial help was scarce, and everything took a while. I noticed an old IBM electric typewriter in one of the storerooms, and after a halfhearted search for its owner, I moved it to my desk. Now I could write my own memos and letters. I lugged that machine from office to office all the years I worked there. Anyone who tried to read my handwriting was grateful for its printed letters. As the only executive who typed, I was considered a little weird, but that can be an advantage in an organization where people strive to not be different. When I did write some memos and trip reports, I found to my amazement that they were actually read by those who received them. In the world of aerospace it was considered bad form to distribute memos widely. At ITT they complained if everyone didn't know what someone had written. Each day, for instance, I received a pile of pink copies of all the telexes sent by anyone in the system, at least ninety of them. When I tried to get off the distribution list, the folks I talked to acted as though I were becoming a Communist or something. Finally I just tossed them out each day.

Looking through the paper-clip closet, where pads and pencils were kept, I discovered a little booklet written by Mr. Geneen. It laid out a way of writing a memo and was entitled *Unshakable Facts*. It stated that the findings of a trip should be listed first and numbered. (I use this example: "1. Burn the plant down. 2. Fire all the management. 3. Plow the ground with salt.") Then a paragraph should be inserted to provide details of and reasons for each of these recommendations. ("Nothing profitable has ever been made here.") Finally, the author's unvarnished opinion should be stated. The findings and recommendations can be fought about and even rejected, but the opinion cannot be altered. Right or wrong writers are entitled to say what they think.

I immediately began to follow this layout and wrote all my reports that way for the rest of my career at ITT. No one else ever did, as far as I know. That always made me wonder. When the big boss lays out a report format that makes sense, why not use it? When I finally got a staff, I had a hard time getting them to do it even though they liked to read my reports. After a few years I finally gave up trying to change people. You can offer them an opportunity to develop, just as you can buy a piano and offer lessons, but you can't make it happen to anyone except yourself. All the money corporations spend on personnel development is wasted, except, of course, for those who get paid to run such programs.

Learning: *people learn only what they are interested in learning.*

My first trip as the ITT quality director was to a pump plant in the Midwest. Before venturing out of headquarters, I had tried to get a feeling about the relationships between the units (as the subsidiary companies were called) and the headquarters staff. I knew that in Martin everyone hated the Baltimore people. These bad feelings may or may not have had a basis in fact; I hardly knew any of the people in Baltimore. At ITT the staffs had the reputation of being tough on the unit people. The old story, which I stole and have used for years, is that people from headquarters are called "seagulls": "they fly in, squawk a lot, eat your food, crap all over you, and then fly away." It seemed to me that a headquarters "expert" who was useful and didn't make trouble would stand out in that environment. I decided to be known as considerate but demanding.

I made certain that I started my visit in the pump plant with the general manager, with whom I had made an appointment. I rejected an offer to be picked up at the airport and made my way over. My feeling was that we could have a stronger relationship if I acted as though I were working for them; there would be no special treatment. The general manager was gracious. After a while I asked whether I could do anything to help him. What was his biggest problem? After some reluctance he decided to share with me that there had been a sudden burst of customer complaints about receiving pumps that were different from those they ordered. I said I would look into it. We talked about the role I planned to play in the corporation and wondered whether it was possible to influence something like quality in a world-wide conglomerate. The general manager then called the quality manager and asked him to come to the office to pick me up.

I spent the morning becoming familiar with the operation. They ran a typical machining and assembly shop. There were a few statistical process-control charts, but basically they just shaped up the little parts and then combined them into big ones. The pumps were well designed, had been proven over the years, and were considered very reliable. The quality manager, Harry, became comfortable with me after a while and began to chat about his problems. The strong marketing group at the plant was always pressuring the shops to produce ahead of the plan. This procedure led to a lot of unnecessary confusion. Also marketing was always changing configurations in order to appear to be offering customers the latest technology.

After a while the general manager called and asked me to come to his office for lunch. Harry delivered me there, and I was led to the executive dining room, where the directors of marketing, manufacturing, and finance were waiting. We all introduced ourselves and sat chatting while the dining staff started to serve the meal. I looked around the room, and when the marketing director asked me what I was looking for, I said I was wondering where Harry was. He didn't belong to the executive dining room, I was told, but they could invite him up. Acting on this afterthought, they made a couple of calls and soon Harry arrived, very nervous about the whole thing.

I chatted up a storm while eating lunch as the rest of them poked around. It was in situations like this that I learned what was really happening in the corporation and in this particular industry. Finally, the subject of quality came up, and I led the conversation around to the problem of the wrong pumps going out to the customers. The marketing manager launched into a condemnation of the manufacturing operation, which was immediately refuted by its director. After a while I asked Harry what he thought caused the problem. He shrugged his shoulders and said that he had included his thoughts in his last report: the problem was that marketing had changed the sales catalogue but had not told manufacturing about it. As a result the plant was shipping the right part number but it related to the wrong part. Harry had been unable to stop it or even to get anyone interested in stopping it. He was not invited to the operations review meetings, and no one seemed to read his reports. He could not help it if no one seemed to care about quality. We finished the meal in silence. The general manager was seething inside, waiting for lunch to get over and me to get lost so he could kill the marketing person. Harry's reports were read with care from that time on, and he was invited to attend a lot of boring meetings. There is a price for recognition.

Learning: *the solutions to the problems of every organization are known by someone in that organization; if you listen long enough, the solutions will emerge.*

This routine seemed to work in every plant. No one paid much attention to quality managers in the "commercial" world unless they had just the right kind of personality, and none of them did. They needed some help, both in organization and in education. In government work the contract required that the quality function report at an organizational level, a requirement that made people at least pretend to listen. Our new corporate policy would bring that practice to ITT. However, we needed to organize the quality managers so they could become a force and we needed to educate them.

The financial people, from timekeepers to accountants to company comptrollers, all reported directly to New York. The local general managers had nothing to say about their activities, policies, or even who they were. The purpose of this policy was to make certain that no one was fooling with the numbers. The corporate comptroller was a senior vice president, was a member of the board of directors, and went to all the meetings. I was sharing a secretary with two other guys, had the worst office in the building, and had zero staff. I could only hope that the corporate comptroller had begun the same way. We were going to have to do quality much differently. I would have refused to have all the quality functions report directly to me anyway. The general managers would be calling to say that "your dummy sent out some very bad stuff; what do you intend to do about it?" Let them be their dummies, not mine.

Learning: *organizational manipulation does not make things happen or not happen.*

In order to turn the quality managers from observers into commandos, I decided to assemble them into quality councils, which would provide education, fellowship, and communication. The quality councils began with the aerospace and defense group. I invited the quality managers of that group, about a dozen people, to meet at one of the plants in the Los Angeles area. Being in government work, they were used to going to meetings and being on committees; they picked up on the quality-council concept right away. I selected one of them as chairman and made it clear that we were going to institute quality councils throughout the corporation in order to make prevention a normal way of life. The quality people would become important and useful if they cooperated with me and learned how to get the right things done. Lack of cooperation could produce the opposite. All of these points sounded reasonable to them, and we began to lay out plans for that group.

The "commercial" people were in another situation altogether. When I sent out a notice inviting the quality managers of one group to a meeting, I was deluged with calls from their bosses saying that they could not be spared from the plant. The concern was that nothing would be shipped if it were not possible to get waivers. I also got a dressing down from my boss, who said I should be out solving problems instead of having quality meetings. My response was that I was solving problems, that our worldwide quality operations were kindergarten grade, and that he should recognize that one guy traveling around the globe was not going to solve anything except some airline's cash shortage. I told him my vision of a stewardess coming to my seat one day to hand me a gold watch. I did promise that every place I went I would solve at least one current problem and save the company enough money to pay for my trip. I described three cases where the comptroller had agreed in writing that my suggestions had saved enough to pay my present salary for the next dozen years. There were so many opportunities it was like picking up seashells, but the regular operations needed to learn how to do what I was doing on their own.

It was becoming apparent to him that I was not going to be influenced by someone who had no experience in managing quality and was not willing to be taught about it. So we smiled together and sat down for a chat. When we began to have an understanding I talked to him about the "quality college." We needed to teach the quality professionals and start on the executives after that. We would bring all the managers to school twenty or so at a time and have classes on how to manage quality. They would learn about management in general, how to deal with executives, and how to implement a quality-improvement process. The goal would be to make ITT the standard for quality worldwide. If that was going to happen, I needed someone to help me. I wanted to bring Bob Vincent up from Martin for that job. To my surprise he agreed to hire Bob on the spot but said I would have to deal with personnel because they were impossible. He would sign the requisition, but the rest was up to me. My experience over the next years proved that he was absolutely right; personnel was impossible.

Hiring me had taken about six months because of what was happening within personnel, but it all had finally occurred. However, that department was a thorn in my side for the next fourteen years. It wasn't that they were picking on me; they just had their own agenda. When hiring at the senior level, they administered a complex series of tests and set up interviews with psychologists. All of this information wound up in a bound booklet that laid out the applicant's assumed personality and history. This booklet was presented to the executive doing the hiring, who then used it to make a decision (or didn't use it). There was no bottom line on the report, no yes or no. My observation over a period of time was that about half of the senior people hired did well and the other half quickly left for one reason or another. I always felt you could tell about a person in a few moments; or you could at least determine how they were going to get along in an organization like ITT. For a while I kept an unofficial scoreboard in my desk, as I did each year during the Miss America telecast. But then I tossed it as being indiscreet.

Learning: *to progress in an organization built around a lot of different departments, it is necessary to utilize the helpful ones and avoid the unhelpful ones.*

Asking for permission is not the way to get things done in a large corporation. No one with authority will ever want to do anything different. No one will understand why you want to start something new or, worse, change what has been there for a while. Questions will be raised about exactly whose approval is needed and how the change will affect other operations. So I learned not to ask but just to go ahead, keeping everyone informed. When you proceed in that way, people think you must have someone's approval and are afraid to ask who that might be. However, your changes have to be presented one day, and that has to be done in a way that does not threaten anyone or any existing programs. It takes a great deal of selling to convince people that your intention is just to make life easier and more productive for them and not to control them.

In late 1965 I went to London and became an unashamed Anglophile. My hobby has always been history, and to walk around actually touching all those treasures was marvelous. It wasn't long before I could almost qualify as a tour guide; the place is like Disney World with real people.

Working with three ITT units in Great Britain, I began to realize that this was an entirely different world of management. There was little contact between those with suits and those with work outfits. It didn't take an expert to see that productivity was low and that it took twice as many people to do about half as much. To make changes in anything, particularly if the suggestion was coming from an American, was not possible. All the people I met thought it was a shame that the system worked this way, but there it was. They would have liked everyone else to adapt.

Learning: *if you want to live a truly frustrating life, try to make everyone as wonderful as you are.*

On this same trip I went to Brussels, where ITT had its European headquarters, to Paris, and to Stuttgart. My purpose was to learn what the corporation was about; my boss thought I should be getting hardware moved. He lived for today; I worried about next year. He was particularly concerned about a plant in southern England that made teleprinters for the British Admiralty. They had not been able to get the machines past the government inspector, and there was a big backlog. Would I go over and see what could be done?

My schedule was to head home after two weeks in Europe. Some of the world staff stayed months on a job; I thought it was not a good idea to start that pattern. However, to work on our relationship I changed plans and went back across the Channel to the plant. They were glad to see me, but then they would have welcomed Hitler back if they thought it would get Brussels off their backs. Their problem was evident in a large room full of teleprinters, all covered with plastic sheets. The government inspector, an elderly gentleman with a great shock of white hair, came by two times a week. He looked at four machines, accepted or rejected them, and then left. Because several hundred units were already made and they were making many more each day, it was not difficult to see where the bottleneck originated. They showed me, on request, exactly what the inspection consisted of. The purpose was to ensure that the machines met the requirements mechanically, but the inspection did not involve hooking up the machines to determine whether they worked. A package of specifications two inches thick described how far apart the keys should be, how much travel should exist in the space bar, and so forth. These specifications had been prepared by our own quality department and were not part of the contract. The contract required only that the machines receive and transmit a certain sized message reliably.

Against everyone's advice I asked to see the Government inspector, who turned out to be a nice person. We went to the pub together, had a Dutch lunch, and discussed the Battle of Hastings, which had occurred nearby. When I asked him why he inspected only four units each time, he replied that those were all they showed him. He was really interested in whether the machines sent messages and got them back. He didn't understand why the quality people were so interested in all the mechanical measurements. We agreed that he would return at the end of the week and spend two days with us.

Learning: *people of good will can work things out.*

Back in the plant I tossed out the mechanical specification and helped take the plastic off the machines. We set up a series of tables and put the machines, all 435 of them, on the tables in neat rows. Then we set up two input/output areas, where a machine could be hooked up and tested. When he returned, the inspector agreed to my plan, which was that he would select machines at random and we would operate them for him or he could do so himself. We agreed that 15 percent of them would make a proper sample. Over the next two days we put 100 units through the testing system. All of them performed to the requirements. He released the entire lot, and they were shipped off to the Admiralty.

We agreed that in the future he would concern himself with the integrity of our test rather than in witnessing a special evaluation. Any time he felt something was lacking, we would stop and conduct special testing. That way a steady flow of machines could leave the plant. It worked that way for many years afterward. I called my boss, and he agreed that I could go back home, which was fortunate because I was already at Heathrow.

The key to getting those machines out was to recognize that the Admiralty wanted them for use and ITT wanted to get paid. The mechanical measurements that had been created for no good reason blocked the whole thing. No one even mentioned them while we were going through the testing, and they never came up again as far as I know. This was a case of people making trouble for themselves and their customers by getting away from the subject. The Europeans like specifications and requirements; they never seem to get enough of them. If none exist, they will create a bunch. Once created they never cease to exist. This is the mentality that produced the International Standardization Organization series on quality. It is sort of like determining the winner of a golf tournament based on whether a person's clubs, clothes, and education meet certain standards. It has nothing to do with playing the game.

During my visit to Europe I learned that each country had a big ITT telecommunications company, all called by initials: SESA, CITESA, CGCT, SEL (Standard Electric Lorenz), TELCOM. The telecommunications business was divided in most countries among ITT, Erickson, Seimans, and a few others. Telephone systems were all run by governments; we just made the equipment for them. But government people were in all the factories and had acceptance stamps, just like the Department of Defense folks in the United States. My goal was for them to have so much confidence in us that they handed over the acceptance stamps and just sat in their offices. At this time they were busy and were not all that happy with our quality. Most of the time our quality people were sitting around arguing about one specification or another rather than solving and preventing problems.

The quality systems inside these companies were patterned after the quality-control methods developed at Western Electric. These were aimed at detection and correction. Inside the operations there was an inspector for each four or five workers. It was obvious that even a modest quality-engineering effort aimed at prevention would pay for itself quickly. The problem was how to get these companies, in a dozen nations with different cultures and languages, to decide that they wanted to go in this direction.

Learning: *it is best to tear down an old house and build a new one; otherwise the floors will still creak.*

Each of these companies had a quality director who worked at the top levels of the organization. They were mostly older than I and had spent their lives in the business. Georges Borel of France, Dr. Behne of Germany, and Dr. Enrique Blanco of Spain were the senior people. They all became close friends. I contacted them and their counterparts in the other countries and asked them to meet with me in Paris during the first quarter of 1966; they agreed. My message was that we would form an executive quality council for Europe, that Borel would be the chairman, and that we would plan how to turn quality around in

Europe. I selected Borel because he was a diplomat and French. The Europeans didn't appear to like each other as nationals all that much, but they didn't dislike the French as much as they disliked the others. I realize that comes out strange, but that is the way it is.

During our first meeting they said we needed a message from Tim Dunleavy, the president of ITT Europe, saying that this quality strategy had his blessing. On the way back home I stopped by the Brussels office between planes, wrote out a sterling letter of support, gave it to Tim, and he signed it happily. As he said, he didn't have anything to lose and had a lot to gain. Tim was not one who signed such letters casually and was known to carefully distance himself from those who wanted him to join their crusade. But he recognized that the company had to improve quality if it was going to survive. I asked his office to distribute the statement, which they did. By the time I got back to the New York office we had telexes from all over Europe saying that the managing directors wanted to come to our meetings and loved us. The same approach had little effect in the United States or South America. Just being in charge got you nothing in those places.

We needed a statement of the new quality concept to work with, to use to get the word out, to hand to people. Using my trusty typewriter, again at home, I wrote a booklet called *Quality Improvement Through Defect Prevention*. It covered the concepts of quality management, plus the fourteen steps of an improvement process. We had to lead people away from the irrelevance of quality control and statistical process control, which were being taught to the profession. They produced no results, just reams of paper and megatons of argument.

Learning: *the basics of any crusade have to be clearly and simply laid out; otherwise horses will be bounding off in all directions.*

To support this understanding I prepared tape recordings of the ZD concept in all the ITT languages. In those days such recordings were on reels of tape (cassette players were not available yet) and were placed in little "handkerchief" boxes for presentation. It was necessary to carry a fifteen-pound player around in order to have someone listen to the concept. But aside from having to learn a dozen languages this seemed to be the only way. The public-relations department pitched in. Rich Bennett, who was an executive vice president, became interested in my efforts and helped me get the money for this project. It didn't amount to much and in fact made little difference; the company had plenty of money and was willing to spend it. The problem was getting it for something that was new. I finally learned to just go ahead and get what I needed. No one seemed to care.

Rich had made a big impact on ITT management ever since he arrived. Geneen (or HSG, as he was known) liked to hire bright people with experience as senior executives and then just toss them into the pits to see what they found to do. Rich realized quickly that few of his colleagues knew much about manufacturing, so he picked up on inventory right away. The company had a great deal of inventory worldwide but did not know how much or of what. Rich arranged for the world staff to calculate it so he could report what terrible shape it was in at the General Management Meeting (GMM). Ed Schaffer, the director of industrial engineering, on the same staff as I, was in charge. As Rich's efforts drove the inventory down, HSG approved, and soon Rich moved into the office of the president. He decided that I was on the right track about quality and became a mentor and supporter. We advised each other many times, but Rich was the master at handling situations.

He developed the idea of taking a company plane and a crew of people to visit several units. Other senior managers never got to these units, so Rich knew more about what was going on than anyone else, except perhaps me. I made a point of visiting several units each month as well as meeting with quality councils. They gave me the real story. Also I went with Rich on his trips.

We worked out a strategy that helped the quality effort in each place. Through my sources in the quality council and my personal relationships with the quality managers I found out what was really going on in each unit, good and bad. I would prepare Rich, and in return he would ask for a comment from the quality manager when the inevitable on-site operations review began. Because the quality manager was hardly ever invited to the review, this caused embarrassment. The lights would go back on, there would be a short break, and when things resumed, there sat Rich, myself, and the quality manager in the front row. After a while the idea went ahead of us, and the general manager could always be found with his arm around the shoulder of the quality guy.

Learning: *managers learn what is important to them by finding out what is important to their seniors.*

When the seven U.S. quality councils were formed, I brought them to New York one group at a time to have lunch in the executive dining room with Rich or Tim Dunleavy, who became president after leaving Europe, or even HSG. After introducing them, I left the room so they were alone with the big boss. One side effect was that ITT top management would remember the quality manager when meeting the staff of a unit and the quality managers could then introduce the really big boss to their boss. All this effort led people to think that they had better things to do than fool around with the quality function.

Learning: *the three most important things in management are relationships, relationships, and relationships.*

The management-development department ran a two-week seminar on the ITT management system, and my boss decided to send me. Later he noted that everyone else was doing something important and I was the only one he could spare. Fortunately, I don't need a lot of love from the business world. The course was run by consultants and was time well spent. They did teach the ITT system, but they also played psychological games that were helpful to me. The meeting was held in a club just outside Atlantic City. I arranged to play golf all by myself with a caddy at the crack of dawn each morning so that I could get to the opening exercises on time. We did the same thing in Brussels during ITT's European Action Committee week. Some of the group played tennis; a few of us went to the Royal Belgian Golf Course and swept the dew.

The first seminar was spent with everyone arguing about the difference between line and staff. This discussion was useless but let everyone become acquainted. Because I had never been to such seminars, this program gave me a good understanding of how to teach executives in a way that would be remembered. Two weeks was much too long, but I had not had any time off for so long that I really enjoyed it.

Learning: *most executives study only what pertains to their present job; if you want them to be interested in a new concept, it is necessary to stage the lesson as an event.*

We needed a movie to explain what ZD was all about, and I persuaded the administrator to slip it into the department budget. I then contacted a film company (this was before videos), and we went to work. My experience at Bendix was a great help here. The producer/director and I both wrote the script; he hired professional actors, whom I recognized from TV commercials; and soon the film, *Zero*

Defects, That's Good Enough, was in the can. It was well received. We made the narration voice-over rather than dialogue so we could dub it in all the ITT languages.

The ITT management system was based on determining the five-year financial goals of each unit early in the first quarter of a year; these goals were turned into a business plan, which was discussed and resolved by the fourth quarter of that year; after that, the staffs monitored compliance. When troubles were foreseen or appeared, the staffs swarmed in to help. It was all right to have problems; it was not all right to ignore them or not ask for help. HSG was a terror when he discovered that information had been withheld or adjusted to shine in a better light. Every month the world status was covered in the General Management Meeting, and then all the senior people went to Brussels to meet with the European executives in the European Action Committee and a bunch of smaller groups. They did this every month, and I did my best to duck out of the trip. It was hard to spend time in those meetings and still do my job. Not being an officer yet, I was not invited to the GMM; my boss went and slept through most of it.

The GMM was the heart of the corporation. It was held in a large conference room on top of the building at 50th and Madison in New York for two or three days each month. Every general manager and staff executive in the corporation wrote a status letter according to a format. These were placed in two leather notebooks and sent to each of the eighty attendees. All I knew about it was that now and then they discussed a "quality problem" that I was supposed to resolve. Through relationships built up in the quality councils, I could call the quality manager from the relevant unit and get the straight story. They knew that I would take time to understand what was going on and that I would not make them look bad because of the problem. They also knew that I would find out eventually what was happening even if they did not tell me. They did not want to be put into that situation. I couldn't fire them, but I could make them wish they were somewhere else.

When executives talk about quality problems, they mean that a product didn't perform correctly. They do not mean that the quality department itself was the culprit, but other people think that is what they mean. So it is essential that corrective-action requests spell out clearly how the problem was caused, how it will be fixed, and how it will be prevented. In the process it is necessary to make certain that individuals are not targeted. "Fight the problem, not the people," said Mr. G., and he was correct. Every problem was different from the way it was described at the meeting, which meant that the information received by the senior people was not complete. From this discrepancy, I learned not to prejudge or get upset or even frown when a problem came down. There was time enough for that later. Also nothing was ever as bad as it had been portrayed.

Learning: *executives are dedicated to communication, but this does not always include listening on their part.*

In mid-1968 I was asked to speak at the European Organization for Quality Control (EOQC) (they dropped the "control" a few years later), which was holding its annual meeting in Madrid. We arranged to hold the meeting of the European executive quality council there and invite the chairmen of the U.S. quality councils to participate also. We held our meetings for two days before the EOQC. When I talked about the ITT corporate program at the EOQC, I was surprised to find my comments challenged by several U.S. quality leaders. They said that trying for zero defects was wasteful and gave people an impossible task. The most vocal of them came to the platform, as was the custom there, to ask me a question. Before he could do so, I asked whether he would mind telling me what ZD was. He described it as a worker-motivation program that deceived managers into believing they could get better products just by getting the workers to sign pledges. I got up from the table and went over to him, put my arm around his shoulder, and said that if that was what ZD was, I didn't want any part of it either. To this day I have never figured out why some people insist that we have to do a few things wrong in order to be human. Their influence has been destructive. Quality professionals are so busy controlling variables they have trouble getting around to the real actions.

Learning: *most professionals become bonded to basic beliefs and do not want to examine anything new; they are afraid change will alter their world.*

My boss had left the company, and they brought in a new one. We had many people on the world staff who could have done the job; but then that person would have to be replaced. It was easier to find someone from the outside to come in as a vice president and run the staff. By following this procedure many corporations lose good people while gaining people other companies are delighted to see leave. This boss was dimmer than the previous one in my opinion, so I decided that ITT was not the place for me. The quality management system was in place; the quality college was operating, I could leave with a clear conscience. My salary was slowly edging up, and I had received a large incentive compensation each year. However, I was still making under $40,000, which was just pocket money in Greenwich. There were no stock options at my level, and I was flying tourist across the ocean and back almost every month. I decided that ITT did not appreciate me, even though they said they did. My new boss let me know that this was about the end of the road for me; he wasn't sure I would be getting a raise this year because I was "pretty high" already.

Learning: *Lincoln's emancipation edict should have included something about corporate executives and the whims of their leaders.*

The Sunday paper had a display ad in the help-wanted section (I read everything) for a vice president of quality. I sent them a copy of *Cutting the Cost of Quality,* which had been published in a new edition the previous year by the now defunct Industrial Education Institute. We used it in some seminars I conducted for the institute on vacation days in order to increase my income. The book didn't sell a lot and was made fun of by the quality press, which only convinced me that my way was the best.

The next week I received a call at home from the head hunter, Elmer Davis, who was delighted that I was interested. He had even heard of me. We arranged for me to come to his office on 42nd Street, which I did. He gave me the most detailed interview I have ever had in my life; when he was done, there was nothing left to know. He passed on this information to his client, which turned out to be RCA, just up the street. After a few interviews at that company, we were positioned for an offer. Going to RCA would have been stepping back in time, beginning all over from a corporate-culture standpoint. However, it was a much less complex company and was not growing like ITT. My plan, one day, was to go out in the world and start a quality education and consulting company. I just didn't know how to make it come off. I read an article that stated that 98 percent of new consulting companies last only two years.

Learning: *when starting a consulting business, it is necessary to begin with customer demand for the services offered.*

My friend George Schmidt had set up his company and had an office on Madison Avenue. We ate lunch a couple of times a month to cheer each other on. When John Delorean was running Pontiac in 1968, he asked me to come and speak to his staff about quality. I got them interested in ZD as a management concept. This was in the days when automakers considered eight or nine defects per car normal quality. When John was interested in doing something about quality, I recommended that he let George, who had been on the original quality committee at Martin, conduct his information program as a consultant. They did well for a while, dropping defects and warranty costs down significantly, but ZD never penetrated the mother corporation. When John moved to Chevrolet, it all stopped.

When RCA was about to make me an offer, Elmer asked me how I thought ITT would react. The thought had never crossed my mind. I said that they would wish me well and that I hoped they would let Bob Vincent take over the controls. I could do nothing else for them while working from a bunker and kept away from the real thought leaders. He made me promise that if they convinced me to stay, I would find him a replacement. I agreed, knowing that it was no problem. When I told my boss that I was going to leave, he said I had to see Dunleavy. I couldn't get near him or Rich or HSG. The personnel people wouldn't talk to me. There was no one to quit to. It was starting to be the holiday season, there was snow and ice, and the family was getting nervous about the situation. So we packed up the kids and drove to Orlando for some warmth and friendship. We checked into a motel with a heated pool and sat around thinking about what to do.

The second day I received a call from HSG, who was in Brussels. He apologized for interrupting my vacation, said that he would like to pay for the family trip because of it and that he hoped I would stay with the company. He said they would make me a vice president, raise my salary to $50,000, give me a large stock option, and put me on the executive bonus role beginning immediately (which meant the whole year). He said that he had been receiving calls from the unit executives telling him not to let me go because I was the only effective seagull in the place. I was overwhelmed and mumbled yes; he thanked me and hung up.

Rich told me later that HSG had said I should have told them I was unhappy, but Rich replied that it was their job to know that. He knew

I would never speak about it. It is true that one of the main jobs of the senior people is to know the attitudes and feelings of those down the line. I was not quitting because of money or even position but because I felt they didn't need me. Sounds kind of silly for someone who is supposed to be tough.

Learning: *don't just sit and mope; do something.*

I had just finished writing a book entitled *The Strategy of Situation Management.* The publisher was about to put it out with my affiliation listed as RCA inside the cover. I had to change that and did after about two thousand copies had been distributed. Every now and then I run into people who have a copy with the wrong affiliation in it; when they ask me to sign, I pretend I am going to swipe it.

After everything quieted down, one of my colleagues went to the office of the president and announced that if he did not become a vice president "like Phil did," he was going to quit. He was sent on his way home that day. As a result of this and other similar instances, I realized that my quitting produced a good result only because I had quit without intending that result. The ITT folks did not feel that I was blackmailing them. I found out later that HSG had called David Sarnoff, the head of RCA, about the incident to make sure the two corporations did not get into a squabble. I was elected an officer of ITT at the December 1968 board meeting and was invited to the annual Christmas luncheon. Many of the units had sent little presents with their logo on them to be distributed to the officers and directors. These were items like key chains, flashlights, and clocks, nothing valuable in themselves. They keep popping up in drawers and boxes. The baking company sent each of us a fruitcake. I am still searching for someone who actually ate some of it. Over the years I have developed the theory that only a dozen fruitcakes exist; they just keep being sent around.

Tim took me aside at the buffet and asked for a proposal of the staff and budget I was going to need in order to do the quality job properly. My request for four people and two secretaries was quickly approved. We were the smallest staff in headquarters, but we became the best known.

HSG liked the ZD film and wanted the board to see it; he felt that it was time to begin taking quality seriously. So I was scheduled to attend the next board of director's luncheon to give a short talk on quality and show the film. Tim suggested that I write out what I planned to say so they could look at it before the session. This was not my usual practice. I never gave a talk without thinking about it and writing it down. However, I never wanted to be held to it and certainly would not read it in front of an audience. But in my tradition of giving unto Caesar I wrote out a couple of pages and sent it to all three of them. Tim and Rich both gave suggestions, which I ignored, but HSG said nothing. Communicating with him was like talking to Mars. Your message went out, and after you thought it had been lost in space, a reply would come back or some action would be taken. He had his own time frame.

At the board luncheon I had an opportunity to listen to a group of heavy hitters chat about the world situation and about the inside of business. They all knew everyone, and it was a delight to just sit there and bathe in this new environment. After lunch HSG stood up and made a few comments about me and the effect I was having on the corporation. Then, with no notes or anything else, he proceeded to give my speech. It had registered in his memory, and he just rattled it off with, I'm certain, no idea of where it had originated. When he got to the end and nodded for me to take over, my mind was blank. I rose, smiled at everyone, and signaled the projector operator to turn on the film. By the time it was over, I had written a new speech in my head, and it turned out all right. The result pleased him, and he invited another officer to make a presentation at the next meeting. That talk did not work out well because the person rambled on and made a poor impression, which no one wants a board to go away with. So John Monaghan was hired to prepare executives for these presentations, and from that date an officer was there each month.

It is a cliche to say that business executives are usually not good speakers. It is also true. When important people speak to those over whom they have power, it does not make much difference how proficient they are. But when those same people speak to strangers or other nonsubordinates, most of the impression comes from the way they appear on a platform. Unfortunately, few business leaders realize the importance of the impression they make, and no one wants to tell them. My observation has been that they can improve with coaching, such as John provides, but that they never get very good at it. They become adequate and avoid embarrassment, but they never realize they had a problem in the first place. This attitude is a mistake. In general, people forget what a speaker has said, although few key remarks might remain implanted. But they never forget whether he or she was interesting and comfortable. They primarily remember only the impression they received. If the speaker stands behind the lectern (it isn't a podium) and mumbles with head down, the audience feels neglected and insulted, as though they are not being taken seriously. The speaker has just a few moments to build a relationship. Life is relationships, and so are speeches.

CHAPTER SEVEN

The Nuts and Bolts
of Reformation

Around February 1969 I became ill; my stomach and insides began acting up for no good reason, and I was often in a great deal of pain. One night I passed out at home, waking to see paramedics peering down at me. The doctors found nothing wrong, and so I kept puttering along putting the new quality department together. I brought three professionals in from ITT units: Jack Hagan, who had worked with me at Martin and had been at our New Jersey unit; Ernie Karlin, who was at West Palm Beach Semiconductors; and Milt Cohen, who became involved in the service operations. Along with Bob Vincent they made up the professional team, and then I was able to obtain Karen Kruger as administrator. Karen made the arrangements for the quality college, conducted corporate quality-awareness activities like the newsletter, and, in her spare time, ran the rest of us.

Now that we had the twenty-seven quality councils working worldwide, I felt the need for us to recognize those employees at all levels, in all departments, who were good examples of quality performance. Most programs of this sort are not successful because the winners are chosen by managers, who always select the wrong people because they judge people by appearance, not by contribution. They have no way to know about contribution. That is why most executive secretaries are attractive.

We had a multinational organization with several hundred thousand people working on all kinds of different products and services from hotel rooms to telephones. There were cultural quarrels, project jealousies, organizational overlaps, and all the other bits and pieces of business relationships. Also there was no corporate award program of any kind and no interest in having one that I could tell.

The key to proper recognition is to have people nominated by those who really know what is going on, their peers. This is the basis for the Oscars, Tonys, Nobel Prizes, Pulitzer Prizes, and other well-respected recognitions. Then, the winners need to be able to show off the award without a great deal of effort. If you have an Oscar on the mantle, all your guests will notice it before the evening is through. A plaque or certificate is not going to meet that test. I finally decided on a ring, the Ring of Quality. When devising something original, I find it of little use to bring it up with the staff. They just water it down or find reasons that it is going to fail. Committees worry that the wrong person will be selected, and they want to have the criteria written down, probably at least three pages of them. I wanted the only criterion to be that someone else thought the person was doing a wonderful job when it came to quality. We would do a check through the quality councils to make sure the person was authentic and a reasonable candidate. Then the executive quality council would make the recommendations to me based on those inputs.

Learning: *a committee will never create a respected award; it has to be conceived by one individual who understands the purpose.*

We designed the ring of 10K gold and also had a "Q" pin for the lapel made of silver. One-page nomination forms were laid out, with the only rule stated clearly on it: you cannot nominate your boss or the corporate vice president of quality. Everyone else was eligible. The nomination forms were sent out around the world, and before long they were returned. We selected about twenty-five ring winners worldwide; the others nominated were given the silver lapel pin and a certificate at a luncheon with their general manager. Some of those sessions turned out to be quite elaborate; units were proud that one of their people had been noticed.

The first Ring of Quality dinner was planned in infinite detail by Karen and myself. For most of the participants this was the most important event of their lives. They came mostly from small towns (one had never been in an elevator) and were impressed by all the attention. I excluded negative things I had learned from the Martin award dinner and included many nice touches. We even rehearsed the ITT executives so they would not be blasé. We in the corporate office lived a special kind of life, traveling most of the time, living well, and expecting people to pay attention when we said something. That lifestyle did not compute in the regular world.

The winners and their spouses were sent to the meeting by their unit, and many ITT executives attended. President Dunleavy handed out rings for the men and medallions with chains for the ladies as I introduced them and read about their achievements. It was a moving experience. Tim even picked up the bill for the dinners, one in Europe and one in the United States each year. We gave out about twenty-five rings or medallions a year, of which five were to executives selected by the councils for obeying us wonderfully. Everyone took the program seriously; we never had a complaint about a winner being unworthy; and it is still being done in the company to this day. At least it was being done until ITT split itself into three parts and then merged some of those parts with others.

Learning: *a noncompetitive award program is taken to heart right away.*

The kids went to horse camp in the Catskills for six weeks during the summer of 1969. They were assigned a personal horse to care for and ride, and Skip was a junior counselor. My insides were still giving me trouble, and Dr. John Lauer, the ITT physician, suggested that I go to the Greenbrier Clinic to get checked out. This was a perk for officers anyway, but I had been putting it off. I called the kid's camp to let them know where we would be and found out that Skip had broken his leg the day before (chasing a co-counselor down the stairs). So I drove up to the mountains to get him and passed him through the family orthopedic group, where they took off his cast and started over. We were good customers of that group. Then the three of us flew to White Sulphur Springs, West Virginia, on a company plane. They had several, of different sizes. This was a small one, but it got there. Personnel was still irritated because I had become an officer, but I figured that was their problem. The little plane was supposed to show me that they were in charge of such things.

Learning: *I am very good at forgiving, but fail forgetting.*

There is no other place like the Greenbrier, and it was great to be back in my home state, which was still poor but beautiful. At the clinic Dr. Morehouse examined me from one end to the other, literally. While he had a long instrument inserted, he asked whether "this" was what I had been feeling. The symptoms were duplicated exactly except that I didn't pass clear out. The next day, after all the tests were in, he explained that I had an inflamed colon, which was caused by "taking yourself too seriously." He said that their experience with corporate people was that when they got a big promotion, they became so intense that this one spot, where the colon took its last bend, became inflamed. He also said I needed to lose twenty pounds and quit smoking. My insides never hurt again, and anytime I felt a little shaky I just remembered that visit. Dr. Morehouse said he was going to "get me ready to be fifty," and he taught me a lot.

Learning: *thinking about being fifty at age forty-two alerts one to become interested in personal wellness.*

In the spring of 1969 I received an invitation to the ITT world meeting that would be held at the Boca Raton Club in Florida. This was the third of these affairs, as I understood it. Everyone who was anyone in the corporation, four hundred people plus spouses, was invited to Florida for the ten-day conference. The Boca Raton Club was taken over completely. The New York contingent traveled on two chartered trains, and others flew in from all over the world. There were serious meetings with well-known speakers, from Gerry Ford (then a Congressman) to Art Buchwald. Every night was Saturday night with carnivals, symphony orchestras, name singers (like Tony Bennett), and a casino night. People had big badges hanging around their necks with their first names in big letters and their last names and companies in smaller letters.

It was a marvelous opportunity for me to meet people and develop relationships that lasted for my time with ITT and afterward. Whatever the event cost, the company got it back right away in people working together. The biggest problem Shirley and I had was digging up a suitable wardrobe; we just did not have the money. In fact I tried to get out of going when I realized the expense we were going to face.

However, Rich let me know that my incentive compensation bonus would have something extra in it for just that reason. As it turned out the bonus was equal to half my annual income. We were even able to pay the baby-sitter and go off relaxed.

Learning: *if you want to get the attention of senior executives, do something original.*

HSG asked me to have lunch and play golf with him. When I came to the meeting place, he already had a game arranged with three other fellows. We were going to be there for several days, so I asked whether we could pick another time (especially since it was raining), but he insisted that I stay with him. After sandwiches and conversation, I was growing nervous about missing our tee time, but eventually we all went out in the rain to the first tee. He pulled out a club, placed a ball on a tee, and at that moment the rain stopped, the sun came bursting through the clouds, and birds began singing. The five of us played together, getting acquainted in the process; when we reached the ninth green, HSG left us to make some calls. We were halfway down the tenth fairway when the heavens opened and chased us all inside, soaking wet. That is the way it always was with Hal.

Let me go back to my first GMM in January 1969. Rich advised me to keep my mouth shut for a year or two until I learned the ropes. I sat next to Ed Schaffer, who was director of manufacturing on a temporary basis but got the real job and became a vice president a year later. Ed did the inventory presentation and was an old hand at these wars. The GMM was notorious in business circles because of the stories about people being destroyed by questioning, particularly from Geneen. He had a b.s. detector with a long antenna built in and was hard to fool. When people did not do what they had said they would do, there was hell to pay. Strong men became pale as their turn in the barrel approached.

The meeting was supposed to begin at 10 A.M., and participants began arriving well before that time. About a third of them were from headquarters, so they had offices they could sit in until they had to appear upstairs. The rest were stuck hanging out in the lounge, which had a dozen telephones and the opportunity for endless conversation. This was a great place to get things done; everyone who could do anything was there. HSG came when he was ready but usually made it before eleven on that first day. He lived in a different time zone than everyone else.

When he went to his seat, the rest of us made our way to the tables, which were shaped like opening and closing parentheses, with a green cloth covering, and sat in the eighty comfortable blue steel chairs, forty on a side. I sat on the staff side six or seven people down from the three people from the office of the chairman. The group executives and product-line managers were on the other side. Everyone knew each other so there was an easy air about the place until the numbers began. Everyone lugged their two big GMM books plus the notes for their own information. I brought nothing except a note pad. No one ever looked inside those books during the meeting anyway.

Learning: *meetings held on a regular basis with the same attendees create their own standards of behavior, which it is wise to understand.*

The meeting began with the comptroller's numbers. Each of us became expert at counting the number of view graphs the three assistants lugged to the tables inside the circle. There were three large screens in the room; the view graphs were set on the tables, and the presentation proceeded through the whole corporation. Revenues, profits, accounts receivable, compensation, inventory, and every other number for the corporation as a whole were displayed. Then we reviewed the numbers for each group and the units within the group. Questions flew back and forth, with the Office of the Chairman or staff people probing and the operations people defending.

About two hours into my first GMM someone brought up a profit exposure caused by a "quality problem." All seventy-nine heads turned toward me. I responded by saying that they should not look at me; I was not responsible for quality. I noted that this particular problem had been caused by a design error that had not been corrected as promised. I also pointed out that the information they were discussing was from my report and stated again that I did not think we could afford to categorize everything that went wrong as a "quality problem" and put it on a list to be handled by someone someday. We had to get serious about corrective action and prevention.

After a silence, the subject was picked up in this new vein. The engineering director agreed that it was his problem and took the assignment, and he gave a date for correction. The next time someone said "quality problem" everyone laughed out loud, and I never heard that expression again for the rest of my days there.

Learning: *speak up firmly and respectfully, but do it about significant topics.*

After all the staff reports, the grilling of the group executives began. The president of ITT Europe (ITTE, which we all said stood for "I Travel, Talk, and Eat") went first. Product-line managers, who worked with one type of item, like switchboards or pumps or insurance, hopped into the conversation now and then. Staff people brought up concerns about their specialty. I made it a solid rule never to raise an issue but to participate when a discussion was going the wrong way.

One had to be careful with HSG. Once he asked me three questions in a row. I answered the first two and then told him we had reached the limit of my factual knowledge and that further replies represented personal opinion. He smiled, and we discussed the subject with those rules. Those who did not separate opinion from fact were always found out. People would get so full of themselves and the encouraging response they were getting to their factual comments that they would keep right on going and fall into a pit. Hal was an information junkie, and he remembered everything. If you told him a number, he might ask you about it a year later.

Most people hated the GMM; it was boring a lot of times but was exciting in bursts—sort of like flying a plane, I imagine. People kept slipping out to make calls or to smoke or just to rest. The trick was knowing when this was safe, when the discussion would not affect you. Unfortunately my stuff could come up anywhere, particularly because we reported cost figures for nonconformance to requirements.

After a few of these events I realized that none of these people had the opportunity to get involved in operations beyond their own. The defense people never went near industrial products; the hotel executives had never been in a plant; the financial officers never went anywhere except corporate meetings. Quality went on in all units, so I found that my exposure to the whole corporation was unique; after a while I had been almost everywhere. Also through the quality-council meetings and the network it created, I knew what would be reported in the GMM. So I became the one to ask about problems and situations. Several times I was assigned to mediate a dispute between two or more units. They accepted my decision without comment. As Geneen said, "We'll let Phil settle it; he is the only one who doesn't care if we make any money."

Learning: *establish a position on a perch above the fray in order to stay out of the political world.*

The GMM was held monthly on the first two and sometimes three days of the first week. The following week all the headquarters people went to Brussels for the meetings there. The quality executive there, who reported to me for functional direction, was part of the manufacturing staff, and I could not get the organization changed to conform to company policy. The ITTE president, Jim Lester, didn't think that quality needed to report at the top. As a result at the meetings there was no real place at the table (which was much smaller than in New York) for me or the ITTE quality director. So I kept appearing at the first meeting for an hour or two and then heading out into Europe to hold council meetings, visit units, and work on real business. Nothing ever happened to affect the quality operation for good or ill in the Brussels meetings.

It took a couple of years for the German units to back away from the thought that their products were marvelous. They translated *Cutting the Cost of Quality* after sending a man over to the States for a few months to learn the real language. Among other things, he came to realize that "prevention" did not mean "condom." I developed a relationship with the managing director of SEL, the biggest ITT company in Germany. He finally decided that I was sincere and agreed to try a quality-improvement process in a couple of plants. SEL had about twenty-five operations making all aspects of telephone systems and electronics.

The company approached quality methodically, doing exactly what I had written in the company procedure booklet. In fact the staff corrected me a couple of times when I made suggestions that were not in the booklet. The results were swift and dramatic, with big reductions in rework and warranty costs. The customer was pleased and wanted to do some of the quality process in its operations. We were able to set up a quality-engineering training course to improve the manufacturing processes. Many of these changes were made possible by the careful leadership of Dr. Behne, who knew the level of resistance to change in the organization.

He set me up to speak to the management board one evening. After a long and large dinner I was asked to explain quality to the board members, who looked as though they were going to send me back to New York. I told them about my background, which was half German and half Irish. "Each morning," I said, "my German side says, 'You will get up and go to work and not come home until everything is done perfectly.' My Irish side replies, 'I'll drink to that.'" There was a forever pause while the translator went through the story, and then they laughed and accepted me. We had a good and honest question session. I never told them what no one knows, which is that the Irish have the lowest per capita drinking rate in Europe. Nobody believes that because of the reputation the Irish have developed over the years. People also believe there are alligators in the sewers of New York City.

Learning: *business schools should have a course in patience.*

The Germans taught me not to try to change a culture that has been around for hundreds of years. For them to become interested in quality improvement, they had to learn that I was not self-serving, and then they had to see the opportunity for themselves. Also, the process of improvement could not be seen as a criticism of what they had been doing in the past. We phrased it as a "rededication to the principles of quality for which we are so well known." As soon as they had a few operations going and were recording successes, I enticed three of the principals to come to the United States and do a road show for the companies there. The Americans ate it up and began doing what we had been trying to get them to do all along.

The year 1972 was quite interesting for a few reasons. First, my publisher had gone out of business the previous year, and I had taken *The Strategy of Situation Management* to McGraw-Hill after a reference from Tom Flynn of the public-relations department. His wife worked at the publisher and got someone to read the book. They liked the first line ("You may have noticed that the world was not designed specifically for you"), and as a result I rewrote the book and changed the title to *The Art of Getting Your Own Sweet Way.* My grandmother used to say, "You can't always have your own sweet way."

The book came out early in 1972 and received a couple of good reviews, which enticed McGraw-Hill to arrange a media tour. We matched schedules so they could set up radio and TV shows in the cities I was visiting. The talk shows liked the subject, and I enjoyed handling problems that the listeners brought up. The process described in the book works. We did noon news, late-night chatting, morning book reviews, and it was a great learning experience. I found that my answers were the most sparkling when I had no idea of the question beforehand.

At the same time, the Sheraton people were finishing construction on their new hotel in San Diego. That city was bidding to host the Republican National Convention in the summer, and the hotel was pushing hard to open in time. To properly open a new hotel by bringing in media and travel people costs around a million dollars. Sheraton management was trying to figure how to get that much money out of ITT when they were approached by the city's convention committee. If Sheraton would make a contribution to the program and if San Diego got the convention, the hotel would be convention headquarters, and the president would stay there. The result would be national—in fact, worldwide—television and other media exposure. As a result Sheraton donated $50,000 to the committee.

One of the ITT public-relations people, who was known to drink a little too much, in fact a lot too much, told a Washington columnist that the money was given as a bribe. The story hit the front pages as a fact. Everyone came down on the company, and the stock began to fall, dropping two-thirds before it was all over. So I was out in this media storm talking about getting your own sweet way and being hit with questions about the company's ethics.

As if this were not enough, ITT was accused of trying to overthrow the government of Chile. That charge was disproved, but the message never got out. Those who have worked for international companies know that they have almost zero influence anywhere. It is only in books and movies that you can bend a nation to your will.

To add one more log to the fire, my publisher got involved with Clifford Irving's pretend biography of Howard Hughes. My book tour became the hottest thing going. I was the only one who could talk about all these situations at the same time. The ITT corporate public-relations people encouraged me because the interviewers seemed not to relate my being employed by the company to the acts that had supposedly taken place. My stock line was "We are a big company, and we do a lot of dumb things, but these dumb things we did not do."

Learning: *don't get in a position where the company feels it owns you; it's better they feel happy that you are willing to work with them, so stay a little aloof.*

My initial stock option when I became a vice president was $62 a share; each year around Christmas I received another one ranging from $55 back up to $62. After all the dust had finished flying on this exposure, the stock was about $20. The company had just completed fifty quarters of profit improvement in a row, had little debt, fifteen billion dollars in assets, and a good future. However, everyone thought we were a bunch of thieves. My children were even snarled at in school.

Investigation showed, finally, that we were not trying to bribe the Republicans and that Geneen was not pulling the strings at the White House. When Richard Nixon's tapes came out, one of the comments that the president made was "Geneen? Hell, he wasn't even a contributor." The remark was engraved on a brass plate and presented to HSG, who had hardly noticed the commotion anyway.

I realized that the company had brought the San Diego scandal on itself by being insensitive. Management has to watch itself when it gets people pumped up about the company. The folks involved were so busy taking care of ITT they never thought about how their decisions were going to look. It would have been much better to have joined a committee and stayed away from appearing to become part of the political process. During a visit to the Washington office the previous year I had noticed signs of this sort of arrogance and had mentioned it to one of the senior executives, who suggested that it was none of either of our businesses. He was wrong because he assumed that our people were following directions. But they were just doing what they wanted to do, and that is worse than having a deliberate plan of deception coming from top management. I learned again that companies make their own image and have to be serious about how they present themselves and how they are perceived.

Learning: *if people are going to represent you, make certain you share the same philosophy.*

One of the problems of international travel is alcohol. The Europeans drink wine at most meals, and it doesn't take long to dive right into that habit. Each wine has a story, and there are hundreds of tastes involved. My colleagues on the executive council were well versed in wine lore and took pains to coach me. They tasted and sipped a lot; I just drank it. I was uncomfortable with the effect alcohol had on me and did not drink beer or whiskey, but I drank a lot of wine. It was not possible to write anything useful after even one glass, so I was not putting out much material. Time changes bothered me too. When I went to Europe, it took me a couple of days to begin functioning again. Consequently, I went over early and spent a day wandering around whatever city I happened to be in. In this way I saw a lot of historical sites and spent time with my colleagues.

In late 1972 I picked up a throat infection and was put on antibiotics. The doctor said not to drink any alcohol as long as I was taking pills. My schedule was to go to Copenhagen for an executive council meeting and the annual Ring of Quality dinner. Flying over from New York I refused all the wine and cordials that were offered, confining myself to Perrier water. These flights usually get in at the crack of dawn, and my custom was to check into the hotel and try without success to get some sleep. This time, however, I dropped right off for a few hours, went out to a nice lunch, and spent the afternoon sightseeing. It was a warm day in Copenhagen, and the secretaries and store clerks were sitting in the park, taking off their blouses and bras in order to grab some sun, a practice that bothers only Americans. That night, after dinner, I slipped into bed and slept without waking until morning, which was a revelation. Alcohol causes time-change problems. If you do not drink it, and you get plenty of daylight when you arrive, there is little effect. I resolved to drink no more and shared that resolve with Shirley on the telephone. She was more relieved than she let on; apparently I was becoming somewhat of a problem in this regard.

Several months before I had been approached by one of the administrative guys in Brussels who bought and sold wine by the case as a sideline. He said that my favorite Graves wine, Oliver, was available in both white and red and asked whether I would like to order some. I told him about the Copenhagen meeting and asked whether we could get a few cases of each sent to the hotel for the Ring of Quality dinner. It was all done, and the wine had arrived. The night of the dinner the steward approached me to taste the wine before they began service. I asked Georges Borel, my Frenchman, to do the honors, and he was suitably impressed. He declared this Graves to be the best he had ever tasted. I realized that I had passed up the best wine anyone had ever had offered to them. But it would not do to fall off my perch. Once my mind is truly made up, the doing is not difficult.

Learning: *there are, or will be, things that need to be removed from our lives; getting rid of them is a matter of intellectual decision and then a firm will.*

My travel schedule at this time was heavy in terms of places to go, but the amount of time I spent away from home was not significant. I never missed a weekend at home except for the ITTE planning meeting at the end of September. Those two weeks were made bearable only by the opportunity to play some golf. On other trips I kept time away to the minimum.

The company sent cars to pick us up at home for travel to the airport and to return us from the airport. And there were also company planes. These were a mixed blessing. We had a 727, set up to carry about twenty-two people, which the chairman used primarily to get to Europe and back. I much preferred to go commercial, as did most of the other people. On the 727 there were only other ITT executives, no movie, and a dull meal. A poker game was always going, but poker interests me only once in a while and never for long. I also don't care about gin rummy, so I spent most of my time reading and avoiding getting into a discussion with Hal. He sat in his little office room with his seven briefcases, wearing an old sweater and working on papers. I did wander in there once and spent the next hour listening to suggestions, some of them good, about things I could do. Later I discovered that he considered these chats to be agreements, and as a result I had a difficult time getting off his to-do list. Most of the other people had a briefcase full of papers to process, but my case contained only books. The great fear of my life was to be trapped on an international trip without something interesting to read. Because I never knew how good a book was going to be, I always brought several. Few bookstores in Europe carry books I want to read. As I noted before, I read only history and biographies.

When it came time for a trip to Brussels, the director of administration in New York started calling those who were going in order to entice them on the plane. He was in a position to dispense or withhold many favors, so we usually wound up doing what he wanted. However, we were able get the meal service changed to an Italian deli menu and a few hot things. If it sounds ungrateful to be complaining about flying a private plane across the Atlantic, accompanied by a dozen good friends, then we should accept that one can get used to anything. It is sort of an "isn't this suite kind of small" mentality. But golden chains are just as binding as those made of steel.

ITT had purchased a company in Massachusetts that made special cables and wire back in 1964. The owner had been unable to get into the local country club for one reason or another, so he decided to create his own golf course in Bolton, Massachusetts. It was the longest in the world, over eight thousand yards from the "tiger tees." There were three other tees, but a good drive for me from the tigers placed the ball right next to the ladies' tee. No one was ever able to stroke a putt across one green, which was an acre in size. The company didn't know about this course until after it had made the purchase. It decided to turn the facility into a place for conferences and thought it perhaps could rent it out one day. Customer groups were taken there regularly by the unit executives, who were often kind enough to invite me to participate. They knew I would come if an event were held at Bolton. We used it many times for quality meetings and as a place to get away. After lodges were built, families were welcome. Bolton is the only part of the company I miss today.

Having realized how successful a place to entertain customers could be, ITT made additional arrangements with a bird-shooting reservation in Georgia, a trout-fishing camp on the Canadian border, and a houseboat anchored in the Florida Keys. I went to these a few times, but my heart was always back in my library. If one must have a master, then ITT was the best. The question that was beginning to form in my mind, however, was, Does one have to have a master?

CHAPTER EIGHT

Implanting the Reformed Quality Philosophy

The family was living better now; we had a good amount of discretionary income, and we were out of debt for the first time in our marriage. We had two cars, a Cadillac for Shirley and an Oldsmobile for me. We had moved (in 1968) two blocks away into a much larger home with two acres of woods and streams. Philip and Phylis liked their schools, we had been able to join the Tamarack Country Club, and we were developing friendships. Most of our friends were not involved with large companies or the international life, which made our relationships relaxing. Shirley and I played in a bridge group in the neighborhood, which was quite pleasant. Our neighborhood association had a golf tournament every year; I won once, but no one could find the trophy.

My ITT life was becoming somewhat routine. The quality college ran continually somewhere in the world; improvement programs existed in most companies; and top managers took their responsibility for the company's integrity seriously. We made a new movie, *Why Me?*, which showed an executive trying to blame everyone but himself for his problems. I made certain that the subject and dialogue were understandable to Asians and Europeans. We used recognizable TV actors, and the film was well received. There were no VCRs in those days, so we used 16 mm projection. Bob Weimer, the producer and director, and I fought tooth and nail over the concept but cooperated smoothly on the script. The film nails executives directly with no room for rationalization.

Learning: *lots of people can work on a creative product like a film, but the road map has to come from one person.*

Systemwide, quality was now in good shape; everyone was aware of it and took personal responsibility for action. The quality-control professionals who would not update had been weeded out, and new, less technically oriented quality managers were coming in. The quality councils were a pleasure to be with; in Europe we had wonderful meetings complete with great meals and fellowship. This was a large move forward from the early days of suspicion and confusion. At one of the first meetings I was told that I would have to work hard to understand all the concepts and concerns that the various quality directors had. My reply was that, to the contrary, they were going to have to learn to understand me if they wanted to have a concrete policy and operating plan. They responded positively to this challenge, and we had a completely apolitical relationship for the rest of our days. They took the lesson of giving the customers what they had ordered to heart.

Learning: *professionals who are viewed as rather dull and reserved blossom as quality becomes a high-level concern in a company; it was as though they have been in a deep freeze—letting the sunlight in melts their reserve.*

The senior operating people were becoming increasingly responsible. We didn't have people trying to slip substandard products out in order to make a date; it just wasn't done. The role model of the resourceful manager who could deliver regardless of the situation began to vanish. Senior management started to appreciate those who did the job properly without a lot of fuss and bother. They did not want to be snatching victory from the jaws of defeat all the time; they wanted a smooth journey. The new system was less painful and made a lot more money. It was also easier to manage.

Sheraton, under Bud James, had launched the first quality management activity in the service area, and soon after that Hartford Insurance began the process. Hartford's merger agreement stated that

ITT Worldwide Conference, 1977, Boca Raton, Florida.
Left to right: F. J. "Tim" Dunleavy, Rich Bennett, Harold Geneen, me.
Hal's way of showing that quality was his friend.

it was to be free from ITT headquarters for a few years, but it asked us quality folks to visit. I always thought Hartford wanted to show that it was not against corporate involvement but also didn't want to get involved with the hard-nose staffs from finance and operations. Our meeting started what became a worthwhile effort inside Hartford.

The chairman, Harry Williams, took me to his office one day and showed me a life-sized painting of an early chairman, complete with watch fob, flowing coat, and stern demeanor. Harry said he never signed anything without looking up to see whether there was approval on the painting's face. He thought the old gentleman would have liked the idea of trying to get things done correctly the first time. These nonmanufacturing companies did not immediately recognize that they spent about half their time doing things over. What the hotels looked at as gracious attention to the guest was actually rework. Insurance companies rarely seemed to get the policy written right the first time. Now that they have computers to help them they do better, but doing things right the first time is still a struggle they often consider inevitable. In those industries the price of nonconformance is 40 percent of the operating costs. The education of the executives who run those kinds of companies has some blank spots when it comes to understanding what is involved in work. They seem to spend more time trying to create a foolproof system than helping people work within the current system.

I found the inspiration for creativity all about me. That was one of the joys of such a large and diverse organization. For instance, at the Mannheim, Germany, SEL plant I reviewed their cost-elimination program (I had learned to teach them to "eliminate," not "reduce") and found they had cut out $250,000 in the last year. The manager told me they had one thousand employees. I figured that the cost cuts came to $250 per person, which meant that each of them had saved one dollar a day for a year essentially. On the way back to Brussels I wrote the BAD program on a cocktail napkin, which had been under my Perrier. BAD stood for "Buck a Day." If we could encourage people to look at their job and determine how to take a dollar a day out of it, we could have a large cost elimination with little effort. My thought was that the form for suggestions should be one page only and that the submitter would receive a coffee cup with the logo "I had a BAD idea" on it. That would be the whole prize. Then management could draw one BAD form a week out of a barrel and give that person the best parking spot. We would have signs that said things like "BAD makes cents" and

"The BAD guys ride again." Real camp. A few groups adopted the idea immediately and ran the program for the suggested thirty days. In every case there was 100 percent participation (as opposed to 5 or 6 percent in suggestion programs), and the cost-elimination goal was exceeded. Some operations would not even consider doing it despite a great deal of testimony and proof that it was worthwhile. After a couple of years George Schmidt asked whether he could make BAD as a product of his company, Industrial Motivation Inc. I agreed, helped him develop some material, and with ITT's agreement was paid a royalty, which made life smoother for the family.

Learning: *a good idea can be explained in just a few sentences.*

I had a heart attack early in 1974 and learned that I was not immortal after all. Everyone was shocked, including me, but it did convince me to stop smoking and to begin to take wellness seriously. I also decided that I was not going to do anything I didn't want to do from then on. I would not go to meetings if they weren't going to be useful; I would not get on committees or do other things that took me away from my family. While in the Greenwich hospital, I didn't even call the office; I just read and watched the news. It was delightful. The whole story of the heart attack and recovery became part of my material and was included in *Quality without Tears: The Art of Hassle Free Management,* which I wrote ten years later. During my recovery I learned that people and companies both have lifestyles that very much determine their health. They also both have attitudes that predict their success or lack of it. This was the seed of an idea that became a book entitled *The Eternally Successful Organization: The Art of Corporate Wellness* many years later.

Learning: *there is nothing like a serious illness to stimulate the creative process.*

During my sick leave we returned to Florida and discovered John's Island at Vero Beach. We decided to see whether we could buy a town house and spend time there during the winter. I could travel out of there as easily as out of New York. Philip Jr. was applying to college to become an accountant, and Phylis would be entering college in two years. I had placed the *Sweet Way* book in a trust for the two of them, and the royalties were going to pay a good part of their tuition. They had worked at Continental Baking headquarters in Rye, New York, during the summers (except when they were at camp) and had saved what they called "pizza money." The royalties from BAD would just about cover the payments on the town house at John's Island. We figured that we had come about as far as we were going to go in life. ITT had an excellent pension program, and with any luck I could take advantage of it in 1981, when I would be fifty-five years old. I was beginning to look for more challenges. A lot that was of interest was still happening. Industry, particularly the automotive and electronic companies, was having trouble with quality. I knew how to get them on the right path, but they were not interested at the time. They were all just doing quality control harder.

Learning: *it is not good to get locked in to one way of doing things; life goes on while we are making plans.*

One of the big telecommunication plants in Europe learned that fingerprints were showing up through the finish of switches after they had been in use for a year or so, particularly in tropical or other high-humidity environments. These installations were large racks of switching units mounted in steel and aluminum frames. Although the metal had been treated and finished, the frames became discolored and eventually deteriorated. The plating procedure was modified and improved, but plant management felt that the problem was not solvable because the reaction was caused by fingerprints, and, according to the plant, menstruating women were particularly prone to producing an acid on their fingertips. I don't know whether this hypothesis is scientifically true, but the plant managers believed it. All that was necessary to produce the reaction was for the metal frames to be touched, and they could not be assembled if they could not be touched.

I suggested to the operations manager that they needed a "zero-fingerprints" program, and he laughed along with the rest of the group. However, about two weeks later he began to have meetings with the employees and staff on the subject of eliminating this problem. The result was the purchase of boxes of cotton gloves and instruction on the necessity of keeping metal surfaces clean. Visitors were handed gloves and were instructed not to touch anything. The operations manager became known as Mr. Zero Fingerprints, and soon people from other plants were coming in to see the operation. The problem went away, and soon the procedure became standard, sort of like wearing safety glasses.

The hardest part was getting top management to cooperate. They never touched anything in the plant anyway but were quite stubborn about not wearing gloves while visiting the work areas. However, when a group of the New York executives came to visit during the European planning meetings, they all got off the bus wearing gloves. That wiped out resistance.

Learning: *if the program had been created and edited at headquarters, it would never have happened.*

After all the media fuss about San Diego, Chile, and Watergate died down the company was absolved of wrongdoing. This information did not find its way onto the front pages. The stock was still lower than it should have been, and some significant problems were arising. HSG seemed, to me anyway, to have lost a little zest. He began to delegate more but never took his finger out of the pot. A new electronic switching system was burning up a lot of money in the development phase and was never going to get off the ground unless strong leadership was applied in that area. But it is difficult for a young tiger to emerge in a structured organization. What I was doing was successful only because it did not threaten anyone or step on any ground that already had footprints on it. The troops were getting restless; several of the brighter officers had gone to be CEOs in another company. Many were looking around.

Learning: *keep the antennas up at all times so you can be in the hills when the floods arrive.*

Most of the officers and other higher-level people had a special stock deal in which the money was borrowed to buy stock and the dividends paid the interest. Unfortunately, all of them were underwater, even though they had been issued at 50 percent of the stock price at that time. In addition, the regular options, which the government was changing the rules for cashing in, were also not worth much. But everyone kept working hard anyway; the ITT people were the hardest workers I ever saw. I worked hard also but in a different way than most others. I kept regular hours, stating firmly that my family came before the company. Many thought I achieved this lifestyle only because I was considered eccentric anyway. Once I was questioned on it by one of my bosses, who said that it didn't present a good image, the business of leaving work on time. I asked whether any departments were more effective than mine, and he had to admit that the answer was no. After that we stopped talking about it, but people did notice. I guess they thought about business the way the Japanese did; they didn't even take vacations. People get to thinking they are doing a lot if they put in long hours. However, much of the time they are concentrating on things that make no difference. Exhaustion is not always an indication of results.

Learning: *executives learn their work style from TV and the movies.*

Jim Purdy, who was running the Far East and Pacific operations, was always concerned that no one loved his area. Everyone was always going to Europe or South America; no one wanted to go to Asia. Jim convinced Tim Dunleavy that he should go show the flag, and Tim convinced Hal that this would be a good idea. Hal, however, secretly did not want Tim to be off on such a long jaunt. He wanted his key people right where he could get at them. He once said that the most important characteristic of an executive was total availability. That is one reason why I took great care to keep him informed. If he knew everything, then he didn't have to chase me down. But he was a fanatic on reaching people; it frustrated him that there were dead spots over the Atlantic Ocean where his phone in the 727 could not reach the States. (We're talking presatellite days.) But the trip was on anyway. Tim invited Bud James (the Sheraton president), me, our wives, and three other couples to join him on the trip in the 727. It was a marvelous opportunity in 1975. We went to Hawaii first, where the Sheraton people had all the hotels on Waikiki Beach. We time-changed, played golf, and made all those hard-working people feel appreciated. I arranged to have a Ring of Quality presentation at each stop. We had been trying to present some of these awards for several years.

Next we went to Wake Island for refueling. This stop turned out to be one of the most memorable parts of the whole trip. The commanding Air Force officer gave us the whole story of the 1941 battle and occupation. We visited their little chapel, and we saw a great many gooney birds, on their way to Midway apparently. When we went over the international date line on the way to Japan, all the ladies stood and looked out the window. But we used to do that on the USS *Kenton* thirty years before.

In Japan we visited a bakery that was in a joint venture with Continental and met with the business community. At a reception I found that I was a celebrity in Japan. Men came with translations of *Sweet Way* and with articles I had written on quality management and zero defects. I signed autographs and even tried to do it in the Japanese script on the front of the books. They all asked whether this was my first visit to Japan. Because my previous one had been as part of the occupation forces, I usually lied and said yes.

I had the opportunity to slip off and see a couple of factories. I was chiefly impressed with the fact that the general managers explained their quality process and plans to me rather than delegating that job to the quality manager as in the United States and Europe. That difference spoke to me of the future. All the companies had quality policies and practices and were involved in training and communication programs. They thought that my ideas on quality management were advanced and knew that I was not generally appreciated by my colleagues in the United States. They all were working toward the goal of zero defects. They had a hard time understanding why anyone would want to start out with the idea of making things wrong. They were delighted that most U.S. and European executives were woefully ignorant of their responsibilities about quality and hoped that no one would ever wise them up. Executives in the United States did not know much about making quality routine, and the quality professionals were just interested in tools like quality circles; when they went to Japan, they looked only at the bottom of organizations.

We went to the Philippines and saw President Ferdinand Marcos, who had more security than I had ever witnessed. In a museum in Taipai I got to speak English to three hundred children one at a time. When I said "good morning" to a little girl and she responded in English, all the kids immediately lined up behind her. Then each of them stepped in front of me and said, "Good morning, sir," we shook hands, and I responded, "'Good morning, young man [or lady].'" It took over an hour, but I got a big kick out of it. This poor nation supported a lot of industry, but the people didn't benefit much. The hotel rooms were bugged in an unsubtle way: a foot-long microphone stuck out of the ceiling. The ladies were uncomfortable, and I wasn't thrilled either. I often wondered what they did with the information they gained.

Hong Kong was worth the whole trip; we shopped until there was some question as to whether the plane would get airborne, and we played golf on a course where the fairways crisscross each other. In Australia we found a lot of ITT people, had a conference and more Ring of Quality presentations, and learned why it was so hard to make any money there. Their market was all the Asian countries, but the Australians did not like the Asians much and so did not build up relationships. The Australians are charming and interesting people, but it sure is a long way down there. They say that no one comes to Australia on their way anywhere else. On the way back we stopped at Fiji for fuel and spent enough time to realize that the main occupation there was going to the airport and watching the jets come and go.

I realized from this exposure to Asia that I was going to have to include these areas if I ever started my own consulting firm. International companies were everywhere in Asia; we would have to deal with them within the context of these cultures. I began to read the newspapers and magazines from that part of the world and to plot my strategy for the consulting business. It began to look like I would be in the business of educating rather than standing around offering advice. Everyone needed to learn.

Learning: *every country has its own culture, but the culture of business is the same everywhere.*

The Spanish, Italian, German, and Belgian companies were doing well with quality improvement but the French were moving slowly. The French companies decided to get me off their back by agreeing to try ZD. As the test site they selected the switching plant in Laval, which is about ninety miles from Paris. I always thought they picked Laval because it was close enough to show off if the concept worked and far enough so no one would ever know if it failed. The plant manager, René Peyraguer, came to the United States and lived with me for two weeks. We went to all the ITT operations so he could see how the quality-improvement process worked. René had learned to speak English from the Germans as a prisoner of war. When you spoke to him, he translated it into German and then into French. Reversing the process brought an answer in a little while. Once when we flew into Dayton for a meeting, I told him that "the two men who invented the airplane lived here." His translation was that "the two men who invented the airplane lived in every city in the world."

After the trip, he went back and started the process in Laval. His approach was just right for his area; he understood what this philosophy meant and did not try to put a coat of paint over an existing way of operating. He went about changing the way people looked at their work. He realized that quality improvement was a leadership problem, not a matter of applying a planned set of techniques and actions.

René met with all the employees in groups of twenty-five. The workers were rural people, primarily young girls, and they were used to the conventional way of working, which almost always required a certain amount of reworking. The prime component produced at Laval was a stacked relay that was put together with its brothers and sisters in the larger frames, which were then wired together one terminal at a time. The rejection rates were large, and rework was well organized. In this culture, the young female workers took most of their wages home to their parents or husbands. If there were problems, the parents or husbands were called.

René started the only incentive program I have ever seen work. The plant would pay, off line, directly to the women a small amount for each box of relays found by the inspectors to be completely correct. Those that were not defect-free would be returned to the workers for correction, and they would receive a minimum rate for the time they spent doing things over. It was to their advantage to get with the movement. The profits of the Laval operation doubled each year for the next several years. However, other French plants did not become interested in the process. They did the system thing and benefited from it, but management would not get close enough to the people to do ZD.

As the 1970s continued, I became concerned with the job and its future. Several opportunities had come and gone because ITT felt I was unique in the position I held. In reality I did not want to become an executive vice president or even president of the corporation. I thought these jobs mostly involved reacting to the problems other people caused and had little to do with real leadership. Corporations could be led, but they needed a culture where leadership mattered. Also I began to realize that my salary was low compared with those of some of the group executives. I began to feel unappreciated again, which is appropriate if one is determined to make a change.

My only option was to set up my own firm. But I had no desire to go building to building asking companies to be my clients. I had to figure out a way to have them come to me. That way was by writing a book that executives would read. I asked McGraw-Hill whether they would be interested, and they gave me support for the idea. So for the next two years I lugged my World War II foreign-correspondent typewriter everywhere I went. All the writing I had ever done up to that time had been away from the office because it is impossible to write there. I can't remember ever writing anything for publication during office hours. But because I did not drink any more, I had plenty of time on the road to sit in my room and write. I have always said that nondrinkers don't have anyone to talk to after eight o'clock while traveling. I also wrote on weekends and in the evenings if the family was doing something else.

In the years since writing *Cutting the Cost of Quality* I had been an executive, living with other executives and answering for any crimes that were committed. This position gave me a view of quality that I had not had when I wrote my other books and articles. Those who wrote and taught about quality management, quality control, quality assurance, reliability, and all the other quality functions had no high-level operating experience. Most of them were college professors, consultants, and statisticians who had advised rather than produced. They also knew little about business management and did not pretend to do so. This lack of operating experience is perfectly all right for those advising professionals, but ordinary people could not understand their books.

Executives in the United States were increasingly under the impression that the problem of quality in the country was the worker. In reality it was the managers, who had become separated from both work and customers through years of success. Companies like IBM, Xerox, General Motors, RCA, and General Electric thought that they were their industry, that whatever they wanted to do would be the standard. Textile manufacturers, faced with defect-free carpets from overseas, still insisted that fifteen defects per hundred yards was the proper standard. They pushed for government regulation in order to stop others from being better at quality. The consumer-electronics business was rapidly flowing to Japan; TV manufacturers refused to use solid-state technology or preventative manufacturing processes; automobile companies would not recognize that their ten defects per car was not what the customers wanted. Having seen that Japanese cars worked as advertised, customers were demanding the same standards from the U.S. companies.

Learning: *people believe the same things at the same time whether they are accurate or not.*

The quality spokespeople were saying that the solution was to work harder at quality control. But that was not getting anyone anywhere; it just made the products increasingly expensive. I thought I could do for the country what I had done for ITT. ITT was far from perfect, but the cost of quality had fallen from 20 percent of sales to well below 10 percent; their integrity was good. But my real hope was to deal with the global problem. If executives could learn to get things right and to quit wasting resources doing things over, then there would be work and jobs for all. Anyway, that is what I thought.

So I wrote *Quality Is Free: The Art of Making Quality Certain.* McGraw-Hill hated the title and looked fruitlessly all through the material for some charts or quality-control stuff. This was not the sort of book they had published in the past, but they were brave. They finally gave in and published it as I wrote it. My plan was that if it were to be a success, I would leave ITT and start Philip Crosby Associates, Inc., in Winter Park, Florida. I would work by myself, with just a few clients and perhaps a part-time secretary. Philip was getting out of college that summer, and Phylis would be in her senior year at Rollins College in Winter Park.

As I turned the book in, looking forward to another eight months or so before it hit the streets, I received a call from an old friend who was on the board of the ASQC. The president-elect had died unexpectedly, and they were wondering whether I would consider taking over the job. My term would start in 1979, but I would go on the board immediately, which would give me time to learn how the organization operated. When I asked why me, my friend said that the board was concerned that the society was falling behind and they thought I might be able to lead them out of the shadows. I wasn't sure I believed that, but he reassured me that the board would give me full support. There didn't seem to be any reason for avoiding this responsibility, so I agreed to do it. My friend was surprised that I didn't have to go to my boss and ask whether I could spend time being president of a volunteer society. "Gee," my friend said, "you don't even have to ask anyone."

This may rank as one of my bigger mistakes. I found no interest among the majority of board members in getting the country straight on quality. They just wanted to make certain that they got to be important in the society. After assuming the presidency, I brought the new board together at ITT's Bolton conference center for strategy sessions; began a public-relations program; and suggested that we change the name of the society to get rid of the "control" stigma, as the Europeans had done, and gain from the emphasis on management. When my book came out, the ethics committee chairman warned me publicly that he was concerned that I had taken the job just to sell books. I tried to resign, but the chairman and new president-elect said they would resign also, which would make the whole thing look like a Mack

Sennett production. The old guard just would not look at what was happening all around them, so I backed off and waited for my term to expire. I announced that I would not serve as chairman, which would normally happen, and asked to be permitted to resign from the ASQC altogether. That was not possible because ex-presidents do not pay dues. Go figure.

Quality Is Free was reviewed in *Business Week* in the spring of 1979 as part of an "America is going down the chute" article. The writer used the logic of my book as the key part of the cover story, and the review itself was better than I could have written. The core of the book was five Absolutes of Quality Management. Quality had always been assumed to be goodness; I defined it as conformance to requirements. That meant that companies should do what they say they will do, that management has to take creating requirements seriously. Other Absolutes were that quality is based on prevention; that the performance standard is zero defects; and that the results are measured in money. Management could understand these concepts. The last Absolute was for quality professionals, and I dropped it from management material; it was that there are no "economics of quality": it is always cheaper to do things right the first time. These Absolutes are correct in every respect, but quality control does not conform to them.

We had joined the Stanwich Country Club in Greenwich, and I began to work a little harder at my golf game. But this club was in the big league of tough courses. The greens were like the top of a dining-room table. Everyone else seemed to have graduated from an Ivy League school; I was the token non-Ivy. But it was a great group of people. Playing there was an introduction to a different world for me. We did little socializing.

HSG thought, I'm sure, that he could stay on as chairman and chief executive as long as he felt fit for the job. After all he turned a $600 million company into a $20 billion one and had a consistent record of profitability in the process. However, the board instructed him to identify some potential successors. He made a short list and told me later that I was on it. From it he picked Lyman Hamilton, the treasurer, and Rand Araskog, who was running the defense-space group. Both were good men, and I felt close to them. They became executive vice presidents; Tim became vice chairman; and Rich Bennett stayed as executive vice president. The idea was that after a year the board would make a choice. HSG apparently wanted Rand, but the board chose Lyman because of his relationship with the financial community. I was making a presentation to the board on the day the choice was made, so I had a ringside seat. It was just like the movies; each candidate was pretending he didn't care that his dreams had been shattered or achieved.

When Lyman and Rand were appointed as potential CEOs, I was getting ready to leave the company. I had not yet decided to write *Quality Is Free;* I just wanted out. I had some vague plan about going to talk to IBM or General Electric, but jobs there would just be more of the same, and I wasn't sure they even wanted me. Lyman persuaded me to reconsider leaving by indicating that there would be a larger and more interesting role for me after he officially took over. Because I had no other plan, this indication of change sufficed to keep me there. However, although he always treated me special, he never mentioned a new role for me after becoming president and CEO. Because he had been the treasurer for most of his career, I helped him learn how to visit plants and offices and look at them from an operations stand-point. We had quality-status charts hanging all over the corporation. These were Bob Vincent's children. They were constructed in a stan-dard format, were about three feet square, and were mounted on a wall or were hung from the ceiling. They were in paperwork areas as well as hardware areas, and they were accurate. All you had to do was ask a question about a chart, and everyone thought you knew what was going on.

Rand and I had a good relationship going back to when he ran his first plant for the corporation. At that time we spent a day together at his request and developed ZD3: zero defects, zero deficit, and zero delinquencies. His unit liked that idea, and its performance, under his direction, grew solidly. From that job he moved up to be group exec-utive of the defense-space group. He was intense, and I know that he thought he was going to become CEO.

HSG was trying to be just chairman of the board and stay out of people's hair, but he was not trying very hard. He and Lyman did not get on well. Lyman went to the outside directors and asked them to tell Hal to quit calling him all the time and sending him orders. They did, and Hal quit interfering. However, he was not happy, and about the time I was getting ready to leave the company the board fired Lyman, who had just returned from a trip to the Far East. Rand was elected CEO. He handled HSG with more care, but it wasn't long before the chairman was asked to retire from the board and move across the street to the Waldorf, where he had an office. After moving there, he made himself a great deal more money than he ever did at ITT. I nudged him into writing a book, and he enjoyed being out on the book tour.

Learning: *don't tie your career to another's coattails.*

We sold the Greenwich house in May and began to move to Winter Park, although I did not get out of ITT for real until the first of July. My leaving ITT was agreeable to everyone. I thought it would be a big shock to me, but it seems that I had already discounted it, like the stock market, some time ago. When we were driving to Florida, I stopped on the New Jersey Turnpike to call the office about something I had forgotten to tell someone. I could not remember the phone number. Rather than look it up, I took that as a sign and never called again.

What I learned in those fourteen years at ITT has filled several books and has provided me with a career that would never have even been in my dreams. I had no information about a career like that, so it was impossible to wish for it. In 1957 I would have sold my life for a guaranteed $10,000 a year. Hal, Rich, and Tim recognized that I could contribute to making their dreams come true, so they gave me an opportunity to create a career for myself. I have not met anyone since with their vision when it came to people. Most executives are so self-centered that they do little to grow their people. After I left the company, the corporate quality job received little attention, but that worked out all right because the culture had been built into the units. They kept right on working at quality management.

The first official day of work for Philip Crosby Associates, Inc., was July 1, 1979.

PART THREE

Teaching the Quality Reformation

CHAPTER NINE

Becoming an Entrepreneur

W hen *Quality Is Free* suddenly became a best-selling book, I began to receive many speaking invitations and media opportunities. The executives for whom I wrote the book related to it and were reading it. Authors can tell when someone has ingested some of their words; they can also tell when the reader has not gotten the message. Quality-control professionals, particularly prominent consultants and teachers, dismissed the book quickly. One said, "The clown has written a book." Most could not get past the title because they considered quality to be goodness and everyone knows that goodness is not free. Actually, because wastrels traditionally spend their money on badness, one would think goodness didn't cost that much. Also they could not forgive the lack of statistical charts and my unremitting emphasis on management's responsibility for quality.

Many speech requests came just because that is the normal way to treat the author of a currently popular business book; those who must arrange for speakers like to pick one who can't lose, at least for a while. But most of the calls were made because quality was becoming a high priority for managers. They were tired of losing market share, and thus revenues, because of it. ITT was good about referring requests to me in Florida. I also received calls from corporations that wanted me to help them get quality right. "Whatever that means," they would say. Soon I had scheduled thirty or so speaking engagements with companies' management teams. Other requests came from associations and professional quality groups. The advice I received from everyone was to not charge for these sessions because holding them would let me build relationships. However, I have always felt that executives do not appreciate what they get for free. So I found out what Peter Drucker charged, around $2,000 at that time, and I did the same. Also, because my company had no money, I asked them to give me the check right after the speech. Most agreed. I would take it home and hand it to my son, the accountant.

Learning: *don't look for advice on how to create a company; do it your own way.*

The typical meeting was held off-site, where the attendees usually were casually dress. Many executive groups plan these "strategy" sessions so they can go to a resort and get in a little golf. I think that is a wonderful way to spend time, I did learn quickly that the speaker is expected to be wearing business attire and should not plan on becoming too friendly with the people. They often invited me to play golf with them and to participate in their meals and entertainment. I soon learned that doing so was not a good idea. There are so many of them that they bury you in questions and comments; it becomes exhausting. This experience gave me a little sample of how a real celebrity must feel. I did learn to do enough socializing to let them understand that there was a warm person behind all that intensity. They could also pick up that I knew as much about the broad content of managing as they did. They did not need a translator.

My first two clients were IBM and Tennant. The entire staff of my company consisted of my son and me. The IBM people were interested in reducing the amount of field service work they had to do to keep their machines running. The company was the most profitable of the Fortune 500 in absolute terms. It was proud of its hard-working, high-tech culture. It thought the world revolved around IBM. In office management it probably did.

The IBM management people who were bringing me into the organization wanted me to become familiar with the company, so we toured six or seven sites across the country. Here was a prosperous, well-organized, computerized giant company with an obedient workforce and tons of well-educated bright people. Its quality operation consisted of regular factory quality control and a product-assurance function. The product-assurance people had great authority and conducted tests and inspections on products. If they didn't like a product, they could make a lot of trouble. They did good work.

The problem as I saw it was twofold. First, managers were very schedule-oriented. They often moved new products out of engineering and into manufacturing before the design was complete in order to meet deadlines. As a result, the engineers were still designing and changing the product while production was trying to learn how to build it. In order to meet the announced delivery dates the machines were shipped to the customers on time, and the field service people finished the job in the customer's office. Second, the quality standard was AOQL (average outgoing quality level). A product did not have to be right; it only had to be no worse than what had gone before. This standard was unmanageable.

IBM was essentially vertically organized. The chip factories shipped to the box factories, as did the screen, keyboard, wire-harness, and other operations. Each of these negotiated their AOQL with the box factory. The component managers received their incentive compensation based on what they had shipped. So the poor folks trying to make main frames in the box factory were receiving materials that did not conform to requirements. Worse, this system was considered to be state-of-the-art management. It produced products that needed constant attention and rework in the field.

We scheduled a senior-management college to last two days in one of the excellent facilities IBM had for training. But before that IBM sent eighteen quality managers, from eighteen plants, to Rollins College in Winter Park, which was our second official college. I was touring and examining IBM by myself because I had no associates. But by the time this class was held Lance Arrington had come from ITT and was ready to help instruct. This one-week class was to determine our future relationship with IBM. The quality professionals did not think they needed any help. I was telling them that the day would come when they could not afford all that field service, that there would be competition. The customers would have to set up the operation and run it on their own. They thought this idea was ridiculous. All week in the Rollins classroom we tussled back and forth about the Absolutes, ZD, and why IBM needed any help at all.

I had about given up hope by Friday morning. In desperation I began a discussion about "biggest problems." The first response was that they had none that weren't under control. I asked the chip-plant quality manager if he had any problems, and he said that everything went out according to the AOQL. Then I asked a box-plant quality manager about his problems, and he said that the chips gave him a lot of trouble because they were not consistent. Manufacturing spent a lot of time replacing and switching them around to make them work.

There was a big silence. Suddenly they began to realize that I was not their enemy, they were their enemy. For the first time in five days they relaxed and began to talk. Within an hour we had put together a plan to educate the quality professionals in the company and start a conspiracy to replace AOQL with ZD. We parted friends.

Tennant, my other first client, was another kettle of fish. It realized it had a problem and wanted help. Tennant made floor sweepers, large and small, for industrial and governmental use. It was an older, profitable company with a lot of competition and was worried about the future. Roger Hale, the president and CEO, had visited the company's joint operations in Japan and found that the customers were complaining about leaks from the engine and hydraulic system that fell on the floor being cleaned. When he got home, he found that the U.S. customers had the same problems but weren't complaining because everyone's machines leaked.

Doug Hoelscher, the vice president of manufacturing, had contacted me while I was in the process of leaving ITT. We arranged for me to visit in Minneapolis and discuss the situation. Their plant was clean and well organized. They had seven assembly lines putting the different machines together. At the end of the lines there was an inspection and test station where the machines were examined and each fault was listed. All the machines had some sort of problem. The wounded were then moved over to a rework station, where several booths were set up. The most experienced workers manned these stations. After rework the units were sent to shipping. The plant was behind schedule, and customers were complaining. There were forty requisitions for new workers.

When we went to lunch the quality manager asked me what I thought. I said that I had a specific suggestion but the company probably wouldn't want to do it. He assured me it would, so I turned the place mat over to draw on it. I made these suggestions:

Close the rework station and assign those workers to the assembly lines as coaches and trainers.

Set up three desks at the end of the line. Put a quality engineer at one, a design engineer at another, and an industrial engineer at the last. Classify each defect found as a supplier item, a process problem, or a design problem. Then insist on corrective action that eliminates the problem forever.

Send machines back up the line for repair.

Establish a performance standard of zero defects.

The marketing director thought they would never ship another sweeper, but the rest of the staff thought my ideas were good. And they did it all. As a result they found many administrative problems such as ordering components based only on price; they found they had not been training the assembly personnel enough; and they found that they had accepted the thought that everything needed rework. After a few weeks they were back on schedule, and they placed a sign at the end of the manufacturing operations that displayed the number of days since the last defect. The numbers that got on that chart as time went by were astounding. They also learned to proof their new products by having workers assemble them as they were developed. Roger Hale wrote a good book about this transformation, and Tennant became a leader in quality education by holding international conferences.

The part that pleased the company most is that it has the largest share of the market because of its reliability. Toyota came into the market for a while and left when it saw the lead Tennant had.

Learning: *looking at an organization as a whole, rather than in pieces, reveals the actions to be taken; it is like holistic medicine.*

All the time I was making speeches in order to convince executives that they did not have to put up with quality problems. IBM sent us a bunch of clients, and the textile companies began to discover us. But I kept speaking, making marketing calls from airport phone booths and keeping track of everything in a little pocket notebook. I loved it.

No staffs, no GMMs, no government inspectors, no bosses. And best of all what I was helping the clients accomplish turned their companies around.

Because of my ITT experience I was comfortable in places like Pinehurst, the Breakers, and Greenbrier. The audiences were respectful and inquisitive but not ready to jump into a completely new way of running their companies. Marketing people, in particular, were suspicious of anyone who thought things could be what they were supposed to be. There was a general understanding, deeply imbedded, that quality was varying degrees of goodness and that the more good you got the more it cost. It was also apparent that these people knew a lot about lightbulbs, washing machines, copiers, pumps, insurance, groceries, medical care, and other products but had no idea of how people operated. They were fixed on strategy planning, financial management, return on investment, and the other tools of conventional management. They often said that if they could, they would run their factories and offices with robots. All of these attitudes resulted from their corporate cultures and the attitude of the big bosses. Because ITT executives were world-oriented, I expected to meet executives with the same information when I started speaking to groups, but it was not to be.

Learning: *most executives know all about their own industry but nothing else.*

I call this attitude, which turns out to be destructive, "mainframe thinking." When companies think that they are the industry, that the customer will follow their lead without question, and that they only need to do more of the same cheaper or with more technology, then they are headed downhill. IBM visualized workers hardwired into a central computer system; Xerox wanted everyone to come to the third floor to get copies; Sears figured that people could get everything they wanted from a ten-pound catalog; General Motors wanted to make just a few kinds of shells and platforms and rearrange tail fins; General Electric was making fifty engineering changes a month in a product that was twenty years old. This attitude was carried out of the big companies to infect smaller companies as managers changed jobs. Big companies automatically rejected the idea that any competition could come from foreign countries unless it was based on artificially low prices—and those would go away one day.

It became possible for me to know early whether a specific company could change its thinking and its culture in relation to quality. I usually found out through a private conversation with the chief. Those who asked questions had a chance; those who gave me an hour lecture on quality were going to be dead in the water. I often feel that something happens to their hearing equipment when people hit the top levels of an organization. They begin to feel that they must generate all the new thoughts and are busy doing that while someone is trying to present them with a new thought.

If it were obviously impossible for me to help, I would tell them that we could get together again when they were ready to deal with the real world. They could be stubborn in thinking that all was well; even showing them their company costs for quality did not make an impression. Usually they just wanted a better class of customer. During my speeches I kidded them about this attitude and the "brain damage" they had suffered. This approach moved many of them to investigate my philosophy further.

Learning: *it is necessary to keep working to find ways of explaining things so they can be understood quickly.*

There were two types of companies in those days: the arrogant and the searching. The corporations that are in trouble today are the ones who were arrogant at that time and would not change. Without exception they thought that they alone understood the customer and the market. They thought that the workers' attention to quality had deteriorated and that quality would be restored if a "level playing field" could be established with the competition. During my talks I explained clearly that this attitude was impractical and that those who would not change had no future. Several senior executive teams made trips to Winter Park for a private one-day meeting to gain an understanding of this point. Most of them went back convinced that they needed help; they sent their managers to school and got on the right track. However, those who had a big training department or quality function usually decided that they could make the necessary changes themselves. It all sounded so easy. As a result they wasted many years trying to change the people rather than managing differently.

When chief executives recognized that a quality-improvement process was not a matter of techniques or cliches and took personal command, their companies were successful. The companies where chief executives delegated quality improvement to the human resource or quality departments just sputtered along. Many of those executives are writing books now about their experiences. Note how long it took them to figure it out, and many have not done so yet. There has been a lot of activity but few solid results and few permanent culture changes.

Learning: *some folks just can't accept concepts that come from others.*

When I went to visit client companies, I always made it clear that the top managers had become isolated from their people and from reality in many cases. I grumbled about executive dining rooms, insisted on meeting the union officers, berated the quality-control people for having low standards, complained about housekeeping, and generally tried to stir up the place. It usually worked. My experience in business had been so complete that it was difficult to fool me or to show me something that did not have a soft spot in it. Even those companies that were doing something about quality were usually just the best of a bad lot. As a result of these visits many executives opened their minds and caused a great deal of progress to be made in their companies. But other executives just became more firmly entrenched in their way of doing things.

Learning: *most executives don't think the other employees mind that they get a free lunch in a nice place.*

One of the most amazing people I ever met called one day when the quality college in Winter Park was about a year and a half old to say he had read *Quality Is Free* and wanted to start his company down that road. This was Roger Milliken, the CEO and owner of Milliken Co., the textile firm. Mr. Milliken had to be the hardest-working executive I ever met. He arranged for all his key people, 241 of them, to meet with us at Pine Isle, Georgia, in February. We had a two-day intense session on quality management. Everything in that session was planned and scheduled right down to the last item. The meals were served on schedule, and everyone was there to eat them. The programs began and ended on time; everyone was attentive. Even though we were miles from civilization everyone dressed in a business suit. Milliken Co. was known for having the best quality in the industry, but management recognized that this was not enough. The company had to forget industry ideas about quality levels and learn how to improve yields by eliminating and then preventing error. It was a joy to see a group that didn't want to argue; they just wanted quality to be free.

They all came to the quality college for a week each over the next year. President Tom Malone drove the thought through the company, and as a result Milliken is the quality leader in its field. He attended the classes with many groups and worked with them after hours to get the message through. Milliken has shared its approach with hundreds of other companies and is always careful to let them know where it all began. We always called Roger our "salesman of the year" because he sent us so many clients.

Learning: *it is easier when the boss wants it to happen.*

CHAPTER TEN

Growing Philip Crosby Associates, Inc.

W̲e had no trouble selling the Greenwich home in early 1979 when we decided to move to Winter Park, as that market was beginning to grow. The buyer got three times what we sold it for about four years later. We purchased a four-bedroom home in Winter Park, and I set up "world headquarters" in one of them. At fifty-three I was independent, with about $30,000 from my ITT thrift plan, a $100,000 mortgage, no health insurance, and no real idea about what the new company should be. I was delighted and having the best time of my life. Our daughter, Phylis, who discovered that her parents had moved in a mile away just as she was starting her senior year at Rollins, was not that thrilled. However, with a full larder and swimming pool available to her on command at the house she began to accept it.

Our son, Philip Jr., having graduated from Bentley College, moved to Maine and tried without success to find a job in accounting. This is not one of the great labor markets of the nation. When his first child, Charles, was born that July, he was working in a chicken-rendering plant on the third shift. In my mind I can hear him telling that story to his children already. He agreed to move to Winter Park and become the comptroller and only worker in the company. He carried the checkbook in his pocket, and I gave him the speech money after each trip. This arrangement paid for our development phase. He also carried all the boxes, the projector, and the refreshments for classes.

As I discuss the development and growth of Philip Crosby Associates (PCA) within this story of my life, ideas, and learning, it is not appropriate to discuss much of what went on with clients, although I will relate anecdotes that aid understanding. Also, I will not talk much about the individuals of PCA by name and their activities. I have purposely not checked the files, so this list is from memory. However, our company newspaper, which was begun when we had about thirty employees, is a good memory jogger for events.

Concerning clients, I have always been proud of the fact that we did no sales work, never made a call; they all came on their own: IBM, Xerox, Tennant, Corning, Milliken, Motorola, Mostek, Cluett-Peabody, J. P. Stevens, Cellulose, General Motors, 3M, Brown and Root, Chrysler, Johnson & Johnson, Federal Prison Industries, Federal Reserve Board, Clark Equipment, Armstrong World Industries, ICI, Seagrams, Allstate, U.S. Navy yards, Westinghouse, General Electric, Armco, British Petroleum, ARCO, Amdahl, Owens Corning, Copperweld, Savin, TRW, Hinkle, Herman Miller, and several hundred others. In some of the larger companies, and all of the smaller ones, the CEO drove the effort; in others a single division or group was the participant. Whatever the source six thousand executives and managers a year were attending the quality college before long, and many thousands more were utilizing the tapes and other material we developed and taught.

As I look at some of the books being written today, I recognize a great deal of my material that has been taken without attribution. But most people who talk about serious quality management, as opposed to Total Quality Management and other shallow efforts, make proper attribution. A couple of our client companies took the material they got from attending the quality college and started firms in competition with us; one took the people we sent to consult with them and helped them set up a consulting firm. After a short while they fell out and sued each other—over the material I created. I could have sued both of them, and the lawyers encouraged us to; but I felt they deserved each other. However, none of these firms were ever serious competition; they concentrated on price rather than results. Companies as a whole were honest with us and diligent. Only one stiffed me on the speech fee; it thought it had given me a great opportunity by having all its people come to a meeting. I said that everyone else there was getting paid. Those few companies that I considered unethical came back to us for help later on and were refused. How's that for a forgiving attitude?

As I started to put PCA together as a company, I wanted to establish a strategy that could be understood. If it were to be a real company one day, then it should be designed so that people would be proud to work there and clients would receive the most help they could stand. For this reason the name Philip Crosby Associates was chosen deliberately. Most similar organizations would have been Philip Crosby and Associates. It was important to me that the employees felt they were an important part of the operation, and the name I chose seemed to be a way of saying that. To my knowledge no one else ever thought much about the difference, but it was always a reminder to me.

Learning: *as the twig is bent, so grows the tree.*

Many new companies flounder early because they become successful right off the bat. The entrepreneur may not know a lot about running a business and is not willing to delegate very much. Suddenly growth is limited. I was determined that we would not suffer this fate. Because of my experience at ITT I knew how to manage finances and people. I also had no problem in delegating. There were two parts to PCA: the quality college and operations management. I served as CEO and creative director and gave others clear roles in the implementation. We had our own GMM, but it only took a couple of hours each month.

During this strategy phase I ran across a comment by Warren Buffett describing a "wonderful business." He listed the following criteria, and I compared PCA on each:

- Has a good return on capital. (PCA would require little capital.)
- Is understandable. (We would educate management and help them educate their people. That is an understandable strategy.)
- Sees profits in cash. (We asked people to pay before they came to school, with no credit, no discounts.)
- Has a strong franchise and thus freedom to price. (No one ever complained about our prices except the quality-control people, and we did not deal with them.)
- Does not take a genius to run. (Within two years everything was delegated except the creative director's role.)

- Has predictable earnings. (We did, but revenues turned out to be subject to recessions, when companies cut back on learning, and recessions are not predictable.)
- Is not a natural target of regulation. (No one cared about us one way or another. We paid our taxes and did not want the government as a client, although it came anyway.)
- Has low inventory and high turnover. (We had no inventory except a few tapes and classroom materials.)
- Has management as the owner-operator. (All employees had stock.)
- Is paid a royalty on the growth of others. (We set up clients to have their own colleges, and they paid us a fee per student.)

I wrote out a strategy at the end of 1979 that combined these strengths with what I had learned over the past few years. I had spent enough time with clients, at the top level of the companies, to know that the executives were ready for change and that we were the ones who would cause that. Management had to understand that it was the cause of the problem, and the employees of the company all had to understand quality the same way. The concepts, not the techniques, were important. Statistical process control, quality circles, and other popular programs had nothing to do with causing and effecting quality. They were just tools, and properly applied they could be useful.

Learning: *you have to think the operation out to the last detail and then help everyone else to understand it the same way.*

I built the Quality College around the four Absolutes of Quality Management as they had evolved over the years:

Quality means conformance to requirements, not goodness.

Quality comes from prevention, not detection.

The quality performance standard is zero defects, not acceptable quality levels.

Quality is measured by the price of nonconformance, not by indexes.

Dean Martin Schatz of the Rollins College business school (Crummer), in Winter Park, offered us a classroom in return for a donation to furnish it. We held our first class there in October 1979 and then did another one in November and another in December. These classes ran for four and a half days, crude by our later standards but effectively integrated in many respects. It didn't take long for us to realize that we needed our own dedicated classrooms and buildings. Philip found a building at the corner of New York and Canton Avenues just off Park Avenue in Winter Park. We were able to obtain 1,600 square feet, which was enough for a classroom called the "gold suite," plus some office space. After years of dealing with buildings and space in millions of square feet and looking at financial charts where they left off the last six zeros, it was another feeling entirely to agree to pay for space for a fixed period of time. Eventually we had the whole building, all 5,000 square feet of it.

One of the oldest ways of evaluating someone who wants to provide advice is to ask, "Has he ever met a payroll?" I always thought meeting a payroll didn't relate to much. After all I had been responsible for millions of dollars of assets and materials; I had organization charts, budgets, and all the other executive concerns. But I have to admit that it wasn't until I had to continually compare receipts with expenses and commit my personal assets to the company's future that I understood business. To this day I always know the accounts receivable, the accounts payable, and the upcoming capital requirements without even studying them.

I invited two people from ITT to join me. The corporate staff in New York and Brussels was being sliced up, and everyone was willing to look at another opportunity. Lance Arrington left a good job to throw in with me, and Bob Vincent was preparing to retire from ITT. Bob came down in the spring of 1980 and became the dean of the college. We obtained the services of a couple of part-time secretaries, and everyone was treated as an independent contractor until we found out how to deal with Social Security, health care plans, and such. On January 1, 1980, we had a real company with real obligations to its employees. I still was not taking any salary, but there was hope. The classroom was scheduled for several months with a class every other week.

Learning: *everything must produce business if it wants to feed at the trough.*

At about this time I was introduced to a lawyer, Bill Grimm, who was part of a new firm downtown. I showed Bill my plan for PCA, which included projections that the company would be able to go public in mid-decade. My estimates and plan didn't mesh with his experience, but he decided I was serious and became our attorney. He guided us through a dozen years of originality. In the same manner we found an insurance agent, a pension and health-plan specialist, and several others who stuck with us through the years. The Lord always provided just the right person for PCA at all levels. We dedicated the company to Him and never forgot that.

To support the once-a-week college class in early 1980 we started what we called the notebook factory; with our little Savin copier we put together the material the students would receive. On Friday afternoon, after the class had left, we took off our shoes, turned on a radio, and filled the new notebooks. We placed the empty binders on the students' tables, and then we took the contents, one page at a time, formed a line, and walked around the room filling the binders. It was fun and memorable.

Before we fed our students lunch, we walked them down Park Avenue in order to have some exercise and absorb a little local character. Two restaurants wanted me to pay in advance for the twenty-five lunches because they had never heard of us. Three others welcomed us with open arms, and over the years we essentially paid their complete overhead with our scheduled lunches. In return they listened to us concerning organizing and planning the meals; with this cooperation we were able to produce zero-defect lunches on schedule. We never did business with the ones who turned us down until they changed management later on. Before much time passed we had a full-time employee who just made arrangements for lunches and meetings.

Learning: *no detail is too small to be carefully arranged.*

The students (executives and managers from client companies) came to the quality college expecting that if we were going to teach them that an operation could be run properly, then we should be a living example of just that. They poked into corners, interrogated the staff, and expected events to happen on time. We also took that objective seriously. Each associate was selected for employment based on his or her desire to get everything done right the first time. All the PCA training was aimed at reinforcing this attitude and helping associates implement it. When something went wrong, we immediately took corrective action and explained to the class exactly what had happened.

Each Friday we had a graduation lunch and told the graduates they were the best class we ever had. And they were; it got better each week. For the first two years we had a buffet at my home on Monday evening for the class so everyone could get to know each other and relax a little. It worked out well because they all wanted to get back to the hotel by 9 P.M. in order to watch football.

My first priority for the company was to select associates carefully based on their personal commitment to contribute and to treat each other, as well as the clients, like ladies and gentlemen. Senior people in business just weren't very nice to the lower-level employees—at least that had been my experience. I conducted orientation programs for all employees, and we set up a "family council" as soon as there were about ten of us. Each month all the associates gathered together for an hour or so. The status of the company was reviewed, special reports were made, questions were answered, rumors were discussed, and everyone had a chance to make comments. It was always a struggle to get the professionals to attend each and every one of these, but I insisted. We had over 120 of these councils before I left.

All the associates appreciated these sessions. After each family council I thought about the years I had spent in companies where management was distant and untouchable. Standing in front of those people, seeing their trusting, expectant faces, and realizing that they were giving their all to the company made me realize each time that this was the right thing to do. It is a rare management that will voluntarily take the time and effort to communicate in this way. Whenever managers do even one, such as a "ZD celebration," they have a good time. They talk about it for months. I do not understand why they don't do it regularly. The refusal usually seems to be based in the human resource department, which is always afraid of starting a precedent. I think they are afraid of the troops.

Learning: *management has to work hard at communicating with employees.*

We never had a dress code as such, but everyone dressed in a manner that was respectful of their fellows and that gave clients a good impression. We did not tell the students what to wear, but most wore jackets and open shirts. In early 1980 one of the tenant companies in our building failed, and the area became available; it was big enough for a classroom for fourteen people, which fit the needs of our new executive college perfectly. We had determined that senior managers did not need to know much about implementation, but they had to understand the concepts. So we began offering a two-and-a-half-day course for senior people, and it was booked quickly. Phylis had just graduated from Rollins and came to work on a temporary basis, until she could "find a real job." We asked her to design and furnish the new room, called the "blue suite." She did a great job, and we used it for a long time.

I selected people to be instructors based on their experience in management and excluded anyone with a quality-control background. We also avoided professors or those who had been teaching. This way we could teach them to instruct properly. The courses were products in themselves and had to be delivered exactly as I had written them. The certification period usually took several months, but the instructors learned quickly and worked hard. In order to help them gain some experience, we set up what I called "barber colleges." The name came from the school in Wheeling where you could get your hair cut for free, or it might have been for twenty-five cents, from those learning the trade. We invited the management of nonprofit organizations to come to school free: hospitals, museums, science centers, homes for boys and girls, and lots of other local organizations. The positive fallout from this program over the years has been visible. We discovered that it was necessary to film some of the material in order to ensure consistent presentation. Also, not all instructors are so interesting they can be listened to for hours. I had been opening each class, which took the first morning, but when we began running parallel sessions, we taught the other instructors how to do that module also.

In this session, we asked the class to rate their own companies on the management grid contained in *Quality Is Free*. Then we passed those ratings out the door to the college secretary. One of the cases I wrote for this session was about the "wheelbarrow company." I used the white board to describe the wheelbarrow the company had planned to make and related how a few compromises here and there turned the project into a financial and organizational disaster. Then students took the roles of the seven officers of the company and read their comments about the situation. At the end they evaluated the wheelbarrow company on the grid. By this time the college secretary had compiled the evaluations of their own companies and slipped them back under the classroom door. The two sets of evaluations were compared by being displayed on the view-graph screen.

Classes always rated the wheelbarrow company at the lowest level on the grid—in sharp contrast with their evaluations of their own organizations. We carried this lesson further by evaluating the comments made by the "top managers" and showing how much money they were wasting by not following their own procedures and requirements. As a result the students began to believe that they knew more about the wheelbarrow company than they did about their own companies. It was always an awakening to them and set up the rest of the course so they could learn how to make changes in their corporate culture.

The wheelbarrow case had become a problem because I was the only one comfortable presenting it. For that reason we decided to put it on film. Phylis found a blue wheelbarrow in a hardware store and we found a new company that had one of those newfangled video cameras. We hired local actors to play the parts of the executives, and I described the original wheelbarrow design up front. It all worked out well, and we began to realize that this was a good procedure for us.

Learning: *teaching has to be taken seriously, particularly when the students have short attention spans.*

Doug Hoelscher of Tennant and I went to Japan early in 1980 to visit his operations and to see what was happening in other areas. As in the 1975 trip I was recognized immediately there; I was treated with much respect and asked many questions, again to my surprise. The Japanese were well versed in my writings and were in the process of translating *Quality Is Free.*

The Japanese Union of Scientists and Engineers (JUSE), which was the group promoting Dr. W. Edwards Deming's work, was interested in doing something with me, as was the Japan Management Association (JMA). We worked out an arrangement with JMA and over the years taught them to teach our material and concepts. I got to meet Dr. Isakawa, who was the real father of quality in Japan. He ran six four-day courses for JUSE each year for Japanese top management. It was heavy on statistics, but all the managers pretended to understand and use them. Suffering is a mark of manhood in Japanese culture.

When I spoke to the Japanese quality-control society, the members were critical of U.S. quality and of the quality-control professionals. They thought I must be very frustrated. I told them that they should not underestimate the Americans, that they were sometimes slow to get interested in what was good for them, but that they would be turned around on quality in a few years. They thought I was being polite.

Learning: *hardly anyone knows much about other nations and their cultures.*

When I returned home, IBM Raleigh, led by Alan Krowe, was beginning a serious quality-improvement process and asked for some help in putting the training package together. Alan was the first senior IBM operating executive to start to change the corporate mind about quality. His unit arranged its product so the customers could put it together themselves. We take this for granted today, but it was a breakthrough then.

We made a twenty-minute film for them of me walking around the quality college talking about the four Absolutes. Soon all our clients wanted one of those films for themselves, so we developed a compact way of doing it. Park Avenue had many nice stores, and the owners cooperated with us, so we used their facilities. I started out in my office talking about quality in general and how important it was to the company. We shot the same scene several times using a different company name each time. We then went to the parking lot, an art gallery, a men's clothing store, and a restaurant covering the four Absolutes of Quality Management. The client company's name appeared three times in their film. This way we could charge them a minimum amount and still make a little money. I began to realize that we were going to have to supply clients with in-house training material.

Learning: *companies have to be permitted to emerge and grow; if they become rigid, the world skips right on by.*

Classroom and office space was getting tight; we arranged to obtain the fourth floor of a building across the street. That let us build one more large classroom (the "silver suite") and three smaller ones. We were growing fast but doing it out of our cash flow. It was getting hard to meet the demands of our clients. The results they were getting led them to refer others, particularly their suppliers, to us. I was busy making speeches and writing new classroom material. At this time I was the creative department, but Phylis began to put together some illustrators and other product people, so she took it over. We were able to standardize view graphs, brochures, and such. It was nice to be able to have material everyone admired. Philip was working on trying to get us some word-processing and computing capability. We often forget how primitive office equipment was in those days, not long ago. When we began PCA there were no VCRs, no video cameras, no personal computers, no faxes.

In September 1980 we went back to Greenbrier for our physicals, and Dr. Morehouse reported that there had been a significant change in my cardiogram during the stress test. In those days that test consisted of running up and down a short flight of stairs. He suggested that I lose some weight and exercise more than I was. When we returned to Winter Park, I went to my family doctor with the report, and he sent me to Dr. Zeb Burton, a cardiologist. He put me on a treadmill hooked up to all the equipment and took me off after about thirty seconds. The upshot was that I went to the hospital and had a heart-catheterization examination followed by an operation in which five bypasses were made of the coronary arteries. In between the two events the doctor let me go back to the office for long enough to tell the staff what was happening.

The courses were laid out well by that time, and I was not needed for teaching. However, the company was still fragile and needed a gentle hand of leadership. It could continue to survive and prosper without me, but it probably would not grow. Several people in the organization could manage the company, but another few could destroy it with their management style. I wanted to make certain that Shirley, Skip, and Phylis knew the difference. I wrote a set of instructions, on my typewriter, suggesting a specific set of actions for the company if something happened to me. I also noted who should not be given positions of authority and gave the family a choice of two people who could become CEO. The letter was sealed and given to Philip with instructions to leave it that way unless I didn't make it. Then all the staff and the students who were there at that time gathered around me, and we said a prayer. The surgery and the recovery went well, and I became a stronger and healthier person. The experience gave me a renewed interest in wellness. I taught a class five weeks after the surgery. Skip returned the unopened envelope, and we shredded the letter.

We added another location, called, not too imaginatively, the PCA building, that housed all our personnel offices. It contained 32,000 square feet. Phylis was busy obtaining furniture for the offices; I was busy demanding that people keep their offices clean; and Skip was busy figuring how to pay for everything. Keeping offices clean is not a natural action. It is a mark of honor for professional people to have papers piled up on their credenzas and desks, but it looked bad to the clients. I toured the offices every day I was in town and left a couple of Hershey kisses on the desks that were in good shape. I placed empty boxes and other stuff that was lying around on top of the desks. People got the message quickly.

A steady stream of companies wanted to come and talk about their strategies. The business was building steadily, and we wanted to reach out to small companies also. In 1979 total revenue was around $400,000; in 1980 it was closer to $2 million; 1981 would be $4.5 million; and 1982 was planned for $8 million.

Bill Sabin, my editor at McGraw-Hill, suggested that I take another look at *Sweet Way* with the idea of adding material on family management. I liked the idea and went to work. My portable typewriter still weighed twenty-one pounds, but I dragged it along on my trips to use in flight and at night. Also, I had a new electric typewriter at my desk (a practice that never failed to embarrass other executives), and it had a new feature that let you see what was going to be typed before it was printed. My grandson, Charlie, and I posed in the computer room for the picture on the back cover of the new *Sweet Way*. The new edition was well received, which made me begin to think about a new book on quality management. It was a couple of years before I got around to it, but I began to think about it. In the meantime I kept writing short pieces called "reflections," which we printed and sent to clients.

The professionals were working hard to become certified to teach in the college. Bob Vincent had broken the material down into modules, and as they learned each one, he checked it off. I wanted each student to hear and see the same things. For that reason the best instructors were those who had no or little quality experience. The conventional wisdom of quality control was bad news; we taught prevention. As I developed each new module, Bob watched me teach it, documented it, and then brought the others on board. Soon he would not let me do that one any more, and I brought forth a different one. After a while he only let me do a weekly question-and-answer session with the classes in the auditorium. He said the modules kept changing under the guise of improvement when I taught them. I think I'm just not good at doing the same thing each time.

Learning: *the boss, even if he or she is the creative source, must step back and let others work; amazingly, things then get better more quickly.*

Qualifying as an instructor was a difficult process. It was necessary to learn the material, of course, but presentation was equally important. John Monaghan, of my ITT days, came down to help us in this area. He was able to show us how to avoid the "noise in the channel"—irritating actions that disturb the student's concentration. He helped organize the material into a logical sequence, and he showed how to show view graphs. Those attending the college often asked whether they could learn all these techniques. As a result we included a half-day communications module designed by John. After all the students had to go back to their companies and explain what was happening. Some of the more arrogant companies looked down their noses at being taught communications. Once in a while there was a revolt, so I would invite those who knew so much about the subject to stand up and tell us what should be done in three minutes. They always flubbed the opportunity, and class went on better than ever.

The associates were putting forth more effort than they had ever done at any other company. This way of working always worries me because I'm afraid home life might get ignored and that those who do the real work in the office might not be appreciated. For that reason I established the Beacon of Quality award for everyone and the instructor-certification plaque for that group. All associates, except the chairman, were eligible for the Beacon award. We just provided a list with everyone's name on it, and people voted. The first year three were selected, and the awards were presented at our company "picnic," an annual black-tie dinner-dance with spouses. The event received that name because when I suggested the dinner, my son, the comptroller, said we couldn't afford a dinner; why didn't we just have a picnic? So we had a dinner and called it a picnic. Each year we had a real picnic too, at Sea World or Disney World. Everyone brought their kids, and it was a wonderful time. These events did not cost much but reaped eternal rewards. People appreciated the company taking them seriously.

Learning: *recognition should please those who receive it, not just those who present it.*

After the certification awards for instructors were given, a local furrier, Art Labellman, came into the room wheeling racks of fur coats.

We asked the wives of the newly certified instructors to select the coat of their choice. They were dumbfounded but pleased. I thought that the wives had given up their husbands for a while and it was only fair that they be compensated. When we certified our first female instructors, we gave their husbands a blazer with PCA buttons.

At the end of 1981 we developed a special program for small corporations. Analysis had shown that this was going to be a big market; millions of these companies were around. It didn't take a deep knowledge of mathematics to know that almost anything multiplied by those numbers would make money. We soon realized that we were way ahead of the market. Small companies thought it was cheaper to deal with nonconformance than to spend money to go to classes. It took us ten years to figure how to do that group correctly.

We also decided to begin making the videos that became the Quality Education System (QES). Clients were complaining that it was difficult to teach employees about their role without some material. This complaint was reasonable, so we had a brainstorming session and arrived at a list of fifteen subjects that would need to be discussed. The idea was to create a fifteen-minute tape on each; the tape would include a lecture led by a trained facilitator using view graphs and then a discussion of how that particular subject applied to the employees in each company.

The next weekend we went to the John's Island house I had bought in 1974, and I wrote all fifteen scripts. They just poured out. We wound up using all of them pretty much as they were. Some changes were made because we writers just cannot keep our hands off the material. We set up a team to produce the support material and made plans to film the scripts. Making these films put us in a whole new business, hard products. It also showed clearly that we had been concentrating on the wrong end of the telescope. I thought the managers and executives we taught would go back and teach. Some did, but mostly they just couldn't handle it. It was going to cost about $600,000 to make QES, but we had revenues of $1,000,000 a month in early 1982, and even though there was a recession it didn't seem to affect us. We were in the process of opening six new classrooms in a new office park about six miles away from the current offices. We also hired five new instructor consultants and had begun training them. Our executive committee was bullish about the way things were going. There was no competition in the quality management field except for a few individual operators, and our clients were achieving success.

More important, they were bragging about it to their friends in other companies.

We had established a line of credit at Barnett Bank, using the PCA building, my house, and my personal guarantee as security. The Barnett people went out of their way to set our folks up with checking accounts, pay depositing, and personal loans. The company had a good cash flow and money in the bank. Furnishing the new offices was a big expense, paying for QES filming added to it, and we had a dozen people in training who were producing no revenue.

Around June the recession began to hit corporations, and true to form they immediately began to reduce what they were spending on education and training. Our revenue dropped by half in an instant. We drew down our line of credit to take care of commitments and devised an action plan. I didn't want to lay people off because we had spent so much time and money training them. We were able to reduce expenses in several ways but needed to cut compensation somehow. We held a family council and explained the situation. I figured we needed to hold out until December or so. My suggestion was that instead of laying off 20 percent of the people we would all take a 20 percent pay cut. I would take zero salary. Everyone agreed right away, and we prayed about it. One of the traditions I started at PCA when it began was to begin each meeting with a word of prayer. Sometimes when I was not at a meeting, they would forget, but overall it helped calm the company and aim it in the right direction.

Learning: *when it comes time to ask for sacrifices, you learn how effective your relationship building has been.*

Our friends at Barnett Bank went ballistic when our revenues began to fall. They shut down my personal line of credit and began to make noises about wanting the company's line paid off in full, right now. We had assets that were of much higher value than our loan even though they were real estate and equipment. These assets did not impress them, of course. Assets are worth nothing if you can't sell them. I did some of my most creative writing in a weekly status report of our progress in increasing revenue and reducing expenses. It was important to not let anyone think we were in a terminal state; that would have been evident to the clients immediately. We kept getting new clients, but we didn't have much to sell the ones who were finishing their management education. Much of the problem came about because companies like IBM, Milliken, and Stevens had put all the folks through quality college that they had wanted to. If we had begun QES earlier, we would have been in good shape.

The bank gave us an "adviser," who immediately suggested that we stop traveling and gave me a lecture on how "marketing types," like me, were impractical when it came to money. He couldn't explain how consultants are supposed to deal with clients without traveling. We got paid for spending time in our client's operations; it was a main source of revenue. I ignored him, and he finally quit calling.

I kept trying to sell the PCA building, which was worth about $2 million, but the whole thing about recessions is that no one wants to buy anything. Each day I went around the company seeing how contacts were going, and every Friday morning we had a "chairman's chat" in the lounge. We picked up several more clients and were beginning to work with them. Unfortunately it takes several months for cash flow to recover. The bank executives called me regularly, and we had a meeting twice a month in which they revealed their complete lack of understanding about the world of business. I kept asking why they were so panicky when we were paying our interest on time. Of course, the auditors had placed our note in the questionable category, and they did not want our blood on their record.

Philip Jr., our comptroller, had the tough part, paying our bills. We could do well if we didn't have to pay for anything. We wrote a letter to each major supplier asking whether they could charge us just for their costs at present and we would make it up after the first of the year. We had established relationships with most of them that provided a positive response. Philip and I went to see several suppliers, and they assured us of their support. Two or three would not have any part of this proposal, so we paid them in full and in keeping with my forgiveness policy they were never permitted to return.

Learning: *stick with the principles that got you where you are.*

One recurring problem was paying for QES. The production costs were hard to meet; the notebooks and graphics were being done by our own people, whom we were paying anyway. We learned to not waste much time doing the videos. The actors all came from the local semiprofessional theater, and most could learn their lines quickly. We filmed them all on location, with the cooperation of the businesses in the area.

Everyone likes show business. I would introduce each segment, usually by talking to the actors in their roles. Then the point of the session would be dramatized. One was about the flypaper company that spent most of its money sending people around the world looking for flies that were weaker than the glue it was making. It was an original way of teaching quality management; the segments were amusing as well as interesting. I thought everyone would be thrilled with them but was concerned to learn that the consultants and instructors were not happy about QES. Apparently they thought that films would replace them. At any rate they were always suggesting that we postpone or eliminate the series. They did not see much of a market for hard material. Because hundreds of millions of people needed to understand quality management, it seemed to me that they were wrong. In fact their attitude ticked me off, and I called everyone together to talk about the future of the company.

I said that we would always have a quality college to teach managers, executives, and client instructors in person, but the college could reach only about 3 percent of a client company's personnel. And it was not a profitable business. I also said that we would continue consulting activities with clients, but even though we charged them well for that, it was not a good way to produce revenue. It was heavy in personnel costs, and clients didn't like to have people poking around their operations. To me, the future was in hard products. If we could provide videotapes and audiotapes that would give the clients the education and direction they needed, then they could do it all at a much lower cost. After their development was paid for, videos were about 90 percent profit. Because I wrote most of the material, the only cost was production.

People have their own agendas, and most of them are not too productive. I let everyone know that we were in survival mode and that although all thoughts and ideas were welcome, we were not doing consensus management. I would make the decisions. If anyone wanted to pledge a house and or provide other personal guarantees on the bank notes, I would give that person an extra listen. I reminded them that we had given everyone stock in the company and that if we were to ever go public with the stock, we had to offer more than a bunch of people standing up in front of another bunch of people. We needed a company, not a gathering. One or two people did not buy this proposal, so I encouraged them to start their own companies. They left but never did anything.

Learning: *never underestimate the inability of individuals to grasp concepts.*

Several times each month I went off to make a speech in order to generate revenue and to get a feel for what was happening. I visited clients and was pleased to see that they were all doing well. It was tight, but we were going to make it; it never occurred to me that we wouldn't.

In 1979 revenues were $320,000 with five associates.

In 1980 revenues were $1,664,000 with sixteen associates.

In 1981 revenues were $5,333,000 with sixty-seven associates.

In 1982 revenues were $7,897,000 with ninety-four associates.

CHAPTER ELEVEN

The Maturing Company

W̶e finished the production of QES in October 1982 and began presenting it to existing clients. It consisted of the fifteen tapes covering the concepts of quality management, individual notebooks, view graphs for the facilitators, and an instructor's notebook. Because QES represented a new concept in quality education, the clients did not absorb the idea immediately. It took a while for most of them to realize that we were offering them the opportunity to be the power behind their process. They could do the "teaching" and be assured that everyone learned the same thing. Our instructors did not like to tell their classes about it because they considered that to be "selling." How they thought our clients would know that we had gone to all this trouble to provide them with an education capability, I'll never know. When you have something everyone wants, it is necessary only to expose them to it; there is no selling.

Learning: *being the boss is not enough to let you have your own sweet way.*

Once clients realized what it was, QES became a big hit even though it didn't produce revenue for several months. We insisted that those who were to be facilitators inside their companies come to school for a week after they had completed the management college. Then they could lead the students through the material using examples from their own organization. We planned to lease the tapes to the clients and sell them the workbooks. Later on we were able to give larger clients master disks from which they could print their own workbooks. The idea was that all participants would have their own notebooks to mark up and keep forever. Some of the training people in client companies duplicated the notebooks or covered the pages with plastic and used them over again. Much of this practice was killed when I explained to their CEOs how cheap and uncommitted it made their companies look to the employees.

We were still struggling with the Barnett Bank people, who were worried about their money, although we had not missed an interest payment.

Learning: *no matter what they say, banks are interested only in getting their loan repaid with interest; get along without them if possible.*

Then two interesting things happened. A local individual made us an offer on the PCA building, which I accepted. The mortgage company he selected came and approved everything; then he decided that he was in a position to beat us out of about 10 percent of the deal. I canceled the sale right there. "Neither a Scrooge nor a patsy be," as they say in West Virginia. The mortgage company said it would finance the building for me personally but would not finance PCA as the owner. All the cash flow I had came from PCA, and my net worth was close to zero. Somehow their proposal didn't make sense, but I eagerly agreed to do it even though I didn't have the $150,000 necessary for a down payment. The Lord would work that out I knew.

The money the company received from my purchasing the building paid off Barnett, and I became the landlord of the company's administrative building. At this time the president of another bank, a smaller one, invited me to lunch. He understood our situation and offered to finance our company as we grew. He also made me a personal loan that let me handle the building deal. So as 1983 dawned we were again financially free and bound to never be in debt again. I went to a golfing buddy's dealership and bought myself a new Jaguar. I also asked Philip to put me back on the payroll. As soon as we were solvent, we gave our employees back the money they had lost because of the pay cut the previous year. Philip decided that he had enough of being comptroller for a while, so we hired a new one and he took over administration. Neither he nor Phylis and I had any problems working together. We did not compete; they didn't write books or teach, and I didn't do their jobs.

Learning: *parents and children can work together if they conduct their relationship on a professional basis.*

At this time Shirley and I had decided that perhaps thirty-six years together was enough. We had no quarrel with each other, but our interests were changing. She was interested in Christian missionary work, and I was wrapped up in changing the philosophy of the business world. We consulted the children and agreed to divide things and separate. I had already given her half the administration building, and we divided my share between Phylis and Philip. I bought a little condo in mid-town Winter Park, with the aid of my new friend the banker, and Shirley took over the house. She already owned a good portion of PCA through stock in her name. All in all it was as friendly a divorce as possible; she helped me furnish the apartment. Both of us felt better once it was over. I have often observed that sometimes people can be together too long, and sometimes they work out well together forever. They need to have the opportunity to make a choice.

The company had a surge of business. Our clients were recommending us to their suppliers and friends. We had an imposing list of clients and were getting a lot of media attention. General Motors asked us to work with them. Jim MacDonald, the president, and I talked about the idea. Jim had been at Pontiac back in the 1960s, when I got to know the General Motors people. He was a quality-oriented executive and even managed to smile when I picked him up in my Jaguar during his time in class.

I suggested that working with General Motors might be a problem for us because we would have to build up our staff in order to handle the increased business and General Motors might change its mind suddenly. As a result, General Motors offered to purchase an equity position in our company in order to make the arrangement more permanent. Jim and I agreed on the price ($4 million for 10 percent with an option for another 10 percent) right then. It took the lawyers several months to work the deal out, but in the meantime we worked together. General Motors was a good partner, sent six hundred or so executives to school, and had us set up a managers' quality college in Michigan. I always remembered Woody Allen's comment that "when the lion and the lamb lie down together, the lamb doesn't get much sleep." But General Motors never gave us any trouble, and we never extended any discounts; the company got exactly the same treatment as other clients and insisted that it be that way.

The stock General Motors received came from the principals of the company. It was nice for us to have some real money for a change. I was able to pay off my condo and car, and for the first time in my life I was debt-free personally. The rest of the family and some of the key executives divided the money. The company had no need for it now that we had learned to manage without debt. Our cash flow was positive, and we were using it to grow. It is harder to manage success than tribulation; people don't listen well when it comes to dividing the spoils, but they do when the lifeboats are being launched.

Learning: *when success comes, it is vital to keep reconfirming the basics of company philosophy.*

We had a management meeting day at PCA once a month, and each member of the executive committee was required to attend. Meetings were scheduled for all day on that Monday, and family council was held on Friday of the same week. This operations review system was based on my experience at ITT, which demanded that everyone look at all the numbers, listen to all the problems, consider all the possibilities, and help make decisions. Everything was covered, and, as at ITT, there was hell to pay only if one was not open and honest. The meetings opened with a prayer, and everyone was nice to each other. We fought the problems, not the people. This tone was evident when I was around and often disappeared when I was not. People do have their own agendas.

One time the European contingent stated that their revenue was below plan because Easter had caused people to not want to do business. They spent twenty minutes explaining to me why the occurrence of Easter had been such a surprise to them. We even got out an encyclopedia and noted that we were able to know exactly when Easter was going to occur for each year in the next century, which should be plenty. We remembered that the purpose of the company was to make our customers and employees successful. It was also not to make trouble for each other. Business should be fun, and we should be the absolute best in the business. I always kept this goal at the front of my mind. I felt that the purpose of organizations was to help people have lives. I ran PCA that way.

In 1984 a BBC producer, Brian Davies, asked whether he could spend some time with us. Brian had produced several notable shows for BBC, one of them a study of lilies worldwide. I was struck by his sensitivity in that piece. After showing the massive and dedicated lily-raising places of the world, he filmed some lilies growing wild on a rocky slope in Greece. They were the most beautiful of all because, as the narrator said, "they chose to grow there." Brian came and lived with us for a month. He went everywhere I went, attended family and company parties, listened to me teach and speak. Then he returned to London and wrote us a proposal for a forty-minute show called *The Quality Man*. He wanted to do it when Peggy and I took a trip to Scotland that June. We had decided to get married in January, and this trip would be a sort of honeymoon. I said we could work it out if they could help me get on the Murfield golf course near Edinburgh. Playing there was generally impossible to arrange, as the club was notoriously difficult. When Tom Watson won the British Open at Murfield, he and Ben Crenshaw went out on the course later that same evening, after the crowds had gone home, to play a few holes just for relaxation. The club manager ordered them off the course because they were not members.

Somehow BBC did arrange for me to play there, paying a fee to Murfield in the process, and we drove down from Gleneagles, where we had been staying. An associate and his wife met us there, and the four of us set out to play a few holes with the cameras and microphone picking up the conversations and action. Women weren't permitted in the clubhouse; however, the manager did unlock a toilet out on the course for the ladies. When he had enough golfing shots, Brian set up in a little valley, next to a shed that blocked the wind, where he had a view of the Firth of Forth. He planted me with my back to the view. Then for several hours on two days he asked me questions and filmed the responses. His month-long visit had taught him more about my philosophy and stories than my staff had picked up. The resulting film was a fine piece of work, interesting and informative. BBC has sold hundreds of the tapes and has shown it several times, making thousands of dollars on it; I got $300 for my efforts. However, it has been a marvelous help in building a business and reputation.

Learning: *some people take time to study others and understand their work.*

I began to work on a book to explain quality management in terms of management action required. My experience as a consultant and teacher for the past four years had convinced me that managers didn't like their employees very much. They continually hassled them and thereby kept the pot boiling. They honestly didn't seem to understand that people were their primary asset. Competitors all around the world could purchase the same equipment and material; the only advantage a company could have was its work force. My personal experience working at low levels had shown me that managers were insensitive and that they assumed people down the line were not too bright. My title for the book was "The Art of Hassle Free Management." However, the publisher hated it, which is fairly normal. But the publisher fought a bigger battle than usual, so somewhat in jest I suggested *Quality without Tears*, and it was accepted. The main emphasis in *Quality without Tears* was the four Absolutes. If one could understand them, the whole secret of quality would be revealed. Managers are so technique-oriented that it is hard to get ideas through to them.

The story chapters in the new book included one on a big corporation's wasted planning effort. Another chapter was a thinly veiled take-off on Dickens's *A Christmas Carol*. I changed it to the "Quality Carol." In my story Marley takes Scrooge to a warehouse where Scrooge is condemned to fix all the shoddy products he had shipped out of his factory during his work life. In the next bin a lady who has been in charge of luggage for a large airline is spending eternity trying to unite all the bags she had lost with their owners. When the book came out, the response to the "Quality Carol" chapter was so strong that I decided to make a training movie out of it. We were able to get Efrem Zimbalist Jr. to play the lead and a fine group of East Coast professionals for the supporting roles. We built a set in Cocoa Beach and spent a fun week shooting the movie. Our star proved to be a fascinating person and a complete professional. He was always ready, knew his lines, and provided a lot of support for us amateurs.

One evening at Cocoa Beach we were all having dinner at a local restaurant when the people at the next table suddenly dropped to the floor, laid on their backs, and wiggled their legs in the air. It turned out that this was a sensitivity group and they had developed this action to bring them together. When someone yelled out "dead ants," they dived for the ground. The next day, in the midst of a critical scene, our script coordinator yelled "dead ants," and the entire organization dropped and wiggled. After that the set became more relaxed. The film was well received, primarily because the production was so good. But I have to note that although people enjoyed it and bought it, they did not seem to get the message.

Peggy and I bought a second house in Savannah, Georgia, out on the islands at The Landings, in order to have a get-away place. It took five hours to drive there or go on the train. We arranged to leave on a Friday and return on the second Monday. This schedule allowed me to write more and have a little less pressure. The house was on the first hole of the golf course, which let me try to regain a little skill at the sport. My golf game had gone south the minute I left ITT and started the company. It was not possible to concentrate for the three seconds it takes to strike a golf ball. I am not an anxious or nervous person, but I do have a tendency to think about a lot of things at the same time—a tendency golf does not permit. In Georgia I hoped to be able to concentrate on the game. Peggy was delighted to have another chance to decorate a house, having just finished our town home in Winter Park. She has a great sense of color and style. The homes are comfortable, and our relationship is marvelous. We get along well and have common interests. Peggy had a hard time dealing with not working after doing it for twenty-five years, but it didn't take long before she was so busy that she had no time for formal work.

Learning: *people can change their lifestyles when they choose to do so.*

For the first time in my work life I was able to write and think during the day. PCA ran on a day-to-day basis in a calm manner. We had thought out the procedures and policies and incorporated them into a strategy that everyone could understand. We made no sudden changes; everything was planned. So the panic calls and noncompleted assignments common in most companies did not exist in PCA. The company was doing so well that I was concerned people would forget to appreciate all the wonderful things that had happened to us. For this reason I established a "Thanksgiving Week" to occur in April each year. The theme was to thank all of those who had made it possible for all of us to be living so well. The quality-improvement team took charge of the event and planned something for each day of the week.

On Monday morning the employees were thanked. Associates received a memento when they came to work; the Thanksgiving Week committee came to the monthly operations review and thanked the executive team, usually by giving each of them a rose or something similar. The outside directors were thanked at the board meeting that day. On Tuesday the suppliers were thanked. They received letters and in some cases a personal visit. On Wednesday we had a prayer breakfast to thank the Lord. A guest speaker was invited, and most of the associates came to the session, which was held by the lake and was over by 8:30 A.M. On Thursday we thanked the clients. Many were called, many received letters, and those who were there in class each received a personal greeting and a memento. On Thursday I usually held an open discussion with the classes for an hour in the auditorium every week. We taped the sessions for distribution and sale later.

On Friday we thanked the families. After work they were invited to the college building for a buffet and some fun and games. One year the kids threw baseballs trying to hit devices that dunked their parents in a tank of water; another year there was a ski show. (We also had the real picnic in the summer.) On Saturday we had the Thanksgiving Ball, our annual black-tie affair, where we presented the Beacon of Quality awards and thanked the organization in general. We had a great band, Marshall Grant from Palm Beach, and everyone danced, even the young folks who were shy about it at first.

Learning: *arranging events properly is a full-time job.*

At this ball I wanted everyone to be comfortable. The events were getting to be large now that there were a couple of hundred associates. Betty Gorenflow, an administrative assistant, had a beautiful voice; she often sang in our church. I asked her to sing a song at the ball while I played the ukulele. Everyone considered the chairman so square that they expected me to wear a suit to the outdoor picnic. Betty didn't know the songs I had in mind, being too young, but we recorded them so she could learn the words. The idea was that after I had presented the Beacon awards and was about to turn the program back to the band, she would rush up and present me with the uke as a gift from the choral group. I would begin to play "Simple Melody," and she would sing. Then I would sing the counter melody, which was mostly a talking kind of voice, and we would then sing both melodies together. We also prepared an encore, "Please Don't Talk about Me When I'm Gone." We practiced in secret for two weeks and almost chickened out on the night itself. However, it was worth all the anxiety to see the reaction when we started. The audience cheered enough for us to do the encore, and they still talk about it. However, I keep waiting for someone to ask us to perform again. So far, no luck.

I had tried several times to set up a bookstore for the quality college where students and others could buy the books, of course, and could also get golf shirts, pens, and other memorabilia with our name on it. Several attempts to have the college personnel set up such a store met with failure; they just could not seem to get the idea even though I personally took them to the Rollins College bookstore and sent them articles on how the major-league teams made money selling logo material. The bookstore was viewed as just another of the chairman's quaint ideas. So one day I asked Phylis to take it over and took it away from the others. Within a few months she had a catalog out and a flow of nice material going through our shop. Within a year it was doing over $200,000 worth of business manned by a part-time attendant. The students were able to get to it between classes, and Phylis advertised in our magazine, which went out quarterly to the mailing list. My thought was that executives all around the world would see others playing golf or relaxing with nice shirts and hats bearing the logos of PCA or the quality college. To me that was advertising and marketing; to many others it was just a diversion. Those who had not lived the life of a corporate executive were not able to market to them. They just did not understand what was important. It is difficult to teach people about things they have not experienced. That is probably why marriage counseling is not all that successful.

When we began to have operations overseas, it was only a matter of time before they needed permanent offices. Clients did not appreciate it when we landed some people and boxes, conducted several classes, and then went back home. They wanted on-site support; at least they said they did. We set up offices in London and Brussels with plans to do the same in France and Germany. As we hired people we brought them to Winter Park for orientation and training. The clerical staff would come for two weeks; the instructors and consultants, for six months. The idea of bringing a secretary across the Atlantic (or from Singapore) seemed like an extravagance to many. However, those people never forgot what they learned at Winter Park, and they built relationships that made them valuable associates.

Learning: *left on their own, branch offices never provide adequate orientation; the need for good orientation is a difficult concept to get into the minds of those who see the world in terms of revenues and profit.*

My best present when traveling is a newspaper. France, 1989.

We started alumni conferences in order to help our clients bring each other up to date. All the speakers were clients talking about their experiences, and the results were wonderful. It was necessary to charge for the conference in order to defray expenses, but each year over two hundred people showed up. We displayed new products, and I had an open discussion with the group. Around 1985 I could begin to see an increased search for tools rather than concepts to implement quality management. This development was disturbing to me; I anticipated that a great deal of effort would be wasted in the field. Business was just beginning to be interested in educating everyone to improve quality. What we taught was a culture change, which required management commitment, education, and action. What most executives would have liked was an action program that could be delegated to a functional department like quality or human resources. Consultants were springing up eager to satisfy this desire. They defined quality any way the client wanted it; they would not insist on management being educated; and they were willing to work for much less money than we were. This change in the field scared the executive committee. But none of these new people had videotapes and other hard material. They did not have the money to compete with us in those areas, and the more material we could create the better off we were. I directed that we would not respond to requests for bids from potential clients. If they wanted to succeed, they would have to do it our way. We kept growing, reaching $20 million in revenues in 1985.

One company program that was being well managed was contributions to charities. Originally I thought that PCA should distribute 10 percent of after-tax earnings to colleges, children's programs, the arts, and other programs. We excluded churches because I felt that the congregations should take care of themselves, and, besides, there were hundreds of churches in central Florida. We finally settled on 5 percent of earnings, which came to be a tidy sum. In 1985, for instance, we gave away around $300,000, and we didn't tell anyone. We had set up a committee early in the company's history to handle these contributions and had hired a consultant to help us out around 1983. Larry Kennedy was a pastor with an MBA; he had a little operation that helped charitable organizations manage themselves better. We asked him to make certain that those who were asking for money were legitimate. We said that we wanted to give money to "real people helping real people." It is not as easy as it sounds.

We bought trucks, funded homeless shelters, gave tuition money to those who did not have it, funded a food bank, bought equipment for a college to teach the blind to read, and in general helped a lot of people to help real people. Our associates knew about this endeavor and were proud to be part of the company. Now and then people would indicate that we should give this money to the shareholders rather than giving it away. My response was that God had made us what we were for this purpose and that we needed to honor our commitment to Him. If they wanted to do it differently, I suggested they start their own company.

If PCA wanted to gain market share, we needed additional material, and that was going to cost money. Also I had given away about 80 percent of the stock in the company to the associates, General Motors, and my family. The family owned less than a third of the organization. I thought we should consider going public. No consulting firm had done that before, and when we discussed it with the people at Dean Witter, they were cautious. They were concerned that we were like an advertising agency, where "the inventory goes down the elevator every night at 5 P.M." We showed them that we were a product company. The college classes were taught by people who had learned how to teach the program, not by professors or individuals doing their own thing. All of the classes were carefully controlled. We also showed that half the revenue and most of the profit came from the hard material. My plan for the future was to reduce stand-up teaching to a minimum and concentrate on hard copy. We began the process of going public. I didn't know how complicated that was until we began.

Learning: *you learn what you know about your business when you have to explain it to hard-nosed Wall Street types.*

"Due diligence" means that everything one says about an organization must be verified, so the person considering a purchase of shares will be told the complete truth. For instance part of the proposal referred to the sales of my books. Books are a fluid asset; thousands of copies are waiting to be sold to someone; some that have been sold have not been reported as sold. As soon as you put a sales figure together, it is not longer valid because someone sold another copy in London. *Quality Is Free* sold around two million copies counting hardcover, paperback, and translations. Several publishers were involved, and it took quite a bit of figuring to arrive at a number everyone could

Granddaughter Jori and I check out the
Orlando Science Center dinosaur exhibit, 1986.

accept. This process seemed like a lot of foolishness to me in many respects, but we stuck to the letter of the law, and there were a lot of letters. We met with security analysts, most of whom had little practical experience in the world of business. However, they were good at investing money.

After more effort than one could believe we were launched on the over-the-counter exchange in October 1985. The stock opened at 13 and worked its way to 34 a few months later. Peggy and I gave shares of stock to several of our favorite charities and funded the Crosby Scholar's Tuition program at Rollins College; each year a gifted student receives a four-year scholarship. We also helped Winter Park Hospital establish the Peggy and Philip B. Crosby Wellness Center. (It now has four thousand members, including us.) I had three reasons for wanting to go public. First, the company needed a sound base for raising funds so that it would not have to suffer the indignities perpetrated by our bank. Second, the associates who owned stock could be on their own, and I would not feel responsible for their having stock that was not marketable. Third, the members of my family could be independent. Shirley, Philip Jr., Phylis, and Peggy all had their own stock. Now they would have their own money. All the associates now had stock worth real money, and several became millionaires. Over the years I had insisted that they learn how to use financial advisers and manage their money. We paid for that advice but had to drag most of them to the sessions.

I didn't start the company to make money, and perhaps that is why we did. I wound up with several million dollars in cash and stock personally and gave away about half of it, but we had launched a quality reformation throughout the world. By the end of 1985 PCA had sent almost fifteen thousand executives and managers through the quality college. Thousands of their employees and suppliers participated through QES and other classes.

1983 revenues were $12,872,000 with 102 associates.

1984 revenues were $20,034,000 with 128 associates.

1985 revenues were $34,333,000 with 182 associates.

CHAPTER TWELVE

Managing a
Public Company

—〜〜— My next book, *Running Things*, was copyrighted early in 1986. It had been written in Savannah the previous year and was the book I'd wished I had when PCA began. It described the purpose of an organization and how to create one. I hoped it would help managers think things through rather than just bumbling along.

Learning: *most companies fail because the management effort is incoherent rather than because the company does not have enough money, but hardly anyone believes that.*

Writing a book is a fine endeavor for me. Everything comes out of my head, so I don't have to plow through other books to lift and document quotes from other writers. It is all me. The books on management that I see today are often a compilation of what different people have said, with the author's opinion placed on top. This practice wouldn't be bad if the authors paraphrased others accurately, at least in my case. I can think of only a couple authors who came close to stating my thoughts correctly. My assumption is that most authors did the same with others' ideas as they did with mine. For that reason I never comment on what others write or do; they can do it better than

I. Often I am asked who writes my books for me. They think that book writing is a sideline to my business. Actually, it is the other way around; I started PCA in order to read my books to people who wouldn't take the time to do it themselves.

Running Things could have been called "The Entrepreneur's Guidebook" because it deals with what CEOs have to do. PCA was a happy company; the people were proud to work there; it was profitable; the customers liked it because it was so professional. All of these results occurred because of actions I had taken or programs I had installed on purpose. These actions were not obvious, and hardly anyone noticed that there was a pattern or intent.

But every person who visited the company remarked within the first half hour that this place was different. Everyone was friendly: to each other, to the suppliers, to the clients. They knew their jobs; they helped each other. The executives and managers who were our students did not recognize at first why PCA was different. They thought it was because the people of central Florida were just naturally soft-spoken and polite. After a day or so, however, they began to see that it was a matter of selection and action. We were able to show them how to arrange their organization to be the same way if they wanted to put forth the effort. This need for change came up often in the coffee-room discussions with executives attending the college. They realized quickly that making similar changes would require them to pay attention to the people and their environment. Usually, doing so did not fit their agenda.

Learning: *corporate attitudes are created either deliberately or by accident; either way everyone in the organization will develop the same ones.*

I realized that the company was going to change after I left and also that I was getting ready to be gone. I was trying to delegate to others even more than I had in the past. I imposed only one rule. "Don't eliminate anything unless you know why it is there; each brick in the wall has a purpose. If you remove it, something must fill its place or the wall will be weakened." This rule had little effect on anyone; it is hard to learn from someone whom you know.

My way of working has always been to create something, develop it, show others how to do it, and then move on. Up to this point that strategy had always worked rather well. All the individual functions of PCA ran without problems. Purchasing was dealing with cooperative suppliers, and we ran seminars for them in order to build up relationships. Each year when it was time to do the supplier workshops, I would wait to see whether anyone began to arrange them. Each year no one would until I suggested it. Then all the arrangements would be made in a professional and effective manner. It was apparent to me that I was becoming part of a problem myself; probably they were waiting for my suggestions. I began to cut myself out of more and more things in order to give the next generation of management a chance to grow and take charge.

I can't stand conflicts where people are unkind to each other or yell and argue. Movies are tough for me; it is hard to sit and watch someone be picked on or beat up or ignored. The ones where dozens of actors are killed or the cattlemen fight the sheepherders don't bother me a bit, but if someone rejects an individual I get upset. I am ready to talk about any subject as long as anyone wants to discuss it, and dealing with problems, no matter how complex or personal, poses no difficulty for me. But I can't stand conflict. For that reason I went out of my way to make certain that the environment of the company was peaceful and purposeful. Supervisors or managers who chewed their people out got a personal lecture from me. Anyone who could not manage like a lady or gentlemen was removed from that post and usually let go. I fired at least three for abusing their responsibility. I can think back over my whole career and identify fifty managers who should never have been put in charge of people.

Keeping quality installed in a company is a full-time job for the senior executive. My daily routine, if I was not traveling, was aimed at ensuring that the proper work environment existed. I wanted to make certain that everyone was proud and productive. Each day I began by processing my mail, which I always stood up to handle, not from respect but because I had learned that it went faster that way. This took at most a half hour. Then I went over to the college and wandered around seeing what was happening. I greeted each individual with a handshake or a hug. Lots of people get little hugging, so it becomes a sort of public service. However, it is necessary to learn to wait for them to come to you, not to go to them. This way if that is not their idea of communication, you do not embarrass them or yourself. While I was touring the college, I never gave anyone directions about their work. I did express a lot of appreciation for obviously good work. Often the visit to the college was planned to coincide with breaks in the classes, when the photograph would be taken; then I could schmooze with the students for a bit. The executive students in particular gave me a chance to learn a lot about what was happening in the real world. Each of them was very up to date on the problems and opportunities in their area of business. We also traveled to the same places and often knew the same people.

Learning: *roles change regularly as a company grows.*

We had, as students, a lot of people entering the quality field who were trying to set up a program for their company. I liked discussing their planned strategy, and they liked the way our philosophy could be taught to all levels of their company. I had to be careful not to keep them chatting past the time class was supposed to begin; if that was a danger, the instructor would come over and give me a not-so-gentle hint.

Then I would visit the administrative areas until each associate had at least been waved to. All of them felt they had a personal relationship with me, and they did; but no one felt that we were buddies. It is dangerous for an executive to get so close to individual employees that there is a perception of special treatment. We have to keep what the psychologists call a "social distance" by being approachable and friendly but never leaving the throne. My opinion is that one is either designed to be able to work this way or not; it is hard to learn. For me it was natural; my life is full of friendly relationships but few friends.

Client companies wanted to know about our experiences in other companies, and just telling them about it didn't seem to satisfy their needs. Actually, people rarely do much differently after being exposed to a case history; they immediately say that it does not apply to their specific situation. However, in order to satisfy this need and also make our clients proud, we began to film activities in their plants and offices. We called the series "Quality in the Twenty-First Century." Each film is about twenty-five minutes long and consists of interviews with people at various levels in that company. Phylis was the master of ceremonies, and I made a few comments at the end. We did Bama Pie, Winter Park Hospital, Green Bay Packaging, General Motors, People's Bank, ICI, and a dozen others.

Learning: *people watch a film of others in the same business talking about their quality-improvement experience and then say, "Well, their business is not exactly like ours"; cases are a waste of time.*

Our Quality Awareness Experience (QAE) film was not going over well in Europe. The middle-class U.S. family we had portrayed appeared to be wealthy there. So we went back to our BBC friends and had the material rewritten with British situations and language. We used the European video format and, while we were at it, added upgraded examples. We did the same thing with QES, dubbing all those films into the various languages involved. I had thought that because the Continent was full of U.S. films, which were shown in theaters all over and didn't seem to bother anyone, why should training films have to be European-compatible? Their purpose was to provide ideas and instruction, not a mood or a good cry. However, the professional audience, the training and quality-control people, wanted to be difficult. So we gave them what they wanted. The QAE film turned out to be much better than the original. We shot my part in the Park Sheraton right down the street from Harrods in London. The clients liked the result, and the QAE program became popular all over Europe. Peggy fell in love with Harrods.

The material was almost exactly the same as in the original, but those ordering it could now say that it was conceived and produced in Europe. Being human, they were not necessarily interested in improving the company; they were more concerned with how their own efforts would be viewed. The result was a much better product, and I had learned once again not to be so certain that I am right about things.

Many PCA associates had children in college, all of whom were looking for summer jobs. It seemed to me that hiring some of them would be good for relationships and would provide us with useful labor over the vacation months. Most PCA people received three weeks of vacation after two years, and we insisted that they take the full time. This policy created a need for folks to fill in while they were gone. In 1986 we had a dozen summer interns. The rules were that they had to have real jobs in the company with real responsibilities and that they would be properly oriented. Over the years we never had problems with any of these kids, and many of them came to work with us after leaving school. One year the human-resources director said that he had budget to cover only nine interns but had eleven applications. I suggested that he decide which two of his fellow associates he was going to disappoint and then go tell them. He found some more budget. The intern program was an example of building goodwill with the employees at a low cost and helping the company at the same time.

When each new associate was being oriented (and we included clients who came for extended instruction also), they had lunch with me for what we called the ADEPT presentation. I gave each of them a little block of walnut wood with a ballpoint pen sticking in a hole. On the top of the block the ADEPT code was engraved. I gave them each the box containing the block and the pen and then took them through what the acronym meant:

A is for accurate. We do what we said we were going to do, and when we give information, we know it is right.

D is for discreet. We do not gossip, and we treat everyone like ladies and gentlemen.

E is for enthusiastic. We try to hire enthusiastic people and then not turn them off.

P is for productive. The more of us there are the less there is to share.

T is for thrifty. We do everything first class, but there is no virtue in throwing money away.

All through the world of PCA, people had these blocks on their desks. They remembered that lunch, and they had a photo of themselves with me too. This is the kind of activity that I had a hard time convincing most of our client executives to undertake. One of the quality-improvement teams turned ADEPT into a recognition system. Each two months the employees voted on who was the most accurate or whichever category was emphasized at that time, and the winner received a little plaque at family council. This reminder and the ceremonies cost virtually nothing but generated large rewards. This sort of activity CEOs should support; they are in charge of all the people things.

While serving on the board of Winter Park Hospital, I had become interested in the concept of wellness, which, of course, is based on prevention. The hospital CEO was interested in beginning a wellness center where people could go to learn how to stay alive and in good shape. Peggy and I donated stock to help the hospital build such a center, and they named it after us. It has been a great source of satisfaction; people keep telling us how much they have improved their joy in life through its services. Every time I go by the cancer center, where there is a great deal of sadness and pain, I am glad we picked wellness. It would be difficult to have people come up to me every day and talk about the loss of a loved one.

My primary effort was making speeches that let me market the company and spread my philosophy. For the most part we charged between $10,000 and $15,000 for these sessions. However, presentations to selected clients or at true public-service events were free. I usually did about seventy-five speeches a year, plus a couple a week at the quality college. This schedule more than paid my salary and expenses, which made me feel that I was earning my money. I have a problem with executives who make a lot of money and don't do any real work.

Each speech was unique, and I prepared it in advance. Usually I worked the Absolutes of Quality Management in, using personal experiences to show their application. I explained that I had realized that the word *quality* had no agreed meaning while I was at Crosley; realized that a commitment to AQLs meant a commitment to doing things wrong while I was at Bendix; realized that I could set a new management standard with zero defects while I was at Martin; and realized, at ITT, that money had to be used to measure quality if executives were ever going to pay any attention to it.

The message was prevention, but it had to be shaped so the audience received it well. People asked me how I could stand to do all these talks on essentially the same subject, and I noted that the audience was different each time. Every actor and speaker figures this out.

Learning: *the responsibility for successful speechmaking lies only partially with the speaker; arrangements play a big part: the comfort of the audience, the comfort of the speaker, their mutual understanding of what the session is all about.*

My experience has been that left to themselves the arranging committee will put the speaker behind a lectern, hemmed in by others sitting on the podium. They will shine a light directly in the speaker's eyes and turn the illumination down on the audience so that the speaker does not see those in front or his or her notes. I need room to roam and despise using a lectern. It is OK for laying some notes on to wander back and review. But the separation from the audience can kill a speech.

Visual aids are also not friendly to the speaker. No matter how well thought out or attractive the view graphs are they detract from the speaker's message. It takes a lot of work to gain the audience's attention and confidence; when those are tossed away, much of the speech goes with them. Let those who deal in numbers rather than ideas use such things. Also, the projection machines often malfunction. I much prefer to deal with the audience by myself. When doing a seminar, it is a good idea to give each student a notebook with the necessary information in it. Then the speaker can refer to a certain page if there is something to share or evaluate. Sending people off in groups to do a workshop is not a useful way for them to acquire knowledge. However, it does use up time and lets people get some exercise while the speaker takes a rest.

All the travel necessary for my work would not have been possible without PCA's Lear 55 airplane. I was able to get around the country rapidly to speak at meetings and to visit clients, and Peggy was able to go along. She shopped and visited often while I was working, but she attended the talks most of the time. I always think no one is going to come to a speech, and during it I feel that I am losing the audience. But a glance at Peggy lets me know what is going on, and she is an excellent critic. When one is the chairman, founder, and chief guru of a company, it is not easy to acquire constructive criticism. Even if you do get a useful suggestion, it may not relate to the thoughts that are going through your mind at that time.

Learning: *we have to do what it is necessary to do, not just what we like to do.*

These thoughts sometimes expand greatly. In *Quality Is Free,* for instance, I talked about "integrity systems," all the functions that produce quality. Nine years later this two-sentence thought became a whole book, *The Eternally Successful Organization,* which was published by McGraw-Hill in 1988, about eighteen months after the original idea occurred to me. This time frame is about par for the book business. It takes most of a year to produce a book after the author submits a manuscript.

The idea for *The Eternally Successful Organization* came on a visit to Bethany College in West Virginia. I was speaking to an industrial-development council and as part of that trip attended a luncheon with some officers of the college. They were talking about how poorly academia was managed, and we were all agreeing. However, it soon emerged that Bethany had existed for almost 150 years, had no debt, and possessed a healthy endowment. It began to occur to me that there had to be a reason for that success. I asked the attendees to identify some corporations that were still around and prospering after 150 years or 100 years or even 50.

When I returned home and went to the wellness center for a workout, two thoughts, of corporate and personal wellness, suddenly merged. People have to die one day, but if they take care of themselves, they can keep from rushing into it. Corporations do not have to die, but they do; in most cases, as a matter of fact, they commit suicide.

I often am criticized by reviewers—and those who write about quality in particular—because they think my ideas and processes are too simple, that nothing works out the way I say it will. Such criticism always amazes me because I write only about what I have actually done. And it always turns out that people who criticize my ideas have not actually done what I have written about. Also they usually have no management experience beyond the department level. They are not looking for a philosophy based on ideas; they are looking for a regime based on techniques and procedures. The ones who relate to me are executives who have had the experience of trying to lead where there were no paths.

To reach both groups I wanted to write about wellness in a way that could not be misunderstood. Personal wellness centers conduct a profile examination of each client. They determine physical status, blood chemistry, food intake, and some details of lifestyle. This examination takes a couple of weeks; afterward, an analyst sits down with the client and explains the status of his or her health. "You have high blood pressure, you are overweight, 60 percent of your diet is fat, you smoke, you have high cholesterol, and you get virtually no exercise. The probability is that you will not live to be sixty years old."

Then they point out that a change in lifestyle could add, for example, twenty or more years to that estimate in addition to greatly improving the client's enjoyment of life. This change involves learning how to be well and taking some actions to stay that way. Most of these are sensible suggestions, and none of them are abhorrent. But it is up to the clients to determine how healthy they are going to be. Corporations have this same problem. They get fat and lazy. Their communication networks become clogged just like human arteries.

In order to make this analogy clear, I built the book around a grid for determining how healthy a corporation is in regard to quality, change, growth, customers, and employees. To show the current status I used terms that are familiar in medicine: comatose, in intensive care, progressing, healing, and well. I explained each status in detail and added stories of people in business who were trying to make their companies eternally successful. I didn't write much about quality management except to show that it was an integral part of general management in every area. The cover of the book said that it contained a "new business philosophy," and that is what I was trying to put forth.

The book did well in both hardcover and softcover, but it took a few years for the idea of wellness to take hold. Even today most people are not comfortable with the concept. It is too connected to prevention and with the idea that current events affect events several years from now. I detect unease with the concept from what people say to me face to face. The good-news part of being an author is that people seek you out to share their feelings about your books. Without exception those who come up to me are courteous and respectful. I don't care if they agree or not as long as my work stimulated them to think about the way they are working.

Learning: *writing books is not for those who need a lot of appreciative feedback.*

About this time we received an invitation from Satcchi and Satcchi to merge with them. They were trying to build the largest advertising firm in the world. They had already picked up a couple of firms and wanted to add PCA, as a consulting group, to their string. They promised that we would be given a free hand as long as we met the agreed performance goals and that we would be bought out in cash. They were offering about $13 for our stock, which was selling at about $6. We agreed to talk with them and discussions were moving along well until the British elections, with which they were deeply involved. This development stalled discussions for six weeks or so, and then they petered out. I think they were beginning to realize that they had a great deal on their plate already. They paid all our expenses, and we parted friends.

After that another advertising agency asked us to consider a merger. It had figured out that PCA was a product-line company rather than a consulting firm. Our courses were taught by people we had taught to teach them, not by those who were themselves experts. We could teach any qualified person to do that. With PCA the product was there all the time. I thought it was astute of the agency to realize our true nature. We were never able to explain it to the financial community.

The deal didn't get anywhere because the offer was not high enough. However, as it turned out we would have done well if we had accepted their stock in exchange. It has increased dramatically over the years.

For PCA to grow worldwide we were going to need a partner. Setting up in a new city—like Sydney, Australia, for instance—required a big investment and a lot of time for us to become known. At this time we had offices in Paris, London, Munich, San Jose, Chicago, and Winter Park. Many clients with worldwide operations wanted us to be near them. We daydreamed about finding a partner who was already in places we were not. They could introduce us around and let us use their phones. We decided to just keep plowing ahead; the company was doing well, although the stock price kept dropping. The financial analysts just couldn't figure us out. Their big problem seemed to be an inability to understand our marketing plan. We had no salespeople and relied on word of mouth; they had difficulty accepting that that strategy worked, even though it obviously did. My speeches and articles brought people in, but most of the inquiries came from suppliers and friends of our clients. What we did for companies worked; it produced results.

Learning: *expect initial public offerings to drop in value in the first few years because of profit taking.*

I was becoming more interested in writing and speaking than in running the company. Larry McFadin, whom the board had elected CEO at my suggestion, and the other executives did a good job of handling operations. They were millions of dollars a year ahead of the competition, which was beginning to emerge. The company was safe, but it looked as though the stock was never going to go up in value again. We discussed buying it all back and even had an informal agreement with a bank to help make it happen. It didn't seem to me that the others had the fire in the belly necessary to make such a buy-out happen. Most of them were comfortable from the sale of stock they already owned. As I noted, we had created a bunch of millionaires.

After my regular prostate checkup I received the news that I was going to need a "Roto-Rooter" job. There were stones in my prostate, and without intervention the next step would be cancer. So I went into the hospital and had the surgery, which is not a big deal except that they give a spinal anesthetic. Recovering becomes depressing when you realize that the big senseless lump you are feeling with your hands is your rear end and hips. However it all passes.

The doctor wanted me to stay settled for six weeks, which meant not traveling; I didn't have any problem about not going to work. This order offered me a great opportunity; I would be forced to spend that time in my library. I could do some radio interviews by telephone, but my main activities would be reading and thinking. Then I received some audiotapes of the open discussions I held each week with the students. These free-for-all question-and-answer sessions had been going on for several years. They seemed to provide the material for a "slam-dunk" book.

I obtained a list of all the questions and picked the ninety-six I considered the most interesting. Then I wrote answers to them without paying much attention to the answers I had given before. Many of the replies were somewhat similar, although I had more information than I had had before. In no case did the philosophy change, but I was often able to offer more practical advice. I didn't tell anyone what I was doing and worked happily along for the assigned time. At the end of four weeks I had the manuscript completed on a computer disk. Debbie Eifert, my assistant, ran through the material and checked my spelling and grammar. This was the first time I had written a book without any hard copy at all. We then transmitted the disks to McGraw-Hill, where my editor, Jim Bessent, rearranged the questions so that they bore some relationship to each other. He made these changes with my agreement, of course. It was a good idea. Because the manuscript was clean, *Let's Talk Quality* appeared on the bookshelves in record time. It was subtitled *96 Questions You Always Wanted to Ask Phil Crosby,* and Lee Iacocca was gracious enough to permit us to use a quote from his book on the cover. The book took right off and had good sales. Readers could turn right to the areas they were interested in. The softcover is now selling in a dozen languages.

Learning: *it is an ill wind that blows no good.*

I had always wanted a house on a Winter Park lake. One day we were offered just the right lot in just the right place, a ten-minute walk from downtown Winter Park. Peggy oversaw the building of our home, which included the library I had always wanted. It had hundreds of books in it and was a comfortable place for me to think and work in. I looked forward to the day when I could have a satellite broadcasting booth nearby and I wouldn't have to travel quite so much.

In 1989 we were approached by the Alexander Proudfoot company, which had just gone from being a partnership to being listed on the

London exchange. The company's roots were American, and it had offices all over the world, including Sydney. Proudfoot offered us twice what our stock was selling for and swore that PCA would remain independent of corporate authority. They agreed to honor all our contracts and were particularly insistent that I remain as creative director and chairman for as long as I wished. I let Larry and our counsel conduct the negotiations except for saying that I thought $60 million was a proper price for the company. I still owned a little less than 10 percent.

Learning: *no one knows how to merge companies successfully because much remains hidden.*

At this time I was writing *Leading: The Art of Becoming an Executive.* Still trying to reach the unreachable, I put it in the form of a novel with a leading character and a recognizable story. I was trying to show what goes on inside the head of a successful executive. I felt that information would be helpful to those who were trying to change a company from within. The book also had a new and practical philosophy about the focus of a leader: finance, quality, and relationships. Quality is the structure, the body of the organization; finance is the nourishment; and relationships are the soul.

Those who read it thought it was solid. However, it had such a poor reception that it didn't make it into paperback, the only one of my books to suffer that fate. It did make money for the publisher however. Later I took the same character and made him the center of a mystery novel. It was rejected. The publisher said, "We like your business philosophy books because they are clear, concise, and logical. Those are the reasons we don't like the mystery. Stick to business." I keep writing the other stuff anyway.

I began working with an agent for the first time, Al Lowman of Authors and Artists in New York. Like all writers I felt that my publisher didn't appreciate me, and like all writers I wanted a larger advance to ensure that the publisher would promote the book enthusiastically. I had been working on the concept that quality management was going to be the most important part of management in the twenty-first century. The book that resulted was *Completeness: Quality for the Twenty-First Century.* It was a little outlandish in some areas, dealing with virtual reality, for instance. It also projected the fall of the U.S.S.R. However, it has done well, and all the things I prophesied are coming true.

With my friend and colleague Bob Vincent (right)
at my PCA retirement dinner, 1991.

The idea of *Completeness* was to encourage management to make employees, suppliers, and customers successful. This task would let them forget all about the Total Quality Management stuff, which was mainly motivation, activities, and manipulation, and also about counterproductive activities like the Baldridge award. With the best of intentions the U.S. government had created an award to be presented to companies that had done well with quality. That in itself was a good idea, but then the creators of the award incorporated some requirements that ruined it. First, they made the process self-nominating. Unlike the Noble or the Pulitzer, for which peers do the nominating, this award required that one put oneself up for honors. Second, they created a forty-four-page list of actions a company should take in order to have "good quality." This requirement was arrogant and misinformed. No one would think of creating such a list for good financial management. Third, the award became a gold mine for consultants who set a company up to meet the criteria and then arranged for it to be audited by examiners. The result of the Baldridge award was to concentrate attention on a lot of quality-assurance procedures that have little to do with helping a company manage quality.

After the merger was complete, we kept working as before. I had felt that PCA needed a package for small businesses and began creating it. However, it was becoming apparent that the Proudfoot executives had a different idea than I did of what consulting and education were about. Because it was their company now, I suggested that we arrange for me to retire early. That way all of us could do what we wanted. I would still be available for counseling, speeches, and such. They graciously permitted me to retire and gave me a nice party. I knew how Harold Geneen felt when his ship was shot out from under him; however, we both sailed away first class. When I left ITT in 1979, I missed the golf course at Bolton; with PCA I missed the people and the airplane. In my last year with PCA, 1990, the revenue was $100 million and the pretax profit was $32 million.

PART FOUR

Careers IV and Five

CHAPTER THIRTEEN

Speaking Out
on Leadership

M y daughter, Phylis, was working for Proudfoot as
a corporate vice president, but she was interested in helping me in a
new venture. We set up a little company called Career IV, Inc., a Subchapter S incorporation. Peggy, Phylis, Philip Jr., and I became the co-
owners. Debbie came to join us from PCA, where people were being
laid off. Each of us made an investment to start the company. Phylis
was CEO, and I vowed never to do another thing from an administrative standpoint. We were not permitted to teach quality management
according to the terms of my noncompete contract, but I had no interest in doing so. My attention was on the subject of leadership. I felt that
the nation was in desperate straits and wanted to change that.

I received many speaking invitations, and although those who
invited me were interested in quality, they seemed more interested in
knowing what I was thinking about. That was an interesting change
from the past; people were becoming interested in me personally not
just in the nuts and bolts of quality. Phylis put this change in perspective, puncturing my balloon in the process, by informing me that
I had become an icon. From iconoclast to icon in a few decades. However, taking her perspective allowed me to become more comfortable

about my new venture; I could talk about anything I wanted to, and it was agreeable to the audience.

Speakers' bureaus provided some of the venues for my speeches, but most invitations came from the organizations themselves. I charged $15,000 and expenses, which seemed to be within everyone's budget. I also did some free speeches for groups that were interesting or that were nonprofits. I started each of these speeches by saying, "Sam [or whoever booked me] said he heard that I was a student of history. What part of the Bill of Rights did I think was the most important? he asked me. 'Free speech,' I replied. 'That's what I want to talk to you about,' he said." This introduction always got a laugh and also let the audience know that I made speeches for a living and that this was a special occasion.

I found that many senior-management teams were concerned that they were not getting anywhere with their self-made quality programs. They would ask me to spend a day with them to see whether I could figure out what their problem was. I had to be careful. Proudfoot kept a close eye on me to make certain I was not competing. The contract specifically called for penalties if I were to do so. Proudfoot seemed paranoid about me. Phylis sent in monthly activity reports for a while; then I just decided to skip them.

Learning: *you never know what is in people's minds; they do what they know is illogical and harmful for their own reasons.*

When I did speak to organizations about leadership, I arranged to spend a day inside their operations so that we could have a good "greenfield" session. In these sessions we looked at an organization as though it had no buildings or other facilities and was without people. Then management could examine the business's requirements and see what was necessary to meet them. Many businesses add resources without giving much thought to what they are doing. It is like packing for a trip and returning home to find that half the clothes have not been worn. People and companies get fat by just increasing their intake a little each day. Doing a "greenfield" lets them keep growth in perspective. I put some examples from these sessions into the text of *Completeness*. Actually the problem always has the same source: managers are trying to delegate something only they can accomplish.

Learning: *the intelligence of the audience changes; they get smarter while you are getting smarter.*

Many groups asked me to describe the differences between Dr. W. Edwards Deming, Dr. Joseph Juran, and myself. I always said that I respected the work of these two men but that we were in different businesses. Deming, whom I had never met, was a statistician and was at the top of his field; Juran, whom I had met years ago, was the leading expert on quality control and quality engineering. Both were worth listening to even if they apparently made unflattering comments about me personally and my work professionally. They would say that I wanted to motivate and "exhort" the workers. Because I had never proposed anything like that in any of my writings or speeches, I wasn't bothered by their misinterpretation. The difference between us was that I was dealing with quality management, which is not quality control or statistics. Also I had learned my trade by fighting my way up through the ranks and by implementing my concepts in many businesses and cultures. I considered their ideas irrelevant to my work. I think they returned the thought. We were not important to each other.

Learning: *arguing with professionals who disagree with you is not a good use of time; your work should speak for itself, and that which deserves to live will live.*

CHAPTER FOURTEEN

PCA Redux

As I thought about Career IV a few things became apparent. I wanted it as a convenient vehicle for managing my professional life, and I would again be the sole source of revenue; my speeches and an occasional seminar would be all we had. This arrangement would work for a few years provided invitations kept coming in. My noncompete contract with Proudfoot and my investments with Sun Bank would ensure that we lived well. Money was not the problem, but I wanted Career IV to pay for itself. The subchapter arrangement would permit transferring a good deal of the revenue to the family.

The speech requests were numerous enough, although the Proudfoot limitations kept me from taking advantage of a lot of opportunities in the quality area. My philosophy was being ignored in many areas because it did not emphasize teams and such. However, basics are basics; I knew that techniques always turn sour after a while, and management goes back to culture. At that time, they were happy to delegate quality to those eager souls who were busily organizing all the lower-level people to make products better.

I was not eager to travel as much and certainly would lose even more interest in the future. We decided to limit my activities to a couple of "gigs" a month. Peggy became testy when I was signed up for what she considered to be too much; so we tried to be selective, although it is difficult for me to pass up an interesting audience. I was in good health and was not concerned about becoming ill; rather we just wanted to enjoy life.

But the activity of a professional speaker varies with the economy. One sure way companies and associations can reduce their budgets is not to have speakers at meetings. Show-business people have understood the relationship between the economy and the size of audiences for years; they schedule themselves for months ahead, and they never know whether the theater will be sold out or empty. Bob Hope, who had more money than anyone, worked somewhere almost every evening. Entertainers seem to have to work every day, or they feel unsuccessful. I just like to get out and see what is happening.

I wanted to make Career IV a revenue-producing organization that took advantage of my work and name but did not require that I keep on the trail forever. We wanted to spend the summer months in our house in Highlands, North Carolina. It seemed that with satellite and other advanced communication systems I should be able to talk from there as well as anywhere. Now that I was not involved with administration, I could follow my thoughts through to their conclusion. It was wonderful to be able to stroll back to my machine after breakfast and write for a few hours. Secretly I felt guilty about feeling good about this arrangement, but the guilt wore off.

The problem with TQM and the conventional quality management process that has evolved over the past few years is that expectations are not high enough. When I talk to people who run programs for organizations, it quickly becomes apparent that they are after an improvement of about 20 percent.

Learning: *you can improve almost anything by 20 percent simply by becoming concerned about it.*

A stern lecture on the need for doing homework promptly and correctly usually raises the grade level one notch. After a while, when the pressure is off, the culprit returns to a normal level. Only a true change of culture will allow people, or companies, to rise to their potential.

U.S. companies should be taking over the world in business; they have a solid economy behind them, the most productive workforce, an unparalleled infrastructure, and freedom of choice. Unfortunately, they are also badly informed about quality from those whom they regard as experts. These folks live in an invisible box that restricts their ability to take proper actions. This box has a lid that says "quality is goodness"; it has one side that says "you can't get things done right all the time"; another side is labeled "people don't really want to work properly"; the third side says "variations are a fact of life, and you can't avoid them"; and the fourth side says "just get better a little at a time."

The bottom of the box is littered with books on the subject written by people who never had to make quality happen for a living. People who have never managed spout management proverbs. Such quality management is a dreadful waste of time. Getting the right things done right the first time is not that difficult. However, I decided that I was not going to let these differences bug me; I would put them all behind and concentrate on trying to help the younger people manage properly. That would be Career IV's mission.

The strategy for accomplishing this mission could not simply be writing books and articles. We needed something more, and I realized that videotapes and audiotapes were the answer. Companies did not want to send their people all over just to learn, and individuals could not afford it. Companies had never attached that much importance to continual education and training anyway. That is one point I emphasized in *Completeness*.

Learning: *the emphasis on education for the twenty-first century has to be relentless.*

If I were starting PCA today, I thought, I would make the quality college a moveable feast. Well-accepted tapes could be advertised and sold by just a few people. After all, QES had provided most of the revenue and income for the company. This idea fit in with my thoughts on teaching the concepts of leadership. I worried about the young people, particularly, who had to fight their way up in organizations and were trying to learn the hard way. There were few good leaders and few people interested in helping them develop. I felt that all workers should be able to do whatever they were able to handle, that they should be able to move up, over, or any other way in their jobs. Establishing a career should not have to mean working one's way through the boxes on an organization chart. Most folks have job skills that offer them the opportunity to be useful. However, they have little insight into what it takes to be an executive. That position is built on relationships with others and a broad knowledge of what makes the world run. This understanding fit with my previous idea that finance, quality, and relationships are the basic topics demanding an executive's attention. Most managers and executives are so narrowly focused that they miss the opportunity to grow programs and organizations. Young Tom Edisons, Henry Fords, Dwight Eisenhowers, or Bill Gateses are usually not noticed by managers, who tend to pick those who are more conventional.

Learning: *the future looks a lot clearer after one leaves the firing line.*

I have always figured that it takes about five years for a real cultural or systemic change to become permanent. When few managerial tenures last even four years, it is easy to see why so little wonderful change happens. That is the main reason why companies have to go through revolutions when they receive a wake-up call from their customers. Ask the veterans of IBM, Sears, Xerox, General Motors, and other companies why their products and management systems had ceased being useful seemingly overnight. For years they had only polished, not really changed. Anyone trying to deal with a company that size is talking with different people continually. While the company is moving people around inside, they forget that the customer would like a little stability. Watch what happens with the enormous conglomerates that contain a television production company, a movie studio, a telephone company, and a cable operation. Who is going to manage those interfaces? Will they let young people with no track records but lots of energy and smarts emerge? Who can have much of a track record today when everything changes dramatically each year?

I was required to work my way up the ladder inch by inch, never being permitted to miss a step unless I changed companies. There was no real reason why I could not have jumped several steps at a time except that I just didn't have the right information. It seemed to me that individuals would like to know how to carve a career for themselves and that I would be able to smooth out a few bumps for them. If I could put together such information in a way that would be accepted, it could change a lot of lives for the better. It would also save many companies from the need to suffer pain in order to mature. In addition, a successful product would provide a financial base for Career IV, which could then develop a whole catalogue of material.

For all these reasons I wrote a series of twelve scripts entitled *To Be an Executive, by Choice.* They laid out what the aspiring executive needed to know in order to make it. I assumed intelligence and ambition; otherwise they would not be interested in the subject. We filmed these at a TV channel after building a library set on one of their stages. I worked with one of the news anchors in order to make certain I was going to present myself properly. Video is hard work, even when you are playing yourself.

We produced the tapes carefully, got professional assistance in advertising, and found that the market was not ready. As I visited MBA schools, I realized that these tapes were exactly what they needed, but since there was nothing like them, they didn't know how to use them. Shades of ZD days. So we changed the marketing strategy, became more patient, and the product is moving now.

Learning: *the bad news about being creative is that sometimes one creates a product no one wants just then.*

I was enjoying life. The pressure of running an organization was gone; the speeches and seminars let me keep up to date and meet new people. There was enough money, and we were healthy. A lot of people still did not agree with my philosophy, but a lot more did. At any rate no one disliked me enough to do anything about it.

I am often asked how it is possible to be a practicing Christian and still be successful in business. I am always surprised at the assumption that the two are incompatible. Most of the people I knew in the business world had integrity; the others were so rare that they stood out and could be avoided. I wrote a reflection on my principles of personal life and used that as the basis for my speeches and for a couple of commencement addresses. These principles are clear, and, best of all for the student, they are brief. I included them in *Completeness* over the objections of the publisher. I receive the most comments, all positive, on that part of the book. These are the principles: love God; love your fellow creatures; keep learning; set goals with numbers in them; and be happy. I put the story of their creation in *Completeness.* All are choices that we can make as individuals. What I have learned over the years is what everyone knows anyway: life is what we make it.

Learning: *starting anew is difficult.*

McGraw-Hill had ideas for a couple of books. One was to take selections from the "Guidelines for Browsers" part of my books and make them into a small book entitled *Reflections on Quality.* This kind of book fits beside a cash register and is purchased on impulse. It also makes a useful gift. McGraw-Hill made selections and sent them to me for review. We worked together on it and settled on 295 different sayings. The book was laid out in an interesting manner and went on sale before the Christmas season in 1996. It was well received, even though McGraw-Hill did almost no marketing of it. People tell me they keep it on their desk or nightstand and open it regularly to read a few items. It is uplifting and contains not a bit of angst.

The other idea was to revisit *Quality Is Free* because it was getting to be twenty years old and was still selling thousands of copies a month in twenty languages, mostly in paperback. I had been thinking about revising it while working on this autobiography, and my brother, David, had offered a title: *Quality Is Still Free.*

I went to work by rereading *Quality Is Free* and observed in the process that it was an interesting book. I had forgotten many of the stories and comments in it. It is fun to look at something one has written as though for the first time. I find I learn from myself this way. During the years I have written so much that once in a while I find a repeat.

Anyway, I went to work on *Quality Is Still Free* in our Highlands home during the summer. The Cullasaja Club development, where we live, is nice and cool at that time of the year, peaceful and quiet. I played golf several times a week, but when you have your own cart and live on the eleventh hole, it doesn't take long. In mid-summer, when the manuscript was complete, I sent it on to New York via e-mail and mailed a disk. This is an interesting way of working. I used to drag three-ring notebooks up to New York; now I just push a few buttons. The book came out late in 1996. It did modestly well and is gaining sales as time goes on. However, it was not received well by the quality reviewers. They seem to think I am a "motivator" because that is what some who didn't know called me years ago. Yet here is a book absolutely not about motivation that would be a big help to their readers. However, management magazines like it.

Learning: *it is hard to teach or reach anyone over thirty.*

During a visit to India in late 1995 I had agreed to work on a CD-ROM that would be designed for the individual who wanted to become successful in his or her professional and personal life. NIIT was putting it together in New Delhi. That summer two people came to Highlands from India and spent a week getting me organized. Nilu Vir had never been to the United States before; her colleague, ("K.K."), was more experienced but had never been in the mountains. We had a good visit and got a lot of work done. They laid out a format for the material I was to create, and that is what I did for the rest of the summer. Each morning I received e-mail from Nilu noting what I had done and what remained to be accomplished. This was not my usual way of writing, but under the whip I produced the work. When Peggy and I returned to India in November, we were greeted with the framework of the CD.

The NIIT team had chosen a mountain-climbing analogy to show the interaction necessary for success. The Absolutes from my leadership book formed the base camps from which the peak was attacked. Determining an agenda, having a personal philosophy, building enduring relationships, and being worldly were the levels of accumulated effort necessary. They also created games and tests that made the student think. It was a good job.

During this visit I saw the effect of the work we had been doing with schoolchildren. Seventy-seven schools were involved. I had written a piece about the "eighth grade and quality management," which was the basis for this work. The students' names had been translated into Hindi from English, but otherwise the words were the same. We went to the Institute of Technology in New Delhi, where I saw a tree I had planted in 1994 that was now nine feet tall. The students demonstrated their work in debates, speeches, plays, dances, and posters. It was charming. I gave my annual lecture, and they asked me questions for an hour. These children are much smarter than the people who are running the nation.

After retiring from PCA, I had the opportunity to be exposed to many different situations, some of which were new to me. I made speeches in Jamaica, Mexico, Brazil, Chile, Argentina, Uruguay, Paraguay, Greece, Saudi Arabia, the United Arab Emirates, Malaysia, Singapore, China, Germany, and all around North America. I had the opportunity to go to several MBA schools and help write a textbook on quality and competitiveness. My part was twenty-two-page "Reflections," each consisting of an anecdote or observation. Often the "Reflections" did not agree with the chapter they graced, but no one seemed to mind.

Phylis and her husband, Nick Wright, decided they wanted to change their lifestyle. They selected a remote location in Tennessee and went to work creating their own home, "Green Acres." At the same time the bank where we had our offices wanted to expand. These developments gave me the opportunity to change the way Career IV worked. We gave up the offices, sold the furniture, and both Debbie and I began working out of our homes. She set up a nice office for herself, and as her youngest child was only six, this arrangement worked well for her. We learned to talk by phone and meet regularly to go over schedules and such. I played golf a couple of times a week at Isleworth, and life went on quite comfortably.

Because we were spending time in Highlands during the hot weather and Proudfoot looked rather shaky to me, I began to think about downsizing. We put the home on the lake in Florida on the market and looked for another Winter Park home. We made offers on two houses that had been on the market for a while only to find that each had been bought out from under us. Then we discovered a nice little home a block away from the lake house. We bought it and worked it over, finishing it just as the big house was sold. Because we did not have enough room in the new home for the contents of the old, I went to an estate-sale shop and asked whether they did estate sales for people who hadn't died yet. They did one for us. We are constantly going to someone's home and finding a familiar piece of furniture or art.

Downsizing included getting rid of debt and other binding obligations. I did not want to drop off the scope one day and leave Peggy to cope with a lot of difficulties. We wrote new wills and cleared up the trust language. I began to send regular distributions to the children so they wouldn't have to wait for us to pass on. With my writing, speaking, golfing, working out, and taking a couple of vacations a year I was enjoying life as 1996 closed out.

Learning: *each person has the responsibility of having an up-to-date will so that loved ones can avoid problems; many people are thoughtless in this regard.*

I had seen it coming for a while, but when Malcolm Hughes, the CEO of Proudfoot, came to Winter Park to see me at the end of 1996, I knew that changes were in store for me. PCA was dead and exhibited no signs of life. Revenue was zero, and all the people were gone. My time of living off a lifetime contract was coming to an end. They had killed PCA by cutting off the management-education part of the operation. The logic was that the books and tapes had a higher margin, but when the quality college died, everything withered. One might wonder why that result could not have been predicted by even a casual observer. I had detected the symptoms four years before. That is when Peggy and I downsized everything and got ready to live on a smaller cash flow. It seemed to me that Proudfoot had a death wish for the organizations it acquired. At least it treated them as though it did.

Malcolm was sincerely depressed by the outcome. I took him to Isleworth for lunch, where he was most impressed by the homes. Young professional athletes and older well-offs live there. I belong as a golf member and play with the "super senior group" a couple of times a week. These are all nice people who earned their own money and have gotten away from the business world. Isleworth is a land of homes ten thousand square feet and up. I think Malcolm expected to find me living in one of them.

We discussed the situation, and while he didn't actually say PCA was going belly up, he did make it clear that there was no future for it. Proudfoot felt that the market for quality management had dried up; I felt Proudfoot had walked away from it. He talked about the leases the company owed money on in Orlando and Chicago and the fact that there was no income. He had made a deal with Organizational Dynamics Inc. (ODI), a Boston consulting firm, giving them exclusive rights to the quality college material in North America. I knew some of the people from ODI; they were professional, but this was not their kind of business. At least PCA would get a royalty if ODI did something with the material.

A couple of weeks after Malcolm's visit I was thinking about the whole business. I was receiving no money from Proudfoot, and I would gain nothing by suing them. My contract was for life; if the insurance tables were right, that should be another eighteen years, or about $9 million. That is a lot of money to give up. Then I had a flash of insight. The Lord speaks to me quietly sometimes in this manner, and I rely on it. The thought was to take PCA back and turn it into what it could still be. I liked that concept and placed a call to Malcolm in London. He was delighted that I would want PCA back and designated Steve Hitchcock, who had originally worked with PCA, to be the go-between. Alex Dombrowski, the Proudfoot lawyer, would also take part in the negotiations. Both of these men proved helpful in making the deal work.

Learning: *stay light on your feet at all times; don't accumulate debt or commitments that you cannot handle.*

I called Bill Grimm, my once and future business lawyer, and told him what was going on. He issued a formal letter, as required by my contract, stating that I was taking my name back. Through experience we had learned not to rely too much on Proudfoot's doing what it said it would do. But working with Steve and Alex showed that spots could be changed. We arranged a meeting in Winter Park at the Interlachen Country Club with Bill, Peggy, and me representing our side. It soon became apparent that Proudfoot was eager to get rid of PCA so it could announce that fact when it talked with analysts in a few weeks. It was ready to just hand over what still existed and was open about it. Proudfoot stock was trading at around 5 percent of the value it had at the time it acquired PCA in 1989. The fall in stock price had been due to loss in the net worth in the company. Two other acquisitions had been self-made disasters.

After separate discussions with Kitty Wrenn, my tax accountant, and Bill, we decided to take back the assets of PCA and form a new company, which we would call Philip Crosby Associates II, Inc. The idea was to avoid being linked to PCA's debts, like the leases and some personnel wages. Also Bill was worried that the shell of PCA might be taken bankrupt one day in order to cancel out the leases. The assets we were taking over contained all the programs and copyrighted material of PCA plus my contract as well as the name-license agreement. They could be dragged back into the company by a bankruptcy judge and put up for sale if they were a gift. For this reason we agreed to pay Proudfoot a small percentage of revenues plus interest.

We established a Subchapter S company with the stock to be owned by the family. We would give employees stock equivalents, but I wanted to keep the stock where I could control it. I kept 51 percent personally and gave Peggy 9 percent, Phylis 10 percent, Philip Jr. 10 percent, our daughter Leyla 5 percent held in trust, and 5 percent in trust for each of the three grandchildren. Phylis agreed to be the trustee of those accounts. She could pay out for the benefit of these family members, but neither Leyla nor the grandchildren would have control until they were older. My idea was that the company would throw off cash over many years, which would let them all have an edge in life. The employees would receive distributions ("virtual shares," I called them) just like the shareholders except that they would have no ownership. Because we never plan to take the company public, getting money was better than holding stock. We would pay distributions as soon as we began to make money.

Learning: *take care of the employees first.*

While negotiations were going on, I kept thinking out and writing down different ways of dealing with the situation. There were a dozen or so licensees around the world. With the exception of ODI they were all people who had worked with the original PCA and were well qualified to deliver our material. However, it soon became obvious that they were not going to produce much revenue for a while. I invited the principals of ODI to meet with me, and they did so. But to them the PCA materials were just a source of revenue that could bolster the rest of their consulting business.

While Bill Grimm and I were faxing back and forth to Proudfoot to finalize the deal, I was realizing that reviving PCA would not be a case of opening envelopes each month and taking out checks. I was going to have to begin PCA all over again. To do that would require a couple of good people and some money. I arranged a $300,000 line of credit with Sun Trust, putting up some bonds as security. The two insurance policies that came with PCA would be worth $125,000 each in cash. I owned one of them and the company the other. There was a third one, for Shirley, and it would need to go on. I suggested that she cash it in since we were about the same age, and she would be able to use the money now. Her lawyer didn't think much of that suggestion, but he never thought much anyway.

Learning: *when something is being put back together, there is no learning curve because you know what to do; driving somewhere unknown is hard, but the return trip is easy.*

With funding available I called Wayne Kost and Sally Kauffman. Wayne was a good administrator, having been executive director of the ASQC at the time I was president, and he had been a PCA associate for ten years as an account executive and instructor. Sally had been with PCA and had worked her way up to QES instructor and then worked on systems integrity. She was having a good career but was glad to help start PCA all over again. She knew all about the materials. They both said they would be delighted to help and would be willing to work for less money than they were making. Debbie would be office manager in addition to being my assistant until we got set up. Then the office could run itself, and she could concentrate on Peggy and me.

Peggy and me at Snowmass, Colorado, 1989.

Learning: *dealing with those you know eliminates a lot of mysteries.*

Once all the papers were signed, we were in business. Wayne found some office space for himself and Sally. Debbie and I would work primarily out of our homes since we were all set up there anyway. It was necessary to buy computer systems for the office, so we took the opportunity to get the latest configuration. We decided that we would operate by e-mail as much as possible. We arranged to meet all the licensees in Madrid in May in order to get the rules straight. Everyone showed up for what turned out to be a reunion. They were delighted that I had taken the company back; all their experiences had been negative under the previous administration. Wayne explained the license agreement, which let them use all the material and receive inquiries from us. They would pay a fee for the use of the name plus a percent of the revenue from college materials. They grumbled a little, but these were primarily Europeans, and that is the way they greet every change. In the end, all agreed. Ashish Basu attended from India, Daniel Kwok from the Far East, as well as Stanley Labovitz from ODI in Boston. The rest were from Europe. Sally, Wayne, and I all went to Madrid in order to show them we were serious.

When we returned, we designed a logo, ordered stationary, and took care of other important details. We examined the possibility of using a public-relations firm in order to let the world know we were back in business. But the ones we talked with just had the same old approach that we could use ourselves if we wished. We wrote letters and contacted people. But we had no way of getting much money except through the funds the licensees sent in. So far we had received little. ODI argued that because Proudfoot owed ODI money, it couldn't send us any until that was paid off. Also ODI was not paying the contractors who were doing classes for them or the hotels. We were getting dunning calls.

It was apparent that we were not going to make ODI and PCA II compatible. There is a long story, but at the end of the day the ODI chairman, an old friend, and I sat down and worked out a deal. They would give up any work in North America and would pay the contractors and hotels. We would give them a nonexclusive license for Europe and anywhere else that was not held exclusive at that moment. They had operations all over and could perhaps do something using our other people in those areas. We would give them money over a two-year period to replace the profit they would have made.

Learning: *when people cannot live together, a divorce that makes everyone content is the best solution.*

Harold Geneen died Thanksgiving week in 1997. He was eighty-seven and still working. He passed away the same week that his company was wiped out by merging with another firm. No more ITT, no more HSG. I'm certain it was a coincidence, but who ever knows. He had designated that there would be no funeral or memorial session, only a viewing. So I hopped on a plane with all the other people who were heading to grandma's house for pumpkin pie and went to New York. All the old ITTers were at the viewing, and June Geneen said, "I knew you would come." That almost broke me up. I was glad to tell her that when I spoke at MBA schools, the students always asked me about Hal.

Many of those who attended the viewing were people I had not seen for eighteen years. They looked older, which is understandable. Tim Dunleavy was right in the center, looking jolly, but broken up about it all. He really loved Hal and had written a memoir about him and the days at ITT. It probably will never get published but it is worth reading and having.

I often think about what my life would have been without Geneen, as well as Tom Willey and Jim Halpin. Hal showed me the world, and he let me be me. He encouraged me to be me actually. In my other jobs I had come in at the bottom of the organization and worked my way up. Thus I was always the boy wonder with the emphasis on the boy. There was a ceiling on my potential. At ITT I came in at the upper level and was seriously considered as a candidate for president one day. I would not have been happy with that job, but it is better than being told there is no future for you, as happened at Martin.

Geneen met the world face to face, and he showed me how to do the same. He was the only one who assumed I would change the world. I will always miss him.

Learning: *when a person of value comes into your life, it must be recognized.*

Becky White joined us after we settled with ODI. She had been working for them from her home in Orlando, taking orders and answering questions. During the mediation we insisted that she be released from her contract without prejudice. (Wayne was chanting, "Free Becky White.") With Becky on the phones and Wayne dealing with our independent contractors, we were billing $65,000 a week right away. Our projection for 1998 was over $4 million in revenue, which meant we could pay some of our debts and have a proper distribution for the shareholders and employees. Under Subchapter S rules the company pays no income tax; everything goes through to the shareholders. So if you make a million and apply it all to loans, the shareholders still have to pay tax on that revenue without getting any of it.

Learning: *designing a company to be a cash cow is the best strategy at this moment.*

Sally had been digging material out of the various places Proudfoot had stored it and by late December 1997 had found all we needed. We now had every product in every language. We had spent millions of dollars creating and producing that material in the original PCA. Around this time we offered Proudfoot a cash payment to settle our obligation. They were delighted to get it, thinking perhaps that there was not going to be much chance to gain the full obligation. We took the money from the line of credit.

PCA II was becoming profitable as we closed out 1998, and we had a profit distribution. Employees as well as shareholders will benefit from the company for a long time. The Lord wouldn't have brought us all this way to let us fail. I am delighted to have my name back along with a second chance to help management throughout the world. I believe that a sound business economy, supported by a well-run education system, will produce peace and progress in the world. If all of this were mounted within a genuine religious framework, then success would be guaranteed. We are concentrating on teaching organizations to be reliable.

To explain being reliable I am working on a new book: *Creating the Reliable Organization.* The content wraps around four topics: policy, education, requirements, and insistence. I have found my creative juices running again as we re-form PCA. Our growth is coming from the calls we get from companies that want to become serious about quality. They realize that they have to learn a philosophy in order to do that. Most of the new clients say they have tried all the "systems" available but see no real improvement. We expect to double our revenue in the next year or so but don't plan on becoming very big. We want to keep expenses low and serve our niche well. PCA II appeals only to those who have given thought to the management process.

Learning: *the more things change the more they remain the same.*

As I look back over my life I see a fortunate person who was offered many opportunities, most of which were not obvious, and had the good luck to be gifted with thought and energy. I always was bright, although I didn't know it or benefit from it for a long time. I always was healthy and active, which I considered normal. And I had an easy time getting along with people; they like me—perhaps because I like them. I have traveled the globe and have been with all kinds of folks with never a cross word. That is a blessing.

I don't know what the future will bring or how long my future is going to be, at least here on earth. But I have left a trail in the writings I have produced, and I have left an organization that should be around for a long time. It will provide a place for those who recognize the need to become educated about quality and reliability. It should provide income for the family and the employees for as long as they pay proper attention to it and respect it.

When I talk with MBA and other college students, they always ask me for advice on how to be successful. I give them all the same answer: *be useful and reliable.*

—ᴡᴡ— Guidelines for Browsers

Everything changes as soon as you change.   20

The war movies are about the fighters, which is
reasonable. But the ones who keep everything going
are the functional people.   20

You can put a couple of thousand men in close
quarters for a long time with no problems if they
are convinced it is for a good reason.   22

If you just accept what everyone else takes as the
way to do things, you soon become brain-dead.   22

If you don't have a plan, someone else will have
a plan, and you probably won't like it.   24

When you decide you are doing the wrong thing,
quit doing it because it probably is not going to
get much more interesting.   24

What is a good idea for one is not necessarily so
for another, but that doesn't make it a bad idea.   24

College is about going to classes, and the real world
is supposed to tread water while the students immerse
themselves in this artificial learning life. As a result
they wind up with blank spots on the experience tape.   25

Father and son have a hard time working together if
they are doing the same thing. If one is the carpenter
and the other is the plumber, they can do well.   26

Little towns don't have many patients in them.   26

You don't need someone else's approval to do what
you want to do.   26

People take advantage of you when you don't have
any money; they equate that with lack of power.   27

If I had accepted the offer made in my first real
conversation with an authority figure, I would now
be retired from the Navy and would have missed the
next couple hundred pages.   27

A confident stride and purposeful look can get you
anything in the service.   28

In a strange place, with unknown people, it is easy to assume that everything is going to be as they say it is going to be. 29

We can never assume that people are prepared to do a job different from the one they have been doing; training is a must for everything. 29

You can deal with anything if you don't have a hidden agenda. 30

Don't question anything that helps you even if the reason seems stupid. 30

The seed was planted in me for helping those who need a little help. 30

There is a defining moment when one takes charge of one's life rather than being part of an organization. 31

The greatest gift my parents placed in my DNA was the gene for being an optimist. 36

When coming to a new place it is good to be quiet and pleasant for a while. If you are smart, they will figure that out. 36

Complex tasks are made up of a concept and a bunch of little steps. If you can understand the concept, the task is yours. 37

Suggestions, to individuals or organizations, have to be made in a context that doesn't make the suggester look too smart. 37

Those who are truly expert in a field live in the past and keep adjusting what they already know in order to meet the needs of the present. They have a mental block about the future. 38

Organizations do not have feelings; they do not actually exist. 39

Quality is conformance to the requirements, not "goodness"—my first Absolute of Quality Management. 39

In an interview one sells oneself; the attitude one
presents is 99.86 percent of the deal.   47

It is a good idea to buy a little more house than you
actually need. It saves at least one later move, and
paying for it motivates the wage earners.   48

The people who are successful with government work
go down in flames doing commercial projects.   50

Bank presidents who want to meet people stand in
front of the bank. Those who don't want to meet people
stay in their offices.   50

People who show up in combat attitude can expect combat.   51

Creating a hard-to-get-to executive area creates hard-to-
get-to executives.   51

It takes only a few moments and some choice words to
impart important concepts. Everyone can understand
and relate to "doing it right the first time."   52

People think that space workers are particularly careful
because of the potential loss of life. But lots more people
die in cars than spacecraft, and the subject never comes
up in auto plants.   52

Those in charge of an area will always defend it.   53

Keeping neat records of incidents of nonconformance
is not quality management.   54

All the actions to organize are often based on opinion
only, "what should work," and are aimed at getting others
to do their part properly. "What actually works" is a
pragmatic program.   55

People who devise a reorganization often have never
worked on a manufacturing floor. They have no idea
what they were bringing about.   55

An operation mimics the attitude of the senior executive. 56

Those who know a lot usually look for someone to mentor,
but the person mentored has to be capable of learning.   58

Because I did not realize what a good idea ZD was,
I lost control of it. 73

There is always a way to make something happen sensibly. 75

If it were easy to have new ideas accepted, life would
be a Disney movie. 76

Zero defects should be the performance standard—
my third Absolute of Quality Management. 77

People have to be carefully instructed to understand
something different from what they know, but they
will not take time to obtain this instruction on their own. 78

It is not necessary to let others define your personal
agenda. 78

You cannot talk people into the need for improvement.
They have to make up their own minds, and then you
must be ready to help. 79

Knowledge and understanding do not always go together. 80

Pick your own people; don't let personnel or the boss do it. 80

People are so concerned about themselves they do not pay
much attention to what others are doing—just like golf. 83

There is little awareness of what goes on inside another
department; outsiders don't know you are conspiring
against them. 83

Management is a one-person job. 84

Anything can be worked out if credit is given and blame
is withheld. 85

I am a good student when the teacher has something
worthwhile to teach. 87

I always figure the Lord has a plan for me, so when an
opportunity arises I just hop right in. 91

Commuting is commuting; it is all solvable. 94

Nobody knows what is going on everywhere in any business. 95

Big, important companies are manned by ordinary people. 96

When starting a consulting business, it is necessary to begin with customer demand for the services offered. 111

Don't just sit and mope; do something. 112

A committee will never create a respected award. It has to be conceived by one individual who understands the purpose. 116

A noncompetitive award program is taken to heart right away. 117

I am very good at forgiving, but fail forgetting. 118

Thinking about being fifty at age forty-two alerts one to become interested in personal wellness. 118

If you want to get the attention of senior executives, do something original. 119

Meetings held on a regular basis with the same attendees create their own standards of behavior, which it is wise to understand. 120

Speak up firmly and respectfully, but do it about significant topics. 121

Establish a position on a perch above the fray in order to stay out of the political world. 122

Business schools should have a course in patience. 123

Don't get in a position where the company feels it owns you. It's better they feel happy that you are willing to work with them, so stay a little aloof. 124

If people are going to represent you, make certain you share the same philosophy. 125

There are, or will be, things that need to be removed from our lives. Getting rid of them is a matter of intellectual decision and then a firm will. 126

Lots of people can work on a creative product like a film, but the road map has to come from one person. 130

⟶ Index

Lightning Source UK Ltd.
Milton Keynes UK
UKOW051812280812

198174UK00002B/10/A